M[...]

for
Manhood

❖

What Every Man Must Know
(Volume 1)

by

Kenneth W. Royce

Published by

JAVELIN PRESS
www.javelinpress.com

Modules for Manhood by Kenneth W. Royce
Common Law Copyright 2007-2014 by Javelin Press.
With explicit reservation of all Common Law Rights without prejudice.
Sold for academic study and informational purposes only.

Read the following disclaimer very carefully and thoroughly!

Modules for Manhood   March 2014

**Printed in the united states of America,
without any 4 USC §§ 105-110 *Federal area* or "§tate."**

10   9   8   7   6   5   4   3   2   1   /   2020 2019 2018 2017 2016 2015

ISBN 1-888766-12-3

www.javelinpress.com

HISTORICAL DEDICATION

For exhibiting consistent and impressive manhood, I would like to recognize two fine American men of days long past:

President Theodore Roosevelt (d. 1919)

U.S. Air Force Brig. General Robin Olds (d. 2007)
(Olds is the 1944 P-51 Mustang ace on the back cover.)

DEDICATION

Modules for Manhood is dedicated to all Men, whatever their current stage in Life. You're never too young nor too old to begin your own unique journey!

ACKNOWLEDGMENTS

I thank my readers who have so enthusiastically supported my thirteen other books (most written under my trademark pseudonym "Boston T. Party"). I have met many hundreds of you throughout the past 21 years, and I hope to have enriched your lives as much as you have enriched mine.

Gratitude to all my instructors, teachers, and coaches who imparted their contributions to manhood.

Finally, I sincerely thank my father and step-father for the quality things they instilled in their son.

Titles by
Kenneth W. Royce
(a.k.a. Boston T. Party)

Modules for Manhood
(2014 Volume 1)

Hologram of Liberty
(2012 second edition)

One Nation, Under Surveillance

You & The Police!
(2009 edition)

Safari Dreams

Molôn Labé!

Boston's Gun Bible
(2002 edition, revised 2003-2009)

Boston's Gun Bible
(2000 edition)

Boston on Surviving Y2K

Boston on Guns & Courage

Hologram of Liberty
(1997 first edition)

Bulletproof Privacy

You & The Police!
(1996 first edition)

Good-Bye April 15th!

by Kenneth W. Royce (Boston T. Party)

Modules for Manhood (2014)
What Every Man Must Know (Volume 1)
What do women want? What does America need? Men! Do you want to become a capable well-rounded man? Learn your unique Purpose in Life, and how to achieve it? Start your exciting journey today!
360 pp. softcover (2014) $27 + $7 s&h (cash, please)

Hologram of Liberty (revised for 2012)
The Constitution's Shocking Alliance with Big Government
The Convention of 1787 was the most brilliant and subtle *coup d'état* in history. The nationalist framers *designed* a strong government, guaranteed through purposely ambiguous verbiage. Many readers insist that it's Royce's best book. A jaw-dropper. Revised for 2012 and Obamacare.
360 pp. softcover (2012) $27 + $7 s&h (cash, please)

You & The Police! (revised for 2009)
The definitive guide to your rights and tactics during police confrontations. When can you refuse to answer questions or consent to searches? Don't lose your liberty through ignorance! This 2009 edition covers the *USA PATRIOT Act* and much more.
168 pp. softcover (2009) $16 + $5 s&h (cash, please)

One Nation, Under Surveillance (2009)
Privacy From the Watchful Eye
Explains precisely how to lay low from snoops of all types. Extremely thorough on computers, data, Internet, VoIP, digital gold, and prepaid cellphones. This is the huge replacement of his 1997 *Bulletproof Privacy.* Boston retired in 2009; this was his last new title.
480 pp. softcover (2009) $27 + $7 s&h (cash, please)

Boston's Gun Bible (new text through 2009)
A rousing how-to/why-to on our modern gun ownership. Firearms are "*liberty's teeth*". No other general gun book is more thorough or useful! Indispensable! Covers the *D.C v. Heller* case. Our best seller.
848 pp. softcover (2002-2009) $33 + $7 s&h (cash, please)

Molôn Labé! (a novel)
If you liked *Unintended Consequences* by John Ross and Ayn Rand's *Atlas Shrugged*, then Boston's novel will be a favorite. It dramatically outlines an innovative recipe for Liberty which could actually work! A thinking book for people of action; an action book for people of thought. It's getting people moving to Wyoming! **www.freestatewyoming.org**
454 pp. softcover (2004) $27 + $7 s&h (cash, please)

Safari Dreams (2008)
A Practical Guide To Your Hunt In Africa
Possibly the most useful "one book" for making your first safari. Thoroughly covers: rifles, calibers, bullets, insurance, health, packing and planning, trip prep, airlines, choosing your PH, shot placement, and being in the bush. Don't go to Africa without it!
352 pp. softcover, 100 color photos (2008) $30 + $5 s&h

www.javelinpress.com

www.javelinpress.com

NOTE: Please verify pricing *and address* from our website *before* ordering!

Prices <u>each</u> copy:	Retail	<40%>	<44%>	<50%>
Boston's Gun Bible 5½"x8½" 848 pp. 1/2009	*1-5* copies **$33**	*6-7* **$20**	*8-15* **$18.50**	*case 16 or more* **$16.50**
Modules for Manhood - 1 5½"x8½" 360 pp. 3/2014	*1-5* copies **$27**	*6-13* **$16**	*14-27* **$15**	*case 28 or more* **$13.50**
Molôn Labé! 5½"x8½" 454 pp. 1/2004	*1-5* copies **$27**	*6-13* **$16**	*14-27* **$15**	*case 28 or more* **$13.50**
One Nation, Under Surv. 5½"x8½" 480 pp. 6/2009	*1-5* copies **$27**	*6-13* **$16**	*14-27* **$15**	*case 28 or more* **$13.50**
Hologram of Liberty 5½"x8½" 360 pp. 5/2012	*1-5* copies **$27**	*6-13* **$16**	*14-27* **$15**	*case 28 or more* **$13.50**
Boston on Surviving Y2K 5½"x8½" 352 pp. 11/1998	*1-5* copies **$11**	*6-17* **$10**	*18-35* **$9**	*case of 36 or more* **$8**
Safari Dreams 5½"x8½" 352 pp. 1/2008	*1-5* copies **$30**	*6-17* **$18**	*18-39* **$17**	*case of 36 or more* **$15**
You & The Police! 5½"x8½" 168 pp. 1/2009	*1-5* copies **$16**	*6-37* **$10**	*38-75* **$9**	*case of 76 or more* **$8**

Mix titles for any quantity discount. This is easiest done as ¼ case per title:
¼ case of: BGB 4   MfM 7   ML! 7   ONUS 7   HoL 7   BoSY 9   SD 9   Y&P! 19

Shipping and Handling are *not* included! Please add below:

non-case S&H within USA for (*BGB   MfM   Molôn   ONUS   Hologram*):
First Class (or UPS for larger orders) add: $7 for first copy, $2 each additional copy.

non-case S&H within USA for other titles (*Y&P!   BoSY   Safari Dreams*):
First Class (or UPS for larger orders) add: $5 for first copy, $1 each additional copy.

CASE orders (straight or mixed) UPS Ground: $35 west of the Miss.; $40 east.

Overpayment will be refunded in cash with order. Underpayment will delay order!
If you have questions on discounts or S&H, please email us through our website.

These forms of payment only:

Cash (Preferred. Cash orders receive pre-signed copies when available.)
payee <u>blank</u> M.O.s (Which allows negotiability.)
silver 1oz. bullion (At today's spot price, found at: www.kitco.com)

Unless prior agreement has been made, *we do <u>not</u> accept and <u>will</u> return* checks,
C.O.D.s, or any other form of tender. (Many of our distributors take credit cards.)
Prices and terms are subject to change without notice (check our website first).
Please send paid orders to the address on **www.javelinpress.com**

TABLE OF CONTENTS

5   Individuality, Courage, Manhood

6   Getting Along (Better With People)

9   Negotiating & Selling

10   Learning & Training

11   Doing (Action!)

"*If —*"

Rudyard Kipling

If you can keep your head when all about you
Are losing theirs and blaming it on you,
If you can trust yourself when all men doubt you
But make allowance for their doubting too,
If you can wait and not be tired by waiting,
Or being lied about, don't deal in lies,
Or being hated, don't give way to hating,
And yet don't look too good, nor talk too wise:

If you can dream — and not make dreams your master,
If you can think — and not make thoughts your aim;
If you can meet with Triumph and Disaster
And treat those two impostors just the same;
If you can bear to hear the truth you've spoken
Twisted by knaves to make a trap for fools,
Or watch the things you gave your life to, broken,
And stoop and build 'em up with worn-out tools:

If you can make one heap of all your winnings
And risk it all on one turn of pitch-and-toss,
And lose, and start again at your beginnings
And never breath a word about your loss;
If you can force your heart and nerve and sinew
To serve your turn long after they are gone,
And so hold on when there is nothing in you
Except the Will which says to them: "*Hold on!*"

If you can talk with crowds and keep your virtue,
Or walk with kings – nor lose the common touch,
If neither foes nor loving friends can hurt you;
If all men count with you, but none too much,
If you can fill the unforgiving minute
With sixty seconds' worth of distance run,
Yours is the Earth and everything that's in it,
And — which is more — you'll be a Man, my son!

INTRODUCTION

What do women want? What does America need? Men. You are merely a male by birth. Only by choice and effort can you become a Man. While 50% of people are male, a male is not necessarily a Man. The transformation of boy-to-man does not happen by accident, but rather through a proven process by fathers, brothers, uncles, grandfathers, and mentors. In the 21st century, most American males haven't access to such character-building role models, so they founder about as soft and incomplete males.

> Among the other signs of times we discover that coping is unfashionable. As far as I can tell, today's young people are taught not to handle problems but rather to call for help. This is very bad conditioning. As a boy, I led a privileged life, but I nonetheless often got into jams beyond reach of assistance. I never called for help, and my father would have sneered at me if had done so. At age seventeen while driving alone I blew a tire. I had never seen a wheel changed but I figured the matter out for myself. This is not to boast but only to point out that young men should be expected to cope.
> **The point is that a young man of 21 should be able to cope with the world around him in a general fashion.** . . . Before a young man leaves home, there are certain things he should know and certain skills at which he should be adept.
> These things should be available before a son leaves his father's household.
> — Jeff Cooper, www.molonlabe.net/Commentaries/jeff13_10.html

> We have not fit men for the times.
> — John Adams

We haven't fit men because today's males cannot *cope* with the world, and coping is what being a Real Man is all about. He handles things. Growing into an internally-ambitious, competent, self-sufficiently productive, self-governed, loving, and pleasant man of honor is a *serious* process. Very little about it is accidental. Good genetics and a quality up-bringing (both are forms of inheritance) help greatly, but they do not guarantee a successful life. (I know many losers with good genetics and good parents. Any inheritance can be squandered, and often is.) The "hardware" of people is all about the same — it's the "software" where the difference lies. Meaning, what you choose to learn and apply is what really matters.

The trouble with most guys today is that haven't grown a "taproot" into the soil of Life. They are not anchored in anything.

A taproot is a very large, somewhat straight to tapering plant root that grows downward. It forms a center from which other roots sprout laterally. Plants with taproots are difficult to transplant.
— wikipedia

Men's best is generally not very good, and most men cannot do their best but sporadically. *Modules For Manhood* will help you:

❶ ability to absorb what's happening
❷ ability to respond correctly (whether tragic or happy)
❸ reflect on what has gone before
❹ ability to share, and thus enlarge yourself

the war against capable citizens

We must stop thinking about the individual and start thinking about what is best for society.
— Hilary Clinton, 1993

At its zenith, the Western way of life encompassed a unique blend of beliefs, characteristics, principles, and philosophies. Numbered among its virtues were honesty, self-discipline, [nonaggression], self-sufficiency, the work ethic, respect for elders, aggrandizement of achievement, planning for the future, respect for the property of others, a stable economic system, reverence for the family unit, courtesy and consideration toward others, and, above all, the right of the individual to be left alone. When I speak of the collapse of Western Civilization, then, it is the literal destruction of this way of life that I am referring to.
— Robert J. Ringer, *How You Can Find Happiness During the Collapse of Western Civilization*

The more narrow your talents, the more you must rely on institutions and government for what you cannot do yourself. For at least the past hundred years, there has been a specific and organized scheme to eliminate talent width amongst people. Why? Because width of skillset increases your self-sufficiency:

A human being should be able to change a diaper, plan an invasion, butcher a hog, conn a ship, design a building, write a sonnet, balance accounts, build a wall, set a bone, comfort the dying, take orders, give orders, cooperate, act alone, solve equations, analyze a new problem, pitch manure, program a

computer, cook a tasty meal, fight efficiently, die gallantly. Specialization is for insects.
— Robert Heinlein, *Time Enough For Love*

Self-sufficiency is toxic to government and institutions. Only the self-reliant can maintain good character over a lifetime. (The dependent, when squeezed, must abandon their own conscience for a job's sake. Try to speak a contrary opinion within a large company or institution, if you dare.) A right-thinking man, with strings attached, cannot be a right-*doing* man. **When you can take care of yourself, you enjoy the privilege of living by what you know is *right*.**

[S]*chooling is a matter of habit and attitude training. It takes place from the outside in. Education is a matter of self-mastery, first; then self-enlargement, even self-transcendence . . . but in schooling, somebody else's agenda is always uppermost.*
You can compensate for a lack of schooling — the human record is full of stories of those who have done so in the past and those who continue to do so in the present — but without education you will stumble through life, a sitting duck for exploitation and failure, no matter how much money you make.
— John Taylor Gatto, *Weapons of Mass Instruction*, p. 61

[Modernity's] *rejection of the* [traditional] *family is based on a rejection of motherhood, and the rejection of motherhood is grounded on a rejection of manliness and fatherhood. No fathers for the country, no patriots. Instead, we are progressively becoming careerists, bureaucrats, and opportunists. A country made of* these *is not a country. Statecraft grows hollow without the proprietary interest of the father. Today, every sort of cheapness and treachery, every sort of circus act and every sort of bizarre nonsense gains access to leadership and the public ear. The people are children and always shall be children. Now, under democracy — orphans.*
— J.R. Nyquist, *Origins of the Fourth World War*, p. 80-81

Theodore Roosevelt remarked a century ago that our society was perfecting its "*cult of nonvirility*" with "*untried men who live at ease*".

I've come to the reluctant but inescapable conclusion that roughly 50% of the adults in this country are simply too ignorant and functionally incompetent to be living in a free society.
— Neal Boortz, *Somebody's Gotta Say It*

Few any longer can fix a car or the plumbing, grow food, hunt, bait a hook or install a new roof. Or defend themselves. To

> *overstate barely, everyone depends on someone else, often the government, for everything. Thus we became the Hive.*
> *Government came like a dust storm of fine choking powder, making its way into everything. You could no longer build a shed without a half-dozen permits and inspections. You couldn't swim without a lifeguard, couldn't use your canoe without Coast-Guard approved flotation devices and a card saying that you had taken an approved course in how to canoe. Cops proliferated with speed traps. The government began spying on email, requiring licenses and permits for everything, and deciding what could and could not be taught to one's children, who one had to associate with, and what one could think about what or, more usually, whom.*
> *Thus much of the country morphed into helpless flowers, narcissistic, easily frightened, profoundly ignorant video-game twiddlers and Facebook Argonauts.*
> — Fred Reed, Your Papers, Citizen
> Gun Control and the Changing American Character
> http://archive.lewrockwell.com/reed/reed250.html

Modules For Manhood will not likely be read in college, which today serves more as remedial high-school education than halls of higher learning. Most college students can neither solve a quadratic equation any more than correctly identify the decade of WWII or explain where price inflation comes from. However, a young man who has self-educated himself with *Modules* can gain several times more education from his college experience, should he choose to attend.

Basically, I'm going to show you how the world really works, and how you can successfully navigate within it. This skill and prowess is no longer routine, but you can still learn how.

ORIGINS OF *MODULES FOR MANHOOD*

My first inspiration for writing was Jeff Cooper, who just a few months before his death in 2006, outlined it all:

> *What should a young male of 21 know, and what should he be able to do? There are no conclusive answers to those questions, but they are certainly worth asking. A young man should know how this country is run and how it got that way. He should know the Federalist Papers and de Tocqueville, and he should know recent world history. If he does not know what has been tried in the past, he cannot very well avoid those pitfalls as they come up in the future. A young man should be computer literate and, moreover, should know Hemingway from James Joyce. He should know how to drive a car well — such as is not covered in Driver's Ed. He should*

> *know how to fly a light airplane. He should know how to shoot well. He should know elementary geography, both worldwide and local. He should have a cursory knowledge of both zoology and botany. He should know the fundamentals of agriculture and corporate economy. He should be well qualified in armed combat, boxing, wrestling and judo, or its equivalent. He should know how to manage a motorcycle. He should be comfortable in at least one foreign language, more if appropriate to his background. He should be familiar with remedial medicine.* **These things should be accomplished before a son leaves his father's household.** *They do not constitute "a college education," which may or may not be a trade school.*
>   — Jeff Cooper; 2006, www.molonlabe.net/Commentaries/jeff13_10.html

His *parents* are responsible for inculcating this, and all *girls* should demand such in their dates. Parents must create the quality young man, and girls are to insist that he *remains* so. Neither has happened for decades. Parents no longer know how, so women must settle for crude and incompetent boys who never became men (and never will). The cycle repeats itself and spirals for each subsequent generation. Thus, the need for this book. Heck, it was needed back in 1933:

> *What are those abilities, skills, or accomplishments, those extra-curricular proficiencies that every man should have in order to be rounded and self-sufficient, and when can he acquire them, and how?*
>   — Robert Littell, "What the Young Man Should Know", *Harper's*
>   www.artofmanliness.com

Parents can make only one of two choices: either they can either turn their children over to TV and public "schools" for baby-sitting (read John Taylor Gatto), **or they can raise a quality human being**. Such a process is very hard work, of course, which is why so few families do it. Also, it cannot be reliably accomplished by single parents or homes with working mothers. **Transmuting adulthood into a child is a full-time job**, and one parent (preferably the mother) must stay home to *be* the parent for her children's first 5-7 years. After that, fatherhood becomes as or more important.

Raising children is far too vital to relegate to public schools, which are purposely designed to create compliant wage-slaves vs. independent thinkers and doers. Paying strangers for important tasks (education, food, self-defense, health, etc.) is now the norm. We are too specialized, and thus have lost the art of becoming complete human beings. From the Wikipedia on functional illiteracy, "*In the*

US, 14% of the adult population is at the "below basic" level for prose literacy . . . and 22% are at that level for quantitative literacy. Only 13% of the population is proficient in these three areas – able to compare viewpoints in two editorials; interpret a table about blood pressure, age, and physical activity; or compute and compare the cost per ounce of food items."

The night closes in. Read the surveys of what children know, what students in universities know. Approximately nothing. We have become wanton morons. As the intellectual shadows fall again, as literacy declines and minds grow dim in the new twilight, who will copy the parchments this time?

No longer are we a schooled people. Brash new peasants grin and peck at their iPods. Unknowing, incurious, they gaze at their screens and twiddle, twiddle. They will not preserve the works of five millennia. They cannot. They do not even know why.

Twilight really does come. Sales of books fall. Attention spans shorten. Music gives way to angry urban grunting. The young count on their fingers when they do not have a calculator, know less by the year. We have already seen the first American generations less educated than their parents. College graduates do not know when World War One happened, or what the Raj was. They have read nothing except the nothing that they read, and little of that. Democracy was an interesting thought.

Ours will be a stranger Dark Age than the old one. Our peasants brush their teeth and wash, imagine themselves of the middle class, but their heads are empty.

And they rule. We have achieved the dictatorship of the proletariat. Hod-carriers in designer jeans, they do not quite burn books but simply ignore them. Their college degrees amount to high-school diplomas, if that, but they neither know nor care.

The things that have forever constituted civilization – respect for learning whether one had it or not, wide reading, careful use of language, manners, such notions as "lady" and "gentleman" – these are held in contempt.

— Fred Reed, http://archive.lewrockwell.com/reed/reed216.html

Life is a continual struggle against *something*, and usually several things at once. Childhood should be a rigorous boot-camp for Life. *Train hard — fight easy!* If parents are soft, their children they will find Life "too hard" and will become collectivists who whine for government to make it easier. Our country has become nearly ruined from sugared lives.

Don't handicap your children by making their lives easy.
— Robert Heinlein

some thoughts on reading this book

Categorizing all these "modules" was a challenge. One way to have done it was in Frank Miniter's excellent *The Ultimate Man's Survival Guide* with its six sections: survivor, provider, athlete, hero, gentleman, and philosopher. My book is somewhat chronological along the path of an individual's personal growth and development. There is much to learn over a lifetime, but the important basics may be grasped by any dedicated young man. An astonishing amount of information you need is freely available at the public library and on the Internet. Nearly everything which you must know won't cost you a dime. Meaning, poverty is no excuse for life-long practiced ignorance. (To get an idea of what people don't know, read *Cultural Illiteracy* and any books by John Taylor Gatto. It's pretty dire.)

Many adult readers will note that I have not written "down" to teenagers or to boys. There are many words which my younger readers will not know — will never have heard of. Solution: buy a large dictionary and learn these words as you go. Begin a notebook and write them out. **Your thinking is only as sophisticated as your vocabulary.** (I learned this from George Orwell's *1984.*) Yes, I know that the average American's speaking vocabulary is only a few thousand words, and that's fine ... if you want to remain *average*.

Before TV, a book like mine could have been easily read by the average high-school student. Back then, they didn't have minds of mush, and could actually read and think! So, I will not write "down" to the current level. My young readers must pull themselves up to what used to be the normal level. (By becoming intellectually "normal" for yesteryear, you will be much brighter than today's peers.) The concepts and ideas in *Modules for Manhood* are timeless, and some of them will take years to really get, much less apply and own.

Be patient, but I've included hundreds of quotations in the hope that a myriad of voices and perspectives will better awaken you (as they did me in my 20s). The right quote can change a life!

I quote others only the better to express myself.
— Michel de Montaigne

Of course everything has been said that needs to be said — but since no one was listening it has to be said again.
— author unknown

Although *Modules For Manhood* was written for young males, older guys can learn much from it. (I did!) Indeed, there is already a sort of remedial men's movement growing. (PromiseKeepers was the first manifestation.) In my studied opinion, the homeschooling and back-to-the-country movements are this nation's only possible salvation — assuming it's not already too late. A Man needs a taproot into Life to anchor himself in the soil for strength and nutrition. This taproot is grown only through intent and dedication.

Yes, you *can* do it!

Reading over Cooper's basic list, it may seem overwhelming to you. *"Where could I possibly find all that time to learn those things?"* **Here's a clue:** by the 12th grade, a boy has spent 8,000 hours in the classroom, and *12,000+* hours in front of videoscreens. Dump that 1,000+ hours/year of video crap, and start learning *real* things! You have but one Life here, and it's no dress rehearsal. Do not waste it! Acquire actual skills which can fulfill your purpose, make you money, help people, and thrill women.

Less than 6 hours/week in a year will achieve any one of these:

- ❒ speak an entirely new language credibly well
- ❒ own basic and reflexive skills in a solid martial art
- ❒ become a confident dancer (ballroom, Swing, etc.)
- ❒ learn to fly a small airplane and become a Private Pilot
- ❒ ride motorcycles (dirt and street)
- ❒ take up sailing and become proficient in a small boat
- ❒ get into public speaking and master this important art
- ❒ learn to write any kind of letter (business, personal, sales)
- ❒ become a credible cook, using ingredients from scratch
- ❒ play guitar or piano decently, with many songs in memory
- ❒ learn dozens of poems to recite from memory
- ❒ totally transform your body through vigorous exercise
- ❒ learn house construction, welding, or how to fix cars

Half of these skills can be learned with next to no money. *Any* of these are available if you'd spend only an hour/day for a year. Three hours/day for a year and you can own *three* of these skills. OK, want to impress the ladies? Get extremely fit, learn to fight and dance. Next year, learn the guitar, a foreign language, and to fly an airplane. **Talk about *studly*, and in just two years!** Everyone will think you've become James Bond. (Meanwhile, your old buddies were playing *Wii* and X-Box And what will they have to show for *that*? Zero.)

"Hey, I'm not even 18 and you're talking about becoming a pilot?! That costs big money!" Well, that didn't stop Illinois

high-schooler Landon Clipp. At 14 he began lessons flying a powered parachute. For 2½ years he mowed some 300 lawns (about 225 acres) to earn the $7,000 for his own vehicle of flight. By 17, he had about 40 hours in powered parachutes. So, if you commit yourself to a definite and worthy goal — and if you don't waste time with videoscreen entertainment and silly people — even teenagers can accomplish very impressive things. Landon, with his own money, became a pilot and bought an aircraft as a high-school sophomore. All a young man needs is a taste of real accomplishment like that, and he *will* succeed in Life.

America will face some very tough times soon and there must be good Men for the future. I hope that you become one of them. You don't need money, good looks, big brains, a prominent family, or even luck. You need only clear thinking, solid goals, and the *will* to become a Man. Think of me as one of your guides.

As the saying goes, the best time to plant a tree is 20 years ago. The next best time is *today*. Resolve to live with all your might, while you do live! Stop wasting time, dump your excuses, get serious about your Life, and let's get started right now!

Kenneth W. Royce
Wyoming, February 2014

CHAPTER LIST

Since the entire text runs to nearly 1,200 pages, I will offer it in three print volumes as well as about 10 e-books.

Volume 1   (published March 2014)
1   Understanding
2   Thinking, Truth, Wisdom
3   Integrity & Character
4   Conquering (Fear, Depression, Laziness, Anger, Impatience, Pride)
5   Individuality, Courage, Manhood
6   Getting Along (Better With People)
7   Communicating
8   Persuading
9   Selling
10   Learning & Training
11   Doing

Volume 2   (due Summer 2014)
12   Teaching
13   Deciding
14   Prioritizing
15   Solving
16   Power
17   Leading
18   Working & Success
19   Savings & Debt
20   Money and Inflation
21   Taxes
22   Government
23   Fighting

Volume 3   (due Autumn 2014)
24   Eating
25   Health
26   Moving
27   Surviving
28   Pursuing a Woman
29   Loving a Woman
30   Husbanding
31   Fathering
32   Believing
33   How To Know God
34   Suffering
35   Living

📁 1

UNDERSTANDING

Rediscoveries are common among philosophers; the human mind moves in a circle around its eternal problems.
— A.J. Liebling

The yearning for comfort prevents understanding. The unawakened individual does not belong to himself. Reality constantly tries to tell us what is right, but the tricky mind distorts the message. Don't accept comfort at the cost of understanding.
— Vernon Howard, *Pathways to Perfect Living*

Understanding is the foundation to *everything*. If you understand poorly, or not at all, you will forever be the pawn of other people and seemingly random misfortune (which you will bemoan as "bad luck").

It's easy to tell these people apart. Those who "get it" understand how things work and have a strategy to create the results they want. Those who don't are stumbling along looking puzzled, and can be found complaining that they never seem to get a break.

You must do what it takes to accumulate enough knowledge to "get it." You need to operate with the information and skills that are necessary to win. Be prepared, tune in, find out how the game is played and play by the rules.

In designing a strategy and getting the information you need — about yourself, people you encounter, or situations — be careful from whom you accept input. Wrong thinking and misinformation can seal your fate before you even begin.
— from Dr. Phil's Life Law #1, www.drphil.com/articles/article/44

There is a knack and formula to the proper understanding of things. Before you can understand yourself, you must fist understand how the world works. Dr. Phil's 10 Life Laws are the best intro:

DR. PHIL'S 10 LIFE LAWS

Dr. Phil is a very wise man, with decades of counseling experience. If I could recommend only *one* self-help book, it would be his *Life Strategies* which describes these 10 Life Laws.

❶ You either get it or you don't.
Strategy: Become one of those who gets it. Break the code of human nature, and find out what makes people tick.

❷ You create your own experience.
Strategy: Acknowledge and accept accountability for your life. Understand your role in creating results.

❸ People do what works.
Strategy: Identify the payoffs that drive behavior, yours and others.

❹ You cannot change what you do not acknowledge.
Strategy: Get real with yourself about life and everybody in it. Be truthful about what isn't working in your life. Stop making excuses and start making results.

❺ Life rewards action.
Strategy: Make careful decisions and then pull the trigger. The world couldn't care less about thoughts without actions.

❻ There is no reality, only perception.
Strategy: Identify the filters through which you view the world. Acknowledge your history without being controlled by it.

❼ Life is managed; it is not cured.
Strategy: Learn to take charge of your life and hold on. This is a long ride, and you are the driver every single day.

❽ We teach people how to treat us.
Strategy: Own, rather than complain about, how people treat you. Learn to renegotiate your relationships to have what you want.

❾ There is power in forgiveness.
Strategy: Open your eyes to what anger and resentment are doing to you. Take your power back from those who have hurt you.

❿ You have to name it before you can claim it.
Strategy: Get clear about what you want and take your turn.

> *Lacking the ability to reason, a person will perceive the world incorrectly. And the person who perceives the world incorrectly will always be a stranger to happiness and success. . . . By perception or insight, I am referring to the ability to interpret*

correctly the events that surround you — the ability to mentally grasp the difference between the real and the unreal; between what is fact and what is myth; between what works and what doesn't work. I am speaking of perception as the foundation of your life. . . . The single most important perception in your life is the your broadview of the way the world works.
  — Robert J. Ringer, *How You Can Find Happiness During the Collapse of Western Civilization*

"WHO AM . . . I?"

You are a little soul bearing about a corpse.
  — Epictetus

You are the lens through which you see and contemplate Life. Your vision and understanding cannot be more clear than that lens. The less you know of yourself, the more inexplicable Life will seem. Have a gut-wrenching, soul-stirring understanding about yourself, and face your issues and shortcomings.

first, understand yourself

We do not deal much in facts when we are contemplating ourselves.
  — Mark Twain

You must see something very clearly. You must see that mankind's game is utterly false. He has false answers, false heroics, false kindness, false intelligence. The whole show is pure nothing. In his vanity a man thinks he is part of the solution, when in fact he contributes to the problem. He lives in a raging madhouse of compulsive desires, which, even if attained, leave him with a tormenting thirst for more. He has no idea who he is unless another deluded human being tells him, and even then he senses the emptiness of a labeled self.

The painful game will stop when we earnestly try to see ourselves as we actually are, and not as we idealistically like to picture ourselves. So we must suspect that we are not who we think we are; we must stop living in dreamland. We can find no better starting point for changing our lives than with a refusal to accept deception, first from ourselves, then from others.
  — Vernon Howard, *Pathways to Perfect Living*

With right self-knowledge, you can cease to be at war with yourself.
  — C.G. Jung

Take some personality tests, such as Enneagram, Briggs-Meyer, etc. to get some deeper insights. Confront and deal with whatever is unpleasant about yourself, before others have to!

> *Be brutally honest with yourself. Don't deny any of your "crimes of living," and don't mince words when you do it. If you're fat, you're fat. If you're lazy, you're lazy. If you're scared, you're scared. You don't have a glandular problem, an energy deficit, and a careful approach to life. You're fat, lazy, and scared.* **Be willing to tell it like it is, or it will stay like it is.**
> — Dr. Phil, *Life Strategies*, p. 124

> *Know your strongest Point, your pre-eminent gift; cultivate that and you will assist the rest. Every one would have excelled in something if he had known his strong point. Notice in what quality you surpass, and take charge of that. In some judgment excels, in others valour. Most do violence to their natural aptitude, and thus attain superiority in nothing.*
> — Balthasar Gracian, *The Art of Worldly Wisdom*

> *Learn to like yourself, or change yourself until you can like yourself.*
> — Guy Kawasaki, of Apple Computers, to a graduating high school class

understand your own values
theoretical (discovery of truth)
economic (what is useful to you)
aesthetic (form and harmony)
social (love of people)
political (power)
religious (your relationship with the Creator)

"There, but for the grace of God, go I!"
There are some people not only born severely handicapped, but under repressive regimes as well. It could have been *you*. If you are a healthy American with a paycheck, about 90% of the world would gladly change places with you. You have no right to complain! You were born on third base! Life is a no-whining zone.

nothing matters unless you *make* it matter
> *Vex not thy spirit at the course of things; they heed not thy vexation.   How ludicrous and outlandish is astonishment at anything that may happen in life.*

If you are distressed by anything external, the pain is not due to the thing itself, but to your estimate of it; and this you have the power to revoke at any moment.
   — Marcus Aurelius (121-180)

I am sometimes taken aback by how people can have a miserable day or get angry because they feel cheated by a bad meal, cold coffee, a social rebuff, or a rude reception. . . . We are quick to forget that just being alive is an extraordinary piece of good luck, a remote event, a chance occurrence of monstrous proportions.
   Don't be like the ingrate who got a castle as a present and worried about the mildew in the bathroom.
   — Nasim Nicholas Taleb, *The Black Swan*, p. 297-298

10% of life is what happens to you, but the other 90% is how you respond to what happens to you. Most of Life really boils down to your choices, especially how you choose to *feel* about things. This is a very difficult lesson to learn, and it usually takes decades. Even then, you will never fully internalize it. So, you may as well get started now. When you hear or read "*It's all in your mind!* ", examine this for truth. Here is a lovely story to ponder:

A 92-year-old, petite, well-poised and proud man, who is fully dressed each morning by eight o'clock, with his hair fashionably coifed and shaved perfectly, even though he is legally blind, moved to a nursing home today. His wife of 70 years recently passed away, making the move necessary. After many hours of waiting patiently in the lobby of the nursing home, he smiled sweetly when told his room was ready.
   As he maneuvered his walker to the elevator, I provided a visual description of his tiny room, including the eyelet sheets that had been hung on his window.
   "I love it," he stated with the enthusiasm of an eight-year-old having just been presented with a new puppy.
   "Mr. Jones, you haven't seen the room; just wait."
   "That doesn't have anything to do with it," he replied."
   "Happiness is something you decide on ahead of time. Whether I like my room or not doesn't depend on how the furniture is arranged . . . it's how I arrange my mind. I already decided to love it. It's a decision I make every morning when I wake up. I have a choice; I can spend the day in bed recounting the difficulty I have with the parts of my body that no longer work, or get out of bed and be thankful for the ones that do.
   "Each day is a gift, and as long as my eyes open, I'll focus on the new day and all the happy memories I've stored away. Just for this time in my life.

"Old age is like a bank account. You withdraw from what you've put in. So, my advice to you would be to deposit a lot of happiness in the bank account of memories! Thank you for your part in filling my Memory bank. I am still depositing."

have an ongoing dedication to reality at all costs

Full credit goes to the late Dr. M. Scott Peck for this perfect maxim. A dedication (not just a passing interest or fad) which must be not only ongoing, but without regards to cost (*i.e.*, time, energy, money, sacrifice). Unreality (*"That can't happen to me!"*) is the most expensive thing in Life, and reality is well worth whatever it costs. Without an ongoing dedication to reality at all costs, you cannot have honest opinions or healthy emotions.

You must always choose to base your actions on *reality*.

While you may be able to (for a time) ignore reality, you will not be able to ignore the *effects* of reality (Ayn Rand).

Reality means reality-based models. Atomic physics was merely a theoretical model long before the first atom was seen, much less split. But, it was a *realistic* model (based on observable and repeatable laboratory phenomenon), and thus worth pursuing.

Quantum physics is another model, and a truly strange one that humans are still trying to wrap their 4-dimensional minds around. Nevertheless, the model does work. We build lasers and many other things from the quantum physics model.

Look into the Interior of Things. Things are generally other than they seem, and ignorance that never looks beneath the rind becomes disabused when you show the kernel. Lies always come first, dragging fools along by their irreparable vulgarity. Truth always lags last, limping along on the arm of Time.
— Balthasar Gracian, *The Art of Worldly Wisdom*

what is your model? what is your mental map?

Models are how humans understand their world. If you want your child to understand how the world works, and how to cope with it successfully, think in terms of teaching models.

Facts are nice, but models are essential. Teach your children to ask for the model. (p. 13)

The more important the model is to you, the higher should be your standard of proof. Where is the evidence? (p. 15)

Experience creates models automatically. (p. 18)
— Richard J. Maybury, *"Uncle Eric" Talks About Personal, Career and Financial Security*

Models. Indeed. Without meaningful models, facts are more confusing than enlightening. (Notice that the public schools do not teach models, and colleges only rarely do.) Richard Maybury has been tremendous in broadcasting these lost core values. He is published by www.bluestockingpress.com and I strongly recommend *all* of his books. TV's Dr. Phil calls models "filters":

> *You know and experience this world only through the perceptions that you create. You have the ability to choose how you perceive any event in your life, and you exercise this power of choice in every circumstance, every day of your life. No matter what the situation, you choose your reaction, assigning meaning and value to an event.*
>
> *We all view the world through individual filters, which influence the interpretations we give events, how we respond, and how we are responded to. Be aware of the factors that influence the way you see the world, so you can compensate for them and react against them. If you continue to view the world through a filter created by past events, then you are allowing your past to control and dictate both your present and your future.*
>
> *Filters are made up of fixed beliefs, negative ideas that have become entrenched in your thinking. They are dangerous because if you treat them as fact, you will not seek, receive or process new information, which undermines your plans for change. If you "shake up" your belief system by challenging these views and testing their validity, the freshness of your perspective can be startling.*
> — from Dr. Phil's Life Law #6, www.drphil.com/articles/article/44

> *There is nothing either good or bad, but thinking makes it so.*
> — Shakespeare

Another important contributor to good mapping was author Ayn Rand, the creator of Objectivism. (The trouble with Rand, however, was that she believed her map to be perfect. Humans cannot create perfect maps. Useful ones, yes, but never perfect.)

> *If they can get you asking the wrong questions, they don't have to worry about the answers.*
> — T. Pynchon

The quality of your own model determines all else. I'd spend a *lot* of time first developing your model before committing to any significant action. For example, before you get involved with girls, develop your model about them. What drives them? What are their goals? What are *their* models? How are their models and your models similar and not?   Understand all this before your first serious relationship. I made a severe mistake on this by letting chemistry carry me away with a very pretty woman. Then, near the end of our short and stormy relationship, I asked her what her goals were. *"To write horror fiction."* I was ashamed at myself for wasting time with somebody of such different goals. It was a painful lesson: Learn much more about a new woman before getting too involved.

GIGO — Garbage In, Garbage Out

You cannot build high-quality products from low-quality ingredients. (Remember this before you're tempted to visit the next fast-food joint.) You cannot become educated by watching TV or reading magazines. You cannot form great relationships from low-quality people. Or, as the memorable line in the movie *Primary Colors* goes: *"Shit begets shit."*

"We see through a glass, dimly." Apostle Paul

You will never see the *complete* picture, or any part of it perfectly. There will always be a significant measure of uncertainty and cloudiness. (Plato's metaphor of the cave wall shadows is appropriate. Look it up.) Know this now and begin to grow comfortable with making plans and decisions based on incomplete knowledge. That is merely one curse of the human condition.

you see what you look *for*, not what you look *at*

Hear hoofbeats. Expect horses, not zebras.
— Robert Heinlein

Try to often challenge your preconceived notions, else you will be blind to the obvious around you.

trust your gut

Your mind is about 10% conscious and 90% subconscious (where most of the real work is done). Your emotions are how your subconscious tries to communicate with your consciousness. Often, these emotions will be too vague to articulate. That's OK. Over time, and through many mistakes, you will learn when to trust them.

Women operate more from their subconscious, which is one reason why they are typically more emotional than men. When something doesn't "feel right" to a woman, it is the equivalent of a man operating on hard evidence. (No kidding. I once asked out a lady for lunch, and she emailed back that it *"felt nice"* to hear from me. This is not language a guy would normally use, and it caught my ear.)

Men can take a clue from women and begin to trust their gut hunches more often, especially in serious matters of business or social relations. If a deal just doesn't seem right, and you cannot understand why, it's probably better to pass. In short, your gut hunch is a form of understanding. Police officers rely on it every day. When something about somebody seems "*hinky*" they are often correct.

Scientists are doing fascinating work in replicating the gut hunch with a branch of mathematics called "fuzzy logic." Very interesting stuff!

we are spiritual beings having a physical experience

Einstein's formula $E=MC^2$ is important here. Energy is just Matter speeded up to the square of the speed of Light. Conversely, Matter (*i.e.*, you and me) is just Energy *slowed down* by (divided with) the square of the speed of Light.

That doesn't mean all Matter is spiritual-being Energy. Humans are more than mere animals for we have a spirit. We operate at spiritual (supernatural) levels more than we understand. Our physical reality is largely a shadow of a higher reality. Truly, we are living in a virtual reality — a kind of software construct. That's why it's vital not to take things *too* seriously down here. See the *Faith* chapter.

whatever you *think* about, you will *do*

The ancestor of every action is a thought.
— Emerson

You are constantly in a state of becoming.   And you do become what you think!
— Mary B. Crowe

Whatever you dwell on, you will eventually do. We can't help it; we were *made* that way. We are spiritual beings currently having a physical experience, and we are constantly devising in one realm to create in another. It is our *nature* to be creators.

Take great care in what you think about, especially things which are temptations. If you nourish your thoughts, they will become too big for you to control. There will be few and faint prior warning signals for that threshold, and once you've crossed it, it's too late. Stamp out early (if not immediately) your bad thoughts.

whatever you *do*, you will *become*

First we form habits, then they form us.   Conquer your bad habits, or they'll eventually conquer you.
— Dr. Rob Gilbert

There are habits which are bad, generically. Habits of laziness, envy, substance abuse, and pride, for example. Squash these early! Avoid anybody who succumbs to them.

Then, there are habits which are neutral, but not necessarily right for *you*:

> *It's no good running a pig farm badly for thirty years while saying, "Really I was meant to be a ballet dancer." By that time, pigs will be your style.*
> — Quentin Crisp

Being a pig farmer isn't a bad habit for those naturally pig farmers. (Jimmy Dean was destined to raise pigs, which is great for those who love bacon!) But for anybody else, it is a bad habit. This is why it's important to early on understand a fitting purpose for your Life, so you don't waste decades raising pigs instead.

My high-school principal put considerable pressure on me to choose a career in my Senior year, but fortunately I had the strength of character to resist. I simply had no idea what I wanted to do. (I knew that college wasn't yet right for me, because it would force me to choose *some* career path.) I'm grateful to my parents for not pushing me into college right after high-school. I didn't want to begin doing something that wasn't right for me, and thus risk becoming somebody else. I'd always sensed my own purpose was unique, and that it wouldn't easily fit in a common occupational cubbyhole.

That summer, I had the idea to begin a very interesting small business which had never been tried in my area. Three years later, after many valuable experiences which did wonders for my maturity and understanding, I sold it for a decent sum and then (with generous parental support) went to university for my BBA.

Take plenty of time in deciding what you shall do, as in doing that you will *become* that. Go to job fairs. Hang around law firms and factories and offices and farms. See what different careers are really like. Travel. Shadow apprentice for a couple weeks different jobs.

you run your day or your day runs you

Sure, some things are out of your control, but you are still in control about how you feel and react to these uncontrollables.

> *[My friend] prevented me from running to catch a subway, "I don't run for trains."*
> *Snub your destiny. . . . In refusing to run to catch trains, I have felt the true value of elegance and aesthetics in behavior, a sense of being in control of my time, my schedule, and my life. Missing a train is only painful if you run after it!*

You stand above the rat race and the pecking order, not outside of it, if you do so by choice.
   You have far more control over your life if you decide on your criterion by yourself.
   Be aggressive: be the one to resign, if you have the guts. It is far more difficult to be a loser in a game you set up yourself.
      — Nasim Nicholas Taleb, *The Black Swan*, p. 297

Let each keep up his Dignity. Let each deed of a man in its degree, though he be not a king, be worthy of a prince, and let his action be princely within due limits. Sublime in action, lofty in thought, in all things like a king, at least in merit if not in might. For true kingship lies in spotless rectitude, and he need not envy greatness who can serve as a model of it.
      — Balthasar Gracian, *The Art of Worldly Wisdom*

eyes + ears vs. 1 mouth = a 4:1 input:output ratio
Drawing on my fine command of the English language, I said nothing.
      — Robert Benchley

Never pass up a good chance to shut up.
      — anonymous

Have you noticed that those who talk the most have the least to say, but when quiet ones open their mouths something very wise is uttered? This is no fluke. The younger you are, the more you need to look, listen, and keep quiet. When you do speak, it should generally be to ask questions. A few presidents ago you were still crapping in your diapers, so it's unlikely that you're now the Oracle of Delphi. Nothing personal; I recall when I was young enough to know everything.

worry never solves anything
F.E.A.R. False Expectations Appearing Real.

Worry is always too early or too late — never on time.

All men should try to learn before they die what they are running from, and to, and why.
      — James Thurber

How will you discern the difference between a genuine fear and worry? A genuine fear will be at least somewhat constructive, and will occur in time for you to do something about it. The rest is mostly likely just worry. I have a friend who had taken worry into the realm of paranoia, and it took years and thousands of miles of western state travel to find the ideal hermit property. He had forgotten to live Life, if he ever knew at all. (I once asked this owner of a bunker home how much more effectively he could possibly prepare for the collapse of civilization. He had no answer to that.)

Whatever you're worried about may never happen, and *then you will later wish you'd lived fully*.

Even if what you were worried about *does* happen . . . and **then you will later wish you'd lived fully**.

The answer is clear: live fully every day. There really is no choice in the matter! Dale Carnegie's book *How To Stop Worrying And Start Living* is a must-read classic, available at any library or used-book store.

"Recognise when Things are ripe, and then enjoy them."
The works of nature all reach a certain point of maturity; up to that they improve, after that they degenerate.
— Balthasar Gracian, *The Art of Worldly Wisdom*

"Drain Nothing to the Dregs, neither good nor ill. "
A sage once reduced all virtue to the golden mean. Push right to the extreme and it becomes wrong: press all the juice from an orange and it becomes bitter. Even in enjoyment never go to extremes.
— Balthasar Gracian, *The Art of Worldly Wisdom*

accomplishment is what creates happiness
Happiness is not the same thing as just having a good day (or lack of a bad one). Such is merely contentment. If you want to be happy, then daily *accomplish* something. (The late Jeff Cooper taught me this.) Winning in Vegas doesn't really bring happiness, at least not the long-lasting kind. An accomplishment, however, *does* last. Learning a language or a musical instrument, wooing the girl of your dreams, building a boat, designing your house, going on your first African safari, etc. will leave you with a glow of pride.

Things won are done; joy's soul lies in the doing.
— Shakespeare

happiness is not the same thing as joy
Joy is a *spiritual* condition regardless of happiness from accomplishment. Happiness derives from what you've *done*. Joy derives from who you've *become* (which is related to what you've been doing all that time). It's a lifelong growth process, with many stages and setbacks. True joy is possible in even the worst of conditions.

Some concentration camp Christian prisoners were actually joyful. (Corrie Ten Boom, for example. Read *The Hiding Place*.)

The Taoist sages said, *"Perfect happiness is the absence of happiness."* It means that those who seek happiness as its own end will not find it, for happiness is the by-product of other things (such as accomplishment, personal growth, giving of yourself, etc.). But, relying on external happenings to "make" you "happy" is just begging for disappointment.

5 simple rules to be happy

❶ Free your heart from hatred.
❷ Free your mind from worries.
❸ Live simply.
❹ Give more.
❺ Expect less.

all things permissible; not all things profitable

A paraphrasing of Apostle Paul from I Corinthians 6:12. Look, you could find someplace on the planet in which nobody cared *what* you did to/for yourself (*i.e.*, permissibility), but such would not necessarily be *profitable* to you. Many 1960s hippies avoided regular bathing (it "cramped" their "style"), but doctors treating their odd skin diseases had to consult medieval textbooks to recognize symptoms not seen in centuries.

Recreational drugs fall into this area to my way of thinking. You can move to Holland or Thailand for the permissive drug culture, but would a life getting high truly be *profitable* for you? If you take drugs, what is it that you are really trying to seek or avoid? And at what cost?

do you want what they have?

If not, then why do what *they* do? Pretty simple, huh? They have what they have by having done — repeatedly — what they did, just like anybody else.

your Life is unique and solely for *you* to live

I always wanted to be somebody, but I should have been more specific.
— Lily Tomlin

We forfeit three-fourths of ourselves to be like other people.
— Schopenhauer

Nobody can be exactly like me.
Sometimes even I have trouble doing it.
— Tallulah Bankhead

When being yourself seems to take effort, that's when you know that you're not only on the right path, but growing.

Often, people attempt to live their lives backwards; they try to have more things, or more money, in order to do more of what they want, so they will be happier. The way it works is the reverse. You must first be who you really are, then do what you need to do, in order to have what you want.
— Margaret Young

A man's true delight is to do the things he was made for.
— Marcus Aurelius

what is it that you are trying to *do?*
Always check your actions with that Question To Self: *What is it that I am trying to do?* Know your goals and keep on track.

constantly examine your own motives
Then ask yourself, *Why do I really want to do that?*

The last temptation is the greatest treason:
To do the right deed for the wrong reason.
— T.S. Eliot

it's likely not about *you*
If you are naturally a suspicious or sensitive type, this will be a difficult maxim to trust. Self-referential people have a very hard time not believing that others' seemingly altered behaviors are not about themselves. For your own mental health, you will have to begin to choose to believe that "it's likely not about *you*." If a friend hasn't called you in a while, it's likely that they are busy and not because their feelings toward you have changed.

if you don't know where you're going, any road will . . .
Ours is a world where people don't know what they want and are willing to go through hell to get it.
— Don Marquis

On the sea of Life, you can hoist your own sails and take the tiller, or you can be a piece of driftwood. If you don't grow a mast and hoist your own sails, then being driftwood is decided for you. The longer you wait, the more difficult it is to make your own course.

You are a life manager, and your objective is to actively manage your life in a way that generates high-quality results. You are your own most important resource for making your life work. Success is a moving target that must be tracked and continually pursued.

Effective life management means you need to require more of yourself in your grooming, self-control, emotional management, interaction with others, work performance, dealing with fear, and in every other category you can think of. You must approach this task with the most intense commitment, direction and urgency you can muster.

The key to managing your life is to have a strategy. If you have a clear-cut plan, and the courage, commitment and energy to execute that strategy, you can flourish. If you don't have a plan, you'll be a stepping stone for those who do. You can also help yourself as a life manager if you manage your expectations. If you don't require much of yourself, your life will be of poor quality. If you have unrealistic standards, then you are adding to your difficulties.

— from Dr. Phil's Life Law #7, www.drphil.com/articles/article/44

anticipate, then participate
Invaluable advice when you are involved in some group setting. Find an oar and begin to *row*. If you cannot find an oar, *make* one.

mind your own business
This becomes pretty easy once you've engaged yourself in your own Life with purpose. Busybodies typically have no Life of their own, and anybody else's is more interesting.

the height of maturity is taking responsibility for yourself
I would say that people's biggest problem is that they refuse to take responsibility for their actions. Then, they look to politicians for "*hope and change*". Be a grown-up!

things are usually not what they seem
Half the work that is done in the world
Is to make things appear what they are not.
— E.R. Beadle

Makeup, wigs, cologne, breast implants, outward displays of wealth, etc. (I think of Gary Larson's cartoon about the cat arching its back to appear larger than it is. The dog cries out, "*Trickery!*")

very carefully choose your battles
Pick battles big enough to matter; small enough to win.
— Jonathan Kozol

Don't go *looking* for trouble. There is plenty enough in this world to find you on its own, and you'll need your strength for that. Thoreau wrote, "*A man is rich in proportion to the number of things he can afford to let alone.*" This is a happy result of not picking fights and minding your own business. Your goal is to not allow the world to sweep you up in its nonsense, foolishness, and lies. Your goal is to be let alone to accomplish your own Life's purpose.

there is evil, generally because of lazy, good people
The world is a dangerous place to live, not because of the people who are evil, but because of the people who don't do anything about it.
— Albert Einstein

There is filth and untidiness because of people too lazy to clean house. It's the same in society: while we'll never eradicate evil any more than dirt, we must keep evil generally at bay.

life means struggling, grief, and suffering
"You mock my pain!"
"Life IS pain, Princess. Anyone who says differently is selling something."
— from the movie *Princess Bride*

The sooner you accept that, the sooner you can begin to place sorrow in its proper perspective. Suffering differs per individual, but *nobody* has a pain-free time down here. Without suffering, there would be no personal growth.

Nobody, as long as he moves about among the chaotic currents of life, is without trouble.
— Carl Jung

A problem is a chance for you to do your best.
— Duke Ellington

Every problem, trial, or tribulation is an opportunity for growth, learning, and victory. How dull and flat Life would be without sudden challenges?

"It's not what you know, but who you know!"

If you are not (yet) a "people-person" then you'd better get cracking and become more of one quickly! Only people matter. Not things, not events, and not even ideas. All of them exist to serve people. If you're not useful to somebody, then you're just useless.

You cannot succeed by yourself, only exist by yourself.

"The price of success is responsibility." Winston Churchill

In the final analysis, the one quality that all successful people have . . . is the ability to take on responsibility.
— Michael Korda

A man may fail many times but he isn't a failure until he begins to blame somebody else.
— J. Paul Getty

As you own up to the responsibility that is (or should be) yours, you will learn and grow from it. That's the only way to become a Man.

You cannot dodge responsibility for how and why your life is the way it is. If you don't like your job, you are accountable. If you are overweight, you are accountable. If you are not happy, you are accountable. You are creating the situations you are in and the emotions that flow from those situations.

Don't play the role of victim, or use past events to build excuses. It guarantees you no progress, no healing, and no victory. You will never fix a problem by blaming someone else. Whether the cards you've been dealt are good or bad, you're in charge of yourself now.

Every choice you make — including the thoughts you think — has consequences. When you choose the behavior or thought, you choose the consequences. If you choose to stay with a destructive partner, then you choose the consequences of pain and suffering. If you choose thoughts contaminated with anger and bitterness, then you will create an experience of alienation and hostility. When you start choosing the right behavior and thoughts — which will take a lot of discipline — you'll get the right consequences.
— from Dr. Phil's Life Law #2, www.drphil.com/articles/article/44

all the mistakes have *already* been made!

Experience is a good teacher, but her fees are very high.
— W.R. Inge

Good judgment comes from experience, and experience comes from bad judgment.
— Will Rogers

Experience is the name everyone gives to their mistakes.
 — Oscar Wilde

About 100 billion people have previously lived and died on this planet before you ever came along. They've not only made all the mistakes *for* you, they described them in thousands of books, letters, interviews, poems, and essays. If you really want to "reinvent the square wheel" yourself, go ahead, but Life is too short to repeat proven mistakes. Meaning, 80 trips around the sun is not enough time to learn and recover from your own nonoriginal mistakes. As they say, "*Experience is priceless; it is paid for by youth.*"

Life must be lived forward, but can only be understood backwards.
 — Kierkegaard

We go through Life backwards, seeing only where we've been. Learn from those who have "*been there — done that.*" You must constantly learn from other people's mistakes. Use their 20/20 vision hindsight as your 20/20 vision *foresight*. Read biographies, in particular. Quotations. Self-help books. How-to-succeed books. Basically, you're looking for shortcuts in the form of models.

don't be *too* hard on yourself!
It is not fitting that I should give myself pain, for I have never intentionally given pain even to another.
 — Marcus Aurelius, Meditations, VIII:42

You will not operate with perfection and seemless grace. You are going to screw up, and repeatedly on some things. Learn, grow, move on.

"*Lies believed are not knowledge.*" (Red Beckman)
Fortunately I read this in my mid-20s. Most powerful! It's saved me a *lot* of wasted time and energy.

The greatest obstacle to discovery is not ignorance — it is the illusion of knowledge.
 — Daniel J. Boorstin

What passes for knowledge in this country is astoundingly based on lies. Money, taxes, health, law, politics — most of it a lie sold to a gullible and lazy public. America lives by the urban legend. Before the Internet, you had to *chance* upon the right book or informed acquaintance to awaken you.

Today, there is no excuse to remain misinformed about anything. True knowledge is out there for the taking. And, by the way, you won't find knowledge and education in public schools. You'll have to become educated through your own independent study.

if you *want* to believe, beware of *having* to later
Meaning, be very cognizant about your own vested interests. What things do you *want* to believe? Caution! Where you want to believe is where you are vulnerable of being fooled or defrauded.

what is the signal:noise ratio?
No signal (truth) is without noise (untruth). While there certainly is truth on the Internet, the signal:noise ratio is horrendously bad. The lower the ratio, the better your filter must be. Confirm all alleged "information" from multiple independent sources.

the map is not the territory
Many have said this. It's wise, regardless of source. The map is "analogous to" the territory, and no map can be as good as the actual territory. Maps suffice until . . . they do not. As long as you keep in mind the limitations of maps and the 100% truthfulness of the territory, your perceived map information will be valid.

what is its *nature?*
People are not complex. They operate from love, hate, anger, laziness, fear, greed, gluttony, pride, guilt, or envy. Truly, that's about it. (Notice that *love* is the only worthy motivation, and that all else is some variant of anti-love.) While it's harsh to declare most people a combination of stupid, lazy, cowardly, or evil — I stand by it.

After many years of experience in all types of social encounters, I can say that people much more often act from fear vs. boldness, envy vs. admiration, greed vs. generosity, deception vs. honesty, laziness vs. industry. They will rarely expose their true motives for doing anything, because their true motives are often pretty shameful. Understand *what* motivates a person, and you can then understand his actions. (Generally, fear and envy are the most likely. Pride and laziness would be next. A good case can be made that all of the anti-love motivations stem from fear and pride. Find out what somebody is *afraid* of and *proud* of, and it likely explains all else.)

Remember the scene in *Silence of the Lambs* where Hannibal Lecter is trying to make Agent Starling understand her hunted serial killer? *"What does he do, this man you seek? What is his nature?"* Starling replies in desperation, *"He kills women!"* Lecter corrects her,

"*No, that is incidental! He covets!*" With that vital psychological clue, Starling soon broke the case.

People rarely operate outside their core nature, at least not for very long. Their nature is what makes them *themselves*. Discover their nature, and you will then understand what model they are using in Life. For example, once you understand that governments *steal* (from greed and laziness), and then *lie* (from fear) to cover up their thefts, it will be difficult for politicians to fool you.

what is the correct *context?*

Nothing can be properly understood outside its proper context. For example, if you heard that in a footrace Jones came in second and Smith next to last, you'd think that Jones beat Smith. The missing context is that they raced only *each other*, which means that Smith actually came in *first*. While the first account is *technically* true, it is *deceptive* because of hidden context.

I once grossly misjudged a very nice person. A lady friend of mine had a gal pal who was overweight. Without understanding her context, I assumed her to be too lazy to work out. Turns out that she was married to a physically abusive husband who was immensely strong. So, she gained weight so that he could no longer throw her across the room. *Context.* Understand it before you judge.

there is no "coincidence"

There are mystic synergies and fateful intersections in life that cannot be the work of coincidence. When they occur, they pierce the soul with an illuminating flash of understanding. At such times, it is impossible not to see the hand of God in them, for blind chance cannot explain otherwise. The odds of random causality are simply too great.
— Mike Vanderboegh

We live in four dimensions (3-D, plus time), but at least *six more* dimensions are mathematically provable. Such can be called the "supernatural" or "paranormal" or the "spirit realm." It has been proven that you can influence things to occur just by *thinking* about them, and that thoughts can be transmitted to others. There is no longer any scientific doubt about this.

Example: I once lost track of for 13 years a girl I knew from college. Then, one day I thought of a funny line we both used to laugh about. I again wondered what had happened to her. *The same week,* I got an email from her. (She'd been thinking of me recently and finally tracked me down through my books.) The subject line of her email had the very words we used to laugh about. Kinda spooky!

This sort of thing has often happened to me. Years ago, when I lived on a rustic ranch without phone, my friends would say, "*It doesn't really matter that you have no phone. All we have to do is think about you, and you call us in a day or two.*"

There is no "coincidence" — only other-dimensional realities affecting our temporal 4-D realm.

> *Coincidences are spiritual puns.*
> — Gilbert Keith Chesterton

there is only "carrot" and "stick"

Motivation falls into one of two categories: pleasure and pain. Know well your own carrots and sticks, and those of others.

don't play at work, and don't work at play

Work and play are different, and have their proper times. Discern when such are, and either work hard or play hard.

everything is negotiable

Human institutions and conventions and standards are created by very malleable and changing beings. Nearly all prices and all terms are negotiable. If human beings are involved — very, very little is "set in stone". If something seems to be "nonnegotiable" then you're not (yet) negotiating with the right person.

there is no "scarcity" — only scarcity at a certain *price*

If you are willing to pay enough, nearly anything can be had. Was there food and water in New Orleans after Katrina? Sure, but not in supermarkets at supermarket prices. Fresh drinking water was selling on the street for $20/gallon. Meaning, at the right price, it was not "scarce." You could drink all you could afford.

Example: the so-called "health care crisis" in America. There was no such crisis before "ObamaCare". True, 15% of people had decided to spend their money on things other than health care insurance, but that was their *choice*. (The fact that such insurance is expensive is a result of government interference in the market.)

broke is a state of *finances* — poverty is a state of *mind*

If you equalized the wealth of all people, in several years the previously poor would be poor again, the previously rich would be rich again. Physical wealth derives from metaphysical wealth — from *thinking* and *acting*. This is why lottery winners lose all their money and then return to the trailer-park. This is why millionaires who go bust come back and remake their fortunes.

needs (necessities) vs. wants (luxuries)

They are not the same things, although people generally confuse their wants as "needs." Humans actually have very few true needs according to Maslow's Hierarchy of Needs. Your real needs are air, water, food, shelter, and some human company. The rest are wants. Necessities are finite; luxuries are infinite. Learn to limit your wants, else your wants will limit you.

almost every "requirement" in U.S. law is *voluntary*

This is *America*, not Russia. The Government cannot force you do things that are required in other countries, because your rights are recognized in the Constitution. But, it is up to you to learn what these rights are. The Government won't tell you!

If you squeeze the truth out of the regulations on such "mandatory" things as "income" taxes (www.losthorizons.com), vaccinations, "selective service", etc. you may be *very* surprised what you learn. The Internet is the place to begin, but beware the low signal:noise ratio. Fact-check from all angles!

> **Neo:**   *The Matrix?*
> **Morpheus:**   *Do you want to know what it is?*
>   <Neo nods his head.>
> **Morpheus:**   *The Matrix is everywhere, it is all around us. Even now, in this very room. You can see it when you look out your window, or when you turn on your television. You can feel it when you go to work, or when go to church or when you pay your taxes. It is the world that has been pulled over your eyes to blind you from the truth.*
> **Neo:**   *What truth?*
> **Morpheus:**   *That you are a slave, Neo. Like everyone else, you were born into bondage, born inside a prison that you cannot smell, taste, or touch. A prison for your mind. (long pause, sighs) Unfortunately, no one can be told what the Matrix is. You have to see it for yourself. This is your last chance. After this, there is no turning back.* <In his left hand, Morpheus shows a blue pill.>
> **Morpheus:**   *You take the blue pill and the story ends. You wake in your bed and believe whatever you want to believe. (A red pill is shown in his other hand) You take the red pill and you stay in Wonderland and I show you how deep the rabbit-hole goes. (Long pause; Neo begins to reach for the red pill) Remember — all I am offering is the truth, nothing more.*
>   <Neo takes the red pill and swallows it with a glass of water.>

CONCEPTS & RULES

These are mini-models, and well-proven over centuries.

The whole world, except for the few awakened individuals, lives from imaginations, which are taken as realities.
The Truth is always introducing itself to us. We fail to see it, because we are looking the other way.
Others can present a truth to you, but no one can confirm it to you but yourself.
Almost all of what is called human enthusiasm is merely a frantic distraction from a sense of inner emptiness.
Your perfect teacher is named Daily Experience.
You need not desperately try to be good, but work to be real, which alone is good.
If you are really in charge of yourself, no one else can possibly take charge of you.
The greatest doctor on earth is honesty, for where there is pure honesty, there can be no pain.
You must be willing to be wrong in the world's eyes, if you are ever to be right in your own.
    — Vernon Howard, *Pathways to Perfect Living*

if you don't ask, the answer is always "*No*"

Take a chance, always. You've nothing to lose but perhaps a bit of pride. And, even if you were turned down, that was a worthy trade-off for your now lessened fear.

take what you want, but *pay* for it

An old Spanish proverb. It doesn't mean to *steal* what you want, because stealing implies willful nonpayment. It means to indeed seek your dreams, but only if you will pay their cost.

Everything I did in my life that was worthwhile I caught hell for.
    — Earl Warren

Things that are worthwhile have a high cost to them. This is just normal. You don't get BMWs for Buick prices.

"*Take what you can use and let the rest go by.*"
— Ken Kesey

Notice that he didn't say take what you *want*, but what you can *use*. Begin to transform your wants into *useful* wants.

The rest? Why take it if it's not useful? Let it go by.

"*Expensive is when the product is not worth the money.*"
This was said by a president of the optics firm Leica, which makes about the best binoculars in the world.

TANSTAAFL — There Ain't No Such Thing As A Free Lunch

Coined by sci-fi author Robert Heinlein in his superb novel *The Moon Is A Harsh Mistress*, TANSTAAFL is one of Life's most important rules. It applies to every sphere: social, economic, and physical. "*There is no free lunch*" in Latin is:

NULLUM GRATUITUM PRANDIUM

What might be free monetarily (*e.g.*, staying over at a friend's house) is not free in other realms (privacy, convenience, schedule, required social graces, etc.). Favors are never "free" and naturally operate from implied reciprocity. Understand the *true* cost of things beforehand. (If it seems "free" then you're not thinking deeply enough into the situation.)
Often, the cheapest way to enjoy something is simply to pay money for it. It's clean, and leaves no further expectations.

pay now . . . truly *enjoy* much more later
however, enjoy now . . . truly *pay* much more later

This is describes "delayed gratification of wants." Sure, you can have nearly anything you want now, but at what higher cost? Convenience and immediacy *always* sell at a premium. This applies to cars and all other depreciating things which people foolishly pay interest on. If, however, you can wait and save/invest your money, you will make interest vs. pay interest — allowing you to buy *more* later of what you want.
It also applies to romance. Guys, if you meet the girl you know you should marry, try not to sleep with her immediately. Wait. Wait a long time, preferably until your marriage night. You will have much better sex throughout your married life.

opportunity costs

These are hidden costs to your choices. When you spend time on a less important project, a more important project can not get done at the same time. (Yes, later, but not as early as it *could* have been.)
Beware especially of "free" things. Nothing is "free". Everything has an opportunity cost. Search for it; it's there. It may be hidden or delayed, but it's there.

diminishing marginal returns (DMR)

Also called marginal returns. This is a term to explain when something has passed its peak in "utility" (*i.e.,* enjoyment, usefulness, convenience, financial advantage, etc.) Your most pleasurable activity, if done long enough, *will* reach a point of diminishing marginal returns. Biking, eating, sex, TV, whatever.

I remember a scene from a WWII novel in which an interrogated Allied agent had been denied water for some time. Finally, he was brought to see an *SS* officer in his office. The officer seemed cordial and concerned for the prisoner's well-being. On his desk was a pitcher of ice-cold water. *"Have a glass of water,"* the officer said. The prisoner gratefully drank it. *Would you like another?* Certainly. Then, with a wicked gleam in his eye, the *SS* officer demanded, *"Have another."* The Allied agent then realized that water, just moments ago his salvation, was about to be used as a form of torture. Water had just reached its point of diminishing marginal returns.

Socially, the concept of DMR is important, as any professional comedian will tell you: *Leave 'em wanting more.* This is vital to understand when dealing with women, especially when you think you've met "the One." (There's no such woman, but I'll explain that later.) Any initial attraction can be ruined by coming on too strong or too quickly or too often. Once you've reached DMR with a woman, it is *very* difficult to regain her former interest. This is because women operate by hope and fantasy. If you chase her too hard, you reach DMR and you pop the bubble of her fantasy and curiosity. (Leave her wanting more, remember? I'll discuss this in greater depth later. *Heh,* now I'm leaving *you* with wanting more!)

the 80/20 Rule (also called "Pareto's Law")

The "trivial many" vs. the "vital few" applies to nearly anything. Basically, you'll derive 80% of your earnings from 20% of your customers. You talk 80% of your time with 20% of your friends. You can get into 80% of physical condition with 20% of the work.

The *converse* is also important: that last 20% of your income comes from 80% of your clients, so they are not the most productive use of your time. We are all limited by Time. So, we must use it efficiently. (Author Taleb of *The Black Swan* makes the point that this law is often expressed even more skewed, such as 50/1 or 97/20.)

Here's an example. Let's say there are five different money-making projects you could do. Each one takes the same amount of time to generate the same amount of income. You could devote all your time to any one of them, but *why*? The input:output ratio is not perfectly linear. Output is peaking after 20% of input because DMR kicks in.

Idea: do *all five things*, but at a 20% level (*i.e.*, 5 x 20% of time = 100% of time), vs. just one thing 100% of time. Your input is still 100%, but your output is *400%* (5 x 80%). This is how I got mostly A's in college. Since a 90% was just as good an A as 100%, I redirected my study time to classes needing to bump up from 88%, and spent less time on classes where I already had a 94% average.

The 80/20 Rule also touches on the increasing price of approaching perfection. The closer you get, the more each additional step costs. Is a $60,000 BMW actually twice the car of a $30,000 Buick? No. Doubling the price gets you a 97% car vs. an 85% car. Perhaps that extra $30,000 for the BMW will pay for itself in social prestige (for business), or for your own contentment. But, as a *car*, the BMW isn't worth the extra coin.

Whatever percentage of perfection you desire is your choice, but the 80/20 Rule will keep you grounded as to the cost. Most things don't require 99.9% or even 90% perfection. 80% is generally good enough, and can be afforded or done *today*.

For example, I've been five times so far to Africa on hunting safaris. Flying to Johannesburg First Class is about $11,000. For 20% of that, I flew fly Economy. If I'd insisted on flying First Class, I could have afforded only a single trip and wouldn't have gained the experience of the four other safaris (and the pleasure of that First Class flight would have worn off).

bell-curve distribution

Few things in Life are evenly distributed. (You probably already know that.) Most are clumped towards the middle or the average, and the rest (the very high and the very low) tapers off. Take IQ, for example. A score of 100 is considered normal, but 25% will score between 90-99 and 25% will score between 101-110. Thus, the "normal range is from 90-110. Slow learners (22% of people) score from 70-89IQ and bright normal (23%) from 111-130IQ. Retarded are 3% of people (under 70 IQ) and only 2% are gifted with 130+IQs.

If this were plotted out on a graph, the line would look like the outline of a bell, hence the name "bell curve distribution." If somebody has what is called "*2-sigma intelligence*" it means they are two "standard-deviations" higher than the normal 100IQ, and are brighter than about 92% of the population.

Author Taleb of *The Black Swan* cautions us, however, to apply this model only to certain things. Much of life doesn't fit there.

Occam's Razor

Amongst answers which all satisfactorily explain a question, choose the most *simple* one. It tends to be correct. Meaning, Life is usually not as complex as we often make it out to be. Start with simple explanations. You can always later add any necessary complexity.

Law of Unintended Consequences

As clever as you may believe you are, nobody is capable of envisioning the ripple effect of their actions. The movie *The Butterfly Effect* is all about this concept. The lesson is that you cannot know or even predict with confidence the effects of what you do (or do *not* do).

Law of Comparative Advantage

Nobody can do everything better/faster/cheaper than everybody else. Meaning, somebody in the world has a "comparative advantage" over you, or your business or your industry. It's why you buy oranges from Florida instead of from Minnesota, and cars from Japan instead of Detroit. Full-color hardback books are often printed in the Orient. Comparative advantage is what makes for an economy, especially an efficient one. (Distance is no longer any real handicap. Shipping is inexpensive, and information travels nearly free.)

People tend to specialize, and that foments "division of labor" and industry. This is a Good Thing. Those who whine about "lost jobs" overseas are those who foolishly had only one comparative advantage of their own to lose. (While I do have sympathy for the unemployed American shoe factory worker, he had a decade of warning that the Orient would soon be competing for our domestic manufacturing jobs. He should have gotten busy acquiring *new* skills for new comparative advantages.)

Whoever thought of outsourcing American software tech-support to *India* was very clever. Indians are very competent technically, work for 20% of our wages, they speak English (of a sort), and work while we're asleep. They have a comparative advantage over software techs in California.

Necessity goods will increasingly be made overseas. Luxury goods, too. Americans have allowed their own taxation and regulations to price their products out of the market. Any comparative advantage any American worker still has is his local *presence*. Thus, he should start to focus on that which can be supplied only by his actual presence. *Services*. Some examples: massage therapy, sales, mechanical repair, home remodeling, etc.

So, what will be *your* comparative advantages?

I'll tell you who simply do *not* understand the Law of Comparative Advantage: American women under 30 who want a career *and* children. They are absolutely foolish to embark on a career first. Why? Because they forsake their comparative advantage of youth, looks, and fertility. It'd be like a college star quarterback about to be drafted into the NFL saying, *"No, thanks, but I think I'll finish law school, open up a practice until my mid-30s, and then come back to play ball."* The scouts would laugh.

Yet that's precisely what most American women do. Then, when they're 38, it dawns on them that the career world wasn't as rewarding as they'd been sold, and that being a stay-at-home mom now sounds pretty good. Well, just how many men prefer a bitter, 38 y/o corporate woman (just 10 years from menopause) over a 25 y/o hottie (who can have more and healthier children, and recover better from pregnancies)?

"But few 25 y/o hotties want to get married and have children!" Nonetheless, there remains a demand for young, pretty, marriageable women. Trouble is, the *supply* no longer exists here. Whenever goods become scarce, substitutes emerge. And they have: *foreign brides.* South American, Asian, and Eastern European women are often gorgeous, well-educated (certainly much better than our own vapid hotties), and *grateful* for a loyal, loving, and employed man. And American men are quickly realizing that their comparative advantage (citizenship, income, wealth) outweigh being 50 y/o, bald, and slightly nerdy (any of which will *repel* American women who never outgrew high-school social politics). I personally know of several American men very happily married to foreign ladies. (And some not.)

Maureen Dowd and her ilk cannot stand it. They had their warning with Taylor Caldwell's *On Growing Up Tough* on how/why Feminism was a raw deal for women. Now, with their looks half gone and their wombs dried up, *now* they will finally condescend dating a stable guy who isn't Randy Red Porsche? Gee, talk about *leftovers!*

Some comparative advantages, once lost, cannot be regained. (Bummer, Maureen!) That is *Life*. However, as long as you capitalized on them *then*, and continue to nourish the newly emerging ones, you'll never be behind the curve.

A NYC female corporate executive read the above and replied:

I understand you are writing for a male audience but my view is that there are two sides to this. Most of the women I know are fully aware that the corporate world is not a particularly satisfying or rewarding place to be, but they feel they have no other choice because approximately 99.95% of men are incompetent and/or untrustworthy. They are afraid of getting involved with someone who will leave them or be unable to adequately provide for the family, and then if this happens once the woman is older and has kids, very few desirable employers want to hire a woman in her 30s with little or no prior experience. If men had their act together a little bit better, more women would reevaluate the choice to marry early!

She has a point, but my view is that the human race being pretty substandard offers very few quality men *or* women. Women need to stop having the children of oafs and morons, and start demanding quality men — even if this boycott means being single for a while. Men generally will only become as good as they must, so women need to demand more in their men. (However, men *do* need to quit stooping for sluts and Man themselves up to deserve a Lady.)

One of your main reasons for success will be to understand *your* comparative advantages. (Yes, advantages — plural. you can and should have more than just one.) The entire world is competing with you for food, fuel, housing, business, friends, and women. Why should anybody choose *you*? For *anything*? What can *you* now do better/cheaper/faster than others?

quality always costs more, and is usually worth it

There are three things a business can offer: quality goods, quality service, low prices. Pick any *two*. In the hunting culture there is a pithy saying: "*Only a rich man can afford a poor rifle scope, because he can pay for a second hunt after his first one was ruined.*"

follow the money

Remember those anti-love human motivations? Greed is one of the most powerful, and following the money of any seemingly complex issue is usually a sure way of unraveling it.

Gresham's Law

"*Bad money drives out good money* (from circulation)." Meaning, people will tender the minimum value possible in any transaction. This is why 90% silver dimes, quarters, half-dollars and dollars had disappeared from circulation by the 1970s. Why spend an intrinsically valuable *silver* quarter when a copper-nickel slug is just as widely accepted?

You're a young man, so you probably have never seen a silver coin accidentally in circulation. OK, well how about a *copper* penny? Pennies minted before 1982 were mostly copper. Before long, the penny became worth *less* than its copper content, and people began to remove them from circulation and selling them to copper smelters. (After 1981, they've been zinc with a copper wash.)

Well, don't despair that you missed out on the copper penny chance. Today's penny *zinc* content is worth *1.3¢*! Either the Government will soon go to the plastic penny, or just dump the penny altogether. Gresham's Law. (Oh, and a nickel is worth 9¢.)

Our dollar has lost so much value since 2005, that it is now worth less than the *Canadian* dollar! Look at any older book; it'll have two prices: US$19.95/$24.95 in Canada. Soon, it'll be the reverse.

"Watch your premises and check your conclusions."

Good advice from Ayn Rand. A faulty premise will take you off-course from reality. And, even when beginning from a valid premise, you can still veer off-course.

the difference between correlation and causation

Just because A and B are somehow related (correlation: the departure of two variables from independence) does not also mean that A causes B (causation). For example, blue-eyed white cats are often deaf, but this correlation doesn't also mean that one caused the other. (Correlation and causation can happen at the same time.)

If you don't want to be fooled by "experts" then you must understand the difference between correlation and causation. Thus, you should often uncover their hidden agendas (such as who pays for their "research" and why). For example, DuPont owned the U.S. patents on Freon and other CFCs. Those patents expired by the mid-1990s, just when "ozone depletion" politics prohibited CFCs. And who was ready with the required "ozone safe" replacements? DuPont. (Mere coincidence . . .)

Understanding correlation vs. causality is an important concept regarding your emotions. Often, somebody is so disagreeable that it seems that they "make" you angry. There seems to be causality. Actually, it's usually more an issue of *correlation*. It's really up to you if you choose to become angry. The direct causality rests with you, not other people. Yes, they can *try* to "push your buttons" but you don't have to always respond as they expect you to.

once is incidence
twice is coincidence
thrice is enemy action

This is not 100% true, but close enough to live by. If something unusual happens to you *three* times, you'd better start paying close attention to it. (Also, examine if you are being your own enemy!)

If there is doubt, there is no doubt. (movie *Ronin*)

Your subconscious *will* give you necessary clues. The duty of your conscious mind is not to reject them. Life is short, and your choices are infinite. There are over 7 billion people on the planet. You can afford to be choosy, so avoid or dump questionable folks, even if you may be wrong.

mala en se crimes versus *mala prohibita* "crimes"

Not all crimes are alike in nature or in moral severity. *Mala en se* (Latin for "evil in themselves") crimes are: aggression, theft, and fraud. Rape, robbery, assault, murder, etc. are prohibited all over the world, with justifiable moral force. **There is *never* any valid excuse for committing *mala en se* crimes.** Those who do so are enemies of peace, justice, and mankind.

Mala prohibita ("wrongs prohibited") are acts that legislatures have outlawed — not by *moral* force, but through sheer political force. They are also called "victimless crimes". These vary not only from country to country, but even from state to state. (Drug laws are a perfect example.) The Libertarian Party (www.lp.org) view is that *mala prohibita* acts are *not* moral crimes deserving fines or imprisonment. This is also my view.

There is a difference between what is *unlawful* (*mala in se* acts) and what is *illegal* (*mala prohibita* acts).

A responsible 18 y/o adult should be able to buy a six-pack of beer, but it is *malum prohibita* for him to do so. A safe and prudent 80mph on the Interstate is *malum prohibita*. Not getting a building permit for your barn is *malum prohibita*. Owning a rifle too short, or a handgun too long, or any gun too quiet, or too fast is *malum prohibita*. These are political crimes, not moral crimes. Myopic regulators are like dogs looking at the pointing finger vs. the object pointed at.

All laws passed in your lifetime have been *mala prohibita*. Kinda makes you think, huh?

It is up to you to decide which *mala prohibita* to abide by or convict others of (www.fija.org).

beginning of wisdom: to call things by their right names

This is a vital part of your ongoing dedication to reality. While it may seem unpleasant or distasteful to call things correctly, to misname them is to sink into fantasyland.

when all else fails . . . read the directions!

Don't jump into something without having first listened to the designer and the engineer!

FALLACIES

A fallacy is falsehood (usually of logic) that is universally acceped as truth. What makes fallacies so harmful is that people build faulty models on them, and then rarely go back to re-evaluate the fallacious foundation of their faulty models. Fallacious foundations can always be understood by the various anti-love natures of people: hate, anger, laziness, fear, greed, gluttony, pride, guilt, or envy.

people are equal   envy
Nature will always separate human beings into strata according to such characteristics as ability, ambition, intelligence, and determination.
— Robert J. Ringer, *Looking Out For #1*, p. 221

seeing is believing   fear
You cannot depend on your eyes when your imagination is out of focus.
— Mark Twain

The fear to exercise faith is strong, yet no growth comes without faith.

there is no 3rd choice   laziness
There is always at least a *third* choice to most any situation. Very, *very* rarely is it truly "either/or." If it seems you've only two choices, then you're not thinking deeply enough.

success is a matter of luck   laziness, envy
Success is a matter of luck. Ask any failure.
— Earl Wilson

The more I practice, the luckier I get.
— Arnold Palmer

There are no "coincidences." Good fortune is either made or enhanced by creating and enjoying opportunities. A key element is to devoutly avoid anybody who seems a magnet for bad luck.

build up the weak by tearing down the strong   envy
Attempted in every society in history, including the USA.

All cries for reform come from below.
Nobody with four aces howls for a new deal.
— Mark Twain

the world "owes" you something   laziness, envy

I used to have a very good friend "A" who believed that his father gave his younger brother all the breaks while denying him. Even if such were true (which I doubt, as I knew the whole family pretty well), what did that matter? "A" let this resentment spiral into outright envy at his (harder-working) brother's success and happiness, while "A" continually moped around from job to job. He used to be a friend, but is so ashamed not to have paid back in eight years an $86 loan that he's ceased contact.

> *Don't go around saying the world owes you a living; the world owes you nothing; it was here first.*
> — Mark Twain

life "happens" to you   laziness

Not nearly as much as you think!   Your attitude is more important than what "happens" to you.

life should be fair   laziness, envy

And rainwater should be beer. It ain't. Get used to it. If you don't like your odds in life, work to better them yourself.

mistakes are bad   fear

> *There is the greatest practical benefit in making a few failures early in life.*
> — T.H. Huxley

> *Aim for success, not perfection.   Never give up your right to be wrong . . .*
> — Dr. David M. Burns

> *Mistakes are the portals of discovery.*
> — James Joyce

Mistakes are Life's most powerful teachers. They can point the way to success, if you allow them to.

> *One of the best ways to properly evaluate and adapt to the many environmental stresses in life is to simply view them as normal. The adversity and failures in our lives, if adapted to and viewed as normal corrective feedback to use to get back on target, serve to develop in us an immunity against anxiety, depression, and the adverse responses to stress.*
> — Denis Waitley

"*If I let you to do it, I have to let everybody do it.*"   envy

Envy that you thought of it at all! That line is usually a cop-out.

"*I'll do ____ when the timing is right!*"   fear

No, you won't. The timing will never be "right" because you're looking to *avoid* _____, not embrace it. If you wanted to embrace it, you would regardless of the imperfect timing. You're the type of person who bitches about the noise when opportunity knocks.

The time to start on anything is *now*. Not tomorrow, not 1 January, but right *now*. You're not guaranteed of tomorrow, *anyway*, but today you *do* have in your hands.

I had another good friend (we went back since 7th grade) who borrowed $3,000 from my mother and promptly avoided repaying it, always with the excuse that he preferred to send her the whole amount instead of smaller payments. (*I.e.*, the "timing" wasn't right.) She may have received a third of the $3,000 in drips in drabs over the years, but grew weary of it all and eventually just wrote it off as a bad debt. Had he sent just $20/month, he'd have paid her back years ago.

God is responsible for human misery   hate

Read what Jesus had to say about this in John 10:10:

> The thief [Satan] *does not come but to steal, and to kill, and to destroy. I have come that my sheep may have life, and that they may have it more abundantly.*

Because God gave free will to human beings, He knew that evil and its suffering would be an unavoidable part of that. Also, we cause our own misery much more than even random "acts of nature".

> *If the world were perfect, it wouldn't be.*
> — Yogi Berra

📁 2

THINKING, TRUTH, WISDOM, & GENIUS

Now, the Truth is more valuable than anything else on earth. This means that everything else is of less value. So, in order to get the Truth you must give up something which you now assume is more valuable. This giving up is your payment. It is like emptying a treasure chest of stones, so it might be filled with jewels.

There is a well of life-saving wisdom, but you must personally lower your bucket.

Every step toward rightness is preceded by the insight that we did not really know what assumed we did.

Knowledge often comes to us beginning with a faint whispering, which eventually turns into clear hearing.

— Vernon Howard, *Pathways to Perfect Living*

The mind of this country, taught to aim at low objects, eats upon itself.

— Emerson (1837)

False ideas may be refuted indeed by argument, but by true ideas alone are they expelled.

— Newman

I want to say something that most Americans will find uncomfortable. Having been to 47 countries in 4 continents, and studied world history and many different ways of living, I've concluded that the USA now does almost everything *wrong*. I've never seen a First World country which has so many things "bass-ackwards": the shallowness of its social life, the junk "food" it craves, the pursuit of money over personal growth, the idolatry of empty celebrities, the jeering at unconventional wisdom, and the continual destruction of young minds through coercive anc corrosive public schooling.

When America goes down a wrong road, she almost never analyzes the matter with a fresh or honest perspective. She never turns back. Instead, she picks up speed and keeps going. After 9/11, instead of arming the pilots and profiling passengers (as did the Israeli airline *El Al*), the obscene TSA gropes and radiates children and the elderly. Instead of holding the sub-prime mortgage banksters accountable in 2008, we allowed Obama and Congress to stick us with the bill. SWAT teams now raid small dairy farms who produce healthy raw milk their customers want. The IRS is about to have the power to invalidate your passport at their whim. The NSA has their Orwellian Thought Police "Utah Data Center" online since 2013, with a million square feet of computers to monitor all our emails and phone calls. Instead of allowing armed parents and teachers, there is a hysterical cry to ban "assault weapons". The feds bought 500,000,000 rounds of .40 caliber (to shoot civilians, as hollowpoints are illegal to use in war). Ayn Rand put it best: *"You can deny reality, but you can't deny the consequences of denying reality."*

We are headed for a colossal train wreck, on *everything*. On the economy, on racial and economic strife, on education, on Social Security, on our depleted soil. Instead of facing up to this early, or even just in time, Americans will continue to entertain themselves away from these critical problems. Nobody thinks anymore. The fact that you're even reading this book — *any* book — is almost a miracle as nobody reads anymore. This country is quickly going down the drain, and the ride is disguised as a waterpark slide with music and colors.

> *The men the American people admire most extravagantly are the most daring liars; the men they detest most violently are those who try to tell them the truth.*
> — H.L. Mencken

For *you*, there may be a chance. You're reading me now; you seem to care about your Life. But you will have fight hard for it. You will have to swim upstream *every* day. This is much more difficult today than when I was your age. People, quite frankly, are dumber now — and their amusements are many times more pervasive. If you will stop (or greatly reduce) your screentime distractions in order to make way for quiet study, thinking, reflection, and growth, you might be able to survive the very Rainy Decade or two ahead. There are no shortcuts, and you'll generally feel alone along the way, but here and there you will encounter kindred souls. I hope I've been one of them.

> *If there is to be an alternative to the culture of distraction, it can only be created one family at a time, by parents and citizens*

---

determined to preserve a saving remnant of those who prize memory and true learning above all else.
— Susan Jacoby, *The Age of American Unreason*

THINKING

I do not feel obliged to believe that the same God who has endowed us with sense, reason, and intellect has intended us to forego their use.
— Galileo Galilei

Think like a man of action; act like a man of thought.
— Henri Bergson

Your whole life is a series of effects, having their cause in thought — in your own thought. All conduct is made and molded by thought; all deeds, good or bad, are thoughts made visible.
— James Allen

The significant problems we face cannot be solved at the same level of thinking we were at when we created them.
— Albert Einstein

Ignorance we can correct. Stupidity is incurable.
— G.W. Ness

Anybody who has begun to think places some portion of the world in jeopardy.
— John Dewey

just because we *can* think doesn't mean that we *do* think

There is no expedient to which a man will not go to avoid the real labor of thinking.
— Thomas A. Edison

There are two ways to slide easily through life; to believe everything or to doubt everything. Both ways save us from thinking.
— Alfred Korzybski

It takes longer to think clearly than it takes to learn rifle shooting, round arm bowling, or piano playing. The great mass of people (of all classes) cannot think at all. That is why the majority never rule. They are led like sheep by the few who know that they cannot think.
— Robert Blatchford, *God and My Neighbor*, 1903

The mind is the womb of ideas. Most childless minds are not sterile, but rather victims of contraception.
— Kenneth W. Royce

A great proportion of the thoughts with which we live are not thought out by us with the evidence in hand.
— José Ortega y Gasset

All that a man does outwardly is but the expression and completion of his inward thought. To work effectively, he must think clearly; to act nobly, he must think nobly.
— William E. Channing

Beware of the half truth. You may have gotten hold of the wrong half.
— author unknown

thinking is a matter of *choice*

He who will not reason, is a bigot; he who cannot is a fool; and he who dares not is a slave.
— Sir William Drummond

It seems reasonable to suppose that idiocy is just an aberration, and that most people do make sense most of the time. But is it true? We have discovered that we very rarely make sense. Almost never. It begins to seem that making sense is a skill not unlike playing the violin. It can, of course, be done; but no one simply falls into the habit of playing the violin. Even those who can do it, do it only by deliberate design; they do not just find themselves doing it without having intended to. It requires some special focusing, a stern singleness of purpose.
— R. Mitchell, *The Underground Grammarian*

Minds are like water. It's the undisturbed, placid ones which turn stagnant.
— Kenneth W. Royce

Truth comes only to a prepared mind.
— author unknown

the power of thought

Our life is what our thoughts make of it.
— Marcus Aurelius

A man is what he thinks about all day long.
— Emerson

where thinking begins

Never ignore a gut feeling, but never believe that it's enough.
— Robert Heller, management consultant

To believe with certainty we must begin with doubting.
— Stanislaus J. Lescynski

The mind knows only
What lies near the heart.
— Norse mythology proverb

Thoughts are butterflies and a pen is the net.
— Kenneth W. Royce

thinking "versus" feeling

One cannot be trusted to feel until one has learned to think.
— Ambrose Bierce

Intense feeling too often obscures the truth.
— Harry S Truman

People don't ask for facts in making up their minds. They would rather have one good, soul-satisfying emotion than a dozen facts.
— Robert Keith Leavitt

the scientific method to find the truth

Research the question.
Form a hypothesis.
Test the hypothesis.
Draw a conclusion.

quality thinking always produces clarity

Everything that can be thought can be thought clearly.
— Ludwig Wittgenstein

The farther backward you can look, the farther forward you are likely to see.
— Winston Churchill

Reality has a bracing clarity about it. It may not be what you expected or wanted, but it's your job to comport yourself with reality — not the reverse. The iron chains of insanity start out as cobwebs. What can be swept away with the hand at the beginning later requires an acetylene torch. Stay real!

All we can do is to search for the falsity content of our best theory.
— Karl Popper

rules for brainstorming

do not criticize or censor your ideas
explore a large quantity of ideas
use an idea to build to another
invent wild, silly, and over-the-top ideas
combine two ideas for the first time, such as Art Fry's Post-It note
— Michael Powell, *Mind Games*

knowing when to stop thinking

A conclusion is the place where you got tired thinking.
— Martin H. Fischer

govern your thoughts, or they will be governed by others

The mind will be governed. If it finds no government within it will embrace whatever government offers itself from without.
— R. Mitchell, *The Underground Grammarian*

You have the right to be ignorant.
If you don't have a philosophy, one will be provided for you.
— Kenneth W. Royce

Much of causation is mental. Your thoughts are creative, and thus become realities. What you think about is what you become. The world around you is generally the physical equivalent of the world within you. A main duty in Life is to create within your own mind the mental equivalent of the Life you want to live. Imagine your ideal Life, in every respect. Hold that thought until it materializes around you. Think continually about the things you really want, and refuse to think about the things you fear or don't want.
— paraphrased from Brian Tracy's *The Great Big Book of Wisdom*

Minds are vacuums, and they *will* be filled — if not by you, then by others. Be in charge of what goes into your own mind!

TRUTH

Truths, Probabilities, Possibilities, Lies
— Thomas Jefferson's newspaper story classifications

Veritas numquam perit.   (Truth never perishes.)

Truth is what stands the test of experience.
— Einstein

To see what is front of one's nose needs a constant struggle.
— George Orwell

Truth lives a wretched life, but always survives a lie.
— author unknown

There is nothing quite so powerful in the world as an idea whose time has come.
— Victor Hugo

All truth is God's truth.
— my pastor

truth vs. "believing"

A man will do almost anything except come face to face with his silent mind.

If we have false values we get false rewards, but will not see them as such. If we have right values, we get right rewards and consciously enjoy them as such. Growth toward true values cannot occur unless there is first the loss of false values. Loss of the false makes room for the true. So, your first aim is to detect what is wrong, not to gain what is right. The true [then] comes automatically . . . If you do not have false values, you cannot have false problems.

How can you end the pain of discouragement? By seeing egotism as the cause of discouragement. Discouragement means you are face to face with the fact that you are not a dictator who can demand that results match your desires. See this, submit your ego to destruction by reality, and discouragement becomes impossible.

Habits are unconscious and mechanical, so you must make them conscious. If you have the habit of nervous haste, deliberately move slowly. This makes you uncomfortable, which forces you to observe the habit. With full awareness, it falls away.

— Vernon Howard, *Pathways to Perfect Living*

As author M.J. "Red" Beckman quips, "*Lies believed are not knowledge.*" Examine what you think you know: do you have firsthand evidence, or do you merely believe it? (Having never been to Antarctica, I do not *know* that it exists, but I do believe that it does.) On what day were you born? Ah, that is something you *believe!* Beliefs are not automatically wrong because they're beliefs, but it is good mental hygiene to recognize what you know vs. believe.

truth contains facts, but facts are not necessarily truth
The truth is more important than the facts.
— Frank Lloyd Wright

He uses statistics as a drunken man uses lamp-posts — for support rather than illumination.
— Andrew Lang

Often the surest way to convey misinformation is to tell the strict truth.
—Mark Twain

Whatever is only almost true is quite false, and among the most dangerous of errors, because being so near truth, it is the more likely to lead astray.
— Henry Ward Beecher

Ignorantia juris, quod quisque tenetur scire, neminem excusat.
Ignorance of the law, which everyone is bound to know, excuses no man.

Truth is always to be understood in its proper context. Some factual elements of truth are important, while others are not, or may even be misleading.

The truth is generally seen, rarely heard; seldom she comes in elemental purity, especially from afar; there is always some admixture of the moods of those through whom she has passed. The passions tinge her with their colours wherever they touch her, sometimes favourably, sometimes the reverse. She always brings out the disposition, therefore receive her with caution from him that praises, with more caution from him that blames. Pay attention to the intention of the speaker; you should know beforehand on what footing he comes. Let reflection assay falsity and exaggeration.
— Balthasar Gracian

there is truth in everything — especially within lies
Give a man a mask, and he'll tell you the truth.
— Oscar Wilde

A lie tells a valuable truth about the liar. God designed the universe for truth, and not even the greatest of liars can avoid communicating the truth about his own pride and insecurities. If what is said is a lie it nonetheless cannot help but form the shape around what is *not* said — the truth.

Everything's got a moral, if only you can find it.
— Lewis Carroll

For nothing is hid that shall not be made manifest, nor anything secret that shall not be known and come to light.
— Luke 8:17

truth is often (but not always!) beauty

When I am working on a problem, I never think about beauty. I think only of how to solve the problem. But when I have finished, if the solution is not beautiful, I know it is wrong.
— Buckminster Fuller

Einstein once remarked on an equation that he instantly knew was either wrong or incomplete, because it was "*ugly*".

truth is simple

Any addition to the truth subtracts from it.
— Aleksandr Solzhenitzyn

The Tax Code represents the genius of legal fiction . . . The IRS has never really known why people pay the income tax . . . The IRS encourages voluntary compliance, through FEAR.
— Jack Warren Wade Jr., former IRS officer in charge of the IRS Nationwide Revenue Officer Training Program, in his book *When You Owe The IRS*

Speaking of income taxes, did you know that the term "*income*" is nowhere defined in the Internal Revenue Code? So, what is "*income*"? Is it "all that comes in" or is it "net profits and gains"? And what does the phrase "*from whatever source derived*" mean? Learn these simple truths, and it's astounding what follows. You might start by scouring the resources of www.losthorizons.com.

truth is often difficult to say

This is because people generally don't want to hear it — especially when they *need* to hear it. Part of your dedication to reality is to promulgate (spread) the knowledge of reality. When truth remains unspoken, a lie continues to be propped up.

truth is often difficult to hear

Truth makes many appeals, not the least of which is its power to shock.
— Jules Renard

All truth passes through three stages. First, it is ridiculed, second it is violently opposed, and third, it is accepted as self-evident.
— Arthur Schopenhauer

It is precisely when people have invested in errors that they are afraid of the truth, and therefore eager to silence those who proclaim it.
— Roger Scruton

The only reason you don't know is 'cuz you don't wanna know.
— All The King's Men

One cannot have an opinion about the truth.
— P.D.Q. Bach

Every man has a right to be wrong in his opinions. But no man has a right to be wrong in his facts.
— Bernard Baruch

Most of the change we think we see in life is due to truths being in and out of favour.
— Robert Frost

I didn't say it would be easy, I just said it would be the truth.
— Morpheus, The Matrix

Humankind cannot bear very much reality.
— T.S. Eliot

If you have (according to Dr. M. Scott Peck) "*an ongoing dedication to reality at all costs*" then new truths will not be so painful for you.

Once you eliminate the impossible, whatever remains, no matter how improbable, must be the truth.
— Arthur Conan Doyle, author of the Sherlock Holmes series

truth is often perilous, and even illegal

Truth uttered before its time is dangerous.
— Mencius

As a circle of light increases, so does the circumference of darkness around it.
— Albert Einstein

In time of war the first casualty is truth.
— Boake Carter

In a time of universal deceit, telling the truth is a revolutionary act.
— George Orwell, *1984*

deteriorated thinking leads to deteriorated institutions

An excellent plumber is infinitely more admirable than an incompetent philosopher. The society which scorns excellence in plumbing because plumbing is a humble activity, and tolerates shoddiness in philosophy because it is an exalted activity, will have neither good plumbing nor good philosophy. Neither its pipes nor its theories will hold water.
— John W. Gardner

Hell is truth seen too late.
— author unknown

be dedicated to learning, hearing, and speaking truth

For here we are not afraid to follow truth wherever it may lead, nor to tolerate error so long as reason is free to combat it.
— Thomas Jefferson

There are three sides to every story — yours, mine, and all that lie between.
— Jody Kern

I keep six honest serving-men
(They taught me all I knew);
Their names are What and Why and When
And How and Where and Who.
— Rudyard Kipling

learn how to effectively tell the truth

Truth often suffers more by the heat of its defenders than from the arguments of its opposers.
— William Penn

The trick is to not emotionalize the matter. Eliminate the story. Tell the truth succinctly, and let the receiver form the proper emotions. This transforms your truth into *his* truth.

WISDOM

Nine-tenths of wisdom consists of being wise in time.
— Theodore Roosevelt

Wisdom is the reward you get for a lifetime of listening when you'd have preferred to talk.
— Doug Larson

Ignorance is a poor substitute for pride.
Pride is a poor substitute for intelligence.
Intelligence is a poor substitute for wisdom.
Wisdom has no substitute.
Knowledge comes and goes, but wisdom lingers.
— Kenneth W. Royce

Only daring speculation can lead us further, and not accumulation of facts.
— Albert Einstein

Wise men don't need advice. Fools won't take it.
— Benjamin Franklin

I define wisdom as the skill and judgment in using the tool of one's own brain. In other words, the brain is a tool of the *mind*. If I had to sum up what wisdom does, **it is the power to discern the *correct* question.** (There is no right answer to the wrong question!)

People tend to confuse wisdom with intelligence. Intelligence means quickness of mind, the ability to make connections and distinctions and to reason fluently in the abstract. Intelligence doesn't necessarily bring wisdom. Wisdom is less an intellectual quality than a spiritual one. It involves the use of intelligence necessary to achieve perspective, but wisdom is more closely identified with an attitude toward life that includes some qualities of character not derived from the brain. There is an element of the intuitive. There are also the patience, humility, and charity that are needed to understand other times and other ways of looking at things. These qualities foster the ability to see events in proper perspective.
— Norman Podhoretz, "Wisdom: What It Is; How To Get It"

Wisdom is also knowing what to *do* with what you know.

. . . to make juxtapositions that elude mere mortals. Call it a facility with metaphor, the ability to connect the unconnected to see relationships to which others are blind.
— "The Puzzle of Genius", 1993 *Newsweek*

the wisdom in trusting

I think that an important value of wisdom is in how it informs proper limits of trust. The peasant, having been cheated once in the marketplace, never trusts any salesman. The heartbroken thereafter never trusts love.

> *We should be careful to get out of an experience only the wisdom that is in it — and stop there; lest we be like the cat that sits down on a hot stove lid. It will never sit down on a hot stove lid again — and that is well; but also it will never sit down on a cold one either.*
> — Mark Twain

the wisdom of seeing from all angles

U.S. Marine Corps officers are trained to constantly "turn the map around" and thus see things from their enemy's point of view. Widening your perspective is a hallmark of wisdom. *"Condemnation before investigation proves ignorance."*

the wisdom of seeing the whole picture

> *You can be strong in one area — but a chain is no stronger than its weakest link. Sooner or later, unless you get your total act together, your Achilles' heel will prevent you from reaching the top. If you don't strengthen that weak link, life will exploit it.*
> — Robert G. Allen, *Multiple Streams of Income*, p. 322

Wisdom keeps listening and digging until it is confident that it understands the entire matter. It doesn't reject unpleasant facts, nor stop at convenient conclusions.

> *Learning without wisdom is a load of books on an ass's back.*
> — Japanese proverb

the wisdom of intentionally growing up

> *I am not young enough to know everything.*
> — Sir James M. Barrie

> *Young men are apt to think themselves wise enough, as drunken men are apt to think themselves sober enough.*
> — Lord Chesterfield

> *Si jeunesse savait; si vieillesse pouvait:*
> *If youth but knew, if age but could.*
> — Henri Estienne

The part of your brain that assesses risk will not (or did not) fully develop until the age of 25, so until then, don't imagine you're Superman. The middle-age stage of Life is probably the most fulfilling, as you've enough youth and health to do what your mature age and wisdom decree as worthy. As a teenager I used to laugh at the country club phrase "*Life Begins at 40*", but now I know it's true.

the wisdom of knowing what to ask
A prudent question is one-half of wisdom.
— Francis Bacon

This is a function of understanding what is and is not relevant. The truly wise know how to zero in on what matters. There is no right answer to the wrong question.

the wisdom of learning from everything and everybody
Wise men learn more from fools, than fools do from wise men.
— author unknown

There are applicable lessons everywhere, and in everyone. This is like food being abundant in the wilderness, if you know where to look.

Every now and then a man's mind is stretched by a new idea and never shrinks back to its original proportions.
— Oliver Wendell Holmes

the wisdom of what to ignore and leave alone
Learning to ignore things is one of the great paths to inner peace.
— Robert J. Sawyer, *Calculating God*

Great minds discuss ideas.
Average minds discuss events.
Small minds discuss people.
— Admiral Hyman Rickover

It is imperative that you learn to ignore or redirect all information and interruptions that are irrelevant, unimportant, or unactionable. Most are all three.
Before spending time on a stress-inducing question, big or otherwise, ensure that the answer is "yes" to the following two questions:
1. Have I decided on a single meaning for each term in this question?
2. Can an answer to this question be acted upon to improve things?

If you can't define it or act upon it, forget it.
— Timothy Ferriss, *4-Hour Work Week*

The art of being wise is the art of knowing what to overlook.
— William James

There are many things of which a wise man might wish to be ignorant.
— Emerson

Life is finite; there is simply not the time to busy yourself with everything. You must pick and choose as you go, with wisdom. Practice not learning certain things, so that you don't have to ignore them within your own mind.

Moderately wise each one should be.
Not overwise, for a wise man's heart
Is seldom glad.
— Norse mythology proverb

the wisdom of what not to do

Don't follow a model that doesn't work. If the recipe sucks, it doesn't matter how good a cook you are.
— Timothy Ferriss, *4-Hour Work Week*

I can't give you a surefire formula for success, but I can give you a formula for failure: try to please everybody all the time.
— Herbert Bayard Swope, first Pulitzer Prize recipient

Even if you unwisely tried something futile, be wise enough to drop it once it proves to be a loser. Never prolong a known mistake.

You should pay close attention to what is known as "providential circumstances". The Lord often speaks through doors that open or close. When you begin to be blocked on all sides in a particular pursuit, you might consider the possibility that God has other plans for you. I'm not suggesting that you give up at the first sign of obstacles but that you attempt to "read" the events in your life for evidence of divine influence.
— Dr. James Dobson, *Life on the Edge*, p. 70-71

the wisdom of what *not* to know

Remain sufficiently confident to be successful.
Remain sufficiently ignorant to be confident.
Remain sufficiently wise to be ignorant.
— Kenneth W. Royce

You shouldn't be overly aware of limitations and risk, as such will sap your confidence. Know enough to take an educated guess, and then dive in. Too much knowledge will tend to increase doubt.

Also, if you know too much about a particular subject you run the risk of being blinded by your own knowledge — of ceasing to consider anything which opposes what you think you know about it. There is a very fine balance between usable knowledge which still leaves room for more, and "expert" knowledge which is deaf to all else.

> *Maturity of mind is the capacity to endure uncertainty.*
> — John Finley

the wisdom of bearing unfairness and injustice

The world is neither fair, nor able to be made so. Get used to it.

> *A lie is halfway around the world before truth is putting on its boots.*
> — Winston Churchill

> *Maturity is the ability to do a job whether you're supervised or not; finish a job once it's started; carry money without spending it and last, but not least, the ability to bear an injustice without wanting to get even.*
> — Fred S. Cook

You cannot "get even" with unfairness and injustice. The thief and the liar are never punished soon enough, near enough, harshly enough, nor long enough. You will have to trust God's universe that *over the long run* thieves and liars receive their justice.

> *For it is in our power to refrain from any opinion about things and not to be disturbed in our souls; for things in themselves have no natural power to force our judgments.*
> *How can our opinions cool down unless the impressions on which they rest are obliterated? But it is in your power continuously to fan your thoughts into a flame. I can have the opinion about anything which I ought to have. If I can, why then am I disturbed? The things which lie outside my mind need have no relation at all to my mind. Be sure of this and you stand erect.*
> — Marcus Aurelius, Meditations, VI:52 and VII:2

the wisdom of giving

> *You make a living by what you get.*
> *You make a life by what you give.*
> — Ronald Reagan

When stolen from, find a way to give. Giving is the ultimate form of retrieving. It's also the ultimate "getting even". Your buoyant spirit stings the Thief, and it helps you get over your own loss.

> *You give but little when you give of your possessions, it is when you give of yourself that you truly give.*
> — Kahil Gibram

the wisdom of not obsessing about "liberty"
> *I was not born to be free. I was born to adore and obey* [God].
> — C.S. Lewis

Besides, you're likely not using even half the freedom you still possess! Having studied and written for 20+ years in the American Liberty movement, I have concluded (for my own peace of mind) that a certain percentage of coercion seems a sociological (if not spiritual) constant. Like gravity, it's an immutable force to which we must daily reckon ourselves. We will always suffer under some measure of oppressive and larcenous government. While it can be minimized and even temporarily suspended, it very probably cannot be eliminated.

This is my theory, and I base it partly on the observation that nothing in life is 100% efficient. Even the best of race-car engines use at most 40% of their fuel's energy. The most efficient type of fossil fueled power plant in commercial operation to date, the combined cycle with heat recovery steam generator (HRSG), has only an efficiency of 58% in "new and clean" condition.

A perfectly libertarian world would have no, for example, economic "gravity" (*i.e.*, coercive misallocation) and hence be 100% efficient in that regard. Even if we managed to reach such a height, I strongly doubt it could be maintained over generations.

So, I've generally come to terms with our difficult world. There will be no perfect liberty, certainly not soon . . . *and likely not ever.*

There will be no gold-backed money not interfered with by rapacious government.

There will be no sovereign right to travel not hampered by the highway patrol.

There will be freedom of diet by the FDA, DEA, etc.

Government is not the problem, as if some outside force. People are themselves the problem, and they make their own problems those of others'. More people are willing to coerce (or indirectly employ coercion) than not. There will always be enough lazy fools to hire enough willing thugs to coerce the laissez-faire productive. Their system of coercion is deeply embedded, reliably funded, and popularly supported. It has acquired, effectively, the status of a force of nature.

Even if Mars were tomorrow colonized by 100,000 libertarians, I'd bet that within just a life-span or three it would devolve to a hybrid statist system similar to what we have today in America. Why? Because libertarianism, though a fine inter-personal paradigm, is notoriously lacking as an intra-personal solution.

People will continue to be people. Thus, they will continue to avoid personal spiritual growth through a variety of well-honed techniques:

- ✗ nondelay of gratification (*i.e.*, pain avoidance)
- ✗ nonacceptance of responsibility (*i.e.*, pain avoidance)
- ✗ denial of uncomfortable truths (*i.e.*, pain avoidance)
- ✗ inability to balance (*i.e.*, pain avoidance)

People will often enough try to take the (seemingly) easier way out to avoid pain, even at the expense of others. (M. Scott Peck's *The Road Less Travelled* is a superb treatise on this.)

There will continue to exist a sufficient number of people who will band together for successful systems of coercion. In America, we once had a very viable country, the product of freedom technology. And Americans messed it up.

Really, the only remaining question is how much political coercion will you accept as a fact of life, in order to enjoy the balance of liberty you *do* enjoy? Railing against the state can become as fruitless as railing against the weather, or gravity. America will never become a libertarian utopia, and likely neither will N.H. nor Wyoming produce free states.

We can, of course, help to improve things and reduce the overall weight of coercion, but we'll never totally free ourselves of that weight. Thus, the trick is becoming strong enough to bear it on our backs, and no longer notice it. I do not notice the weight of my body as I walk. We walk without conscious effort. We must become strong enough to make the omnipresent weight of government an unconscious matter.

> *Everywhere and at all times it is in your power to accept reverently your present condition, to behave justly to those about you, and to exert your skill to control your thoughts, that nothing shall steal into them without being well examined.*
> — Marcus Aurelius, Meditations, VII:54

The best revenge is not merely "living well" but living *joyfully*. Root out what steals your joy, for that is the real enemy of life. Excessive dissatisfaction with the world is corrosive. Daily strive to:

✔ delay immediate gratification for a deeper one later
✔ accept responsibility
✔ dedicate yourself to truth and reality, at all costs
   (change your "map" when necessary)
✔ keep all things in balance

. . . and endeavor to associate only with others who do. That done, the burdens and coercions and inefficiencies of this life simply must be accepted and thus ignored. But they cannot be made moot until you've first recognized them for their relentless existence.

And until one rejects utopian notions (either on this planet or on others) regarding essentially dystopian beings, one will continue to chew one's elbows over government, the police, regulations, taxes, etc. Meanwhile, one's life passes by, second by frustrated second, joyless. No coercive system or their agents deserve such a thorough victory, so easily won by default. While I still urge you to do what you reasonably can to remain free, chalk the rest of it up to a cost of living on this planet — and then go enjoy your day!

the wisdom of what to let go

Remembering that you are going to die is the best way I know to avoid the trap of thinking you have something to lose.
— Steve Jobs, CEO of Apple Computer

Forgiving is the ultimate letting go of something. What you let go of ceases to have power over you. A classic story in AA lore is about a guy who is drowning while clutching a heavy rock. People on the bank implore him to drop the rock and swim. The drowning guy yells back, "*But it's my rock!*" If you're holding onto to something so big that it's harming you, drop it!

the wisdom of dependency

The Lord works from the inside out. The world works from the outside in. The world would take people out of the slums. Christ takes slums out of people, and then they take themselves out of the slums. The world would mold men by changing their environment. Christ changes men, who then change their environment. The world would shape human behavior, but Christ can change human nature.
— Ezra Taft Benson

The writer you quote was very good at the stage at which you met him; now, as is plain, you've got beyond him. Poor boob — he thought his mind was his own. Never his own until he makes it Christ's; up till then, merely a result of heredity, environment, and the state of his digestion. I became my own only when I gave myself to Another.
— C.S. Lewis, 17 July 1953

the wisdom of frequent silence

Be wiser than other people — if you can; but do not tell them so.
— Lord Chesterfield

We have a pair of eyes and ears and one mouth to naturally maintain the proper input:output ratio of 2:1. Keep quiet and learn.

When circumstances have compelled you to be a little disturbed, return to yourself quickly, and do not continue out of tune longer than the compulsion lasts; for you will be more the master of the harmony by continually returning to it.
— Marcus Aurelius, *Meditations*

the wisdom of having a versatile nature

A man should be both a fox and a lion — a fox so that he can deal with other foxes; and a lion in case he should fall among wolves.
— Machiavelli

The best way to have a good idea is to have a lot of ideas.
— Linus Pauling

Versatility enriches your Life experience, makes you less vulnerable to the predators, and increases your resiliency.

the wisdom of knowing when to stop thinking

We must not cease from exploration.
And the end of all our exploring
will be to arrive where we began
and to know the place for the first time.
— T.S. Eliot

And *that* place is exactly where to stop. Upon (re?)discovering pillars of truth — *Stop* — else you risk thinking right through such "first principles" (as C.S. Lewis calls them). Do not let your brain take over your mind.

the wisdom of "failing fast"

Beware being committed to an idea or a person that is overly painful to abandon. Admit your mistake and "fail fast". Never prolong a known error.

final thoughts on wisdom

The problem basically is theological and involves a spiritual recrudescence and improvement of human character that will synchronize with our almost matchless advances in science, art, literature, and all material and cultural developments of the past 2,000 years. It must be of the spirit if we are to save the flesh.
— Douglas MacArthur, *Reminiscences*, p. 459

We are not human beings having a spiritual experience.
We are spiritual beings having a human experience.
— Teilhard de Chardin

[T]he thing is to rely only on God. The time will come when you will regard all this misery as a small price to pay for having been brought to that dependence.
— C.S. Lewis, 1949

GENIUS

Genius is only a superior power of seeing.
— John Rushkin

Genius does what it must, talent does what it can.
— Bulwer-Lytton

Genius is the power of lighting one's own fire.
— John Foster

It is easier to perceive error than to find truth, for the former lies on the surface and is easily seen, while the latter lies in the depth, where few are willing to search for it.
—Goethe

The purpose of genius is not to give new answers, but to pose new questions which time and mediocrity can resolve.
— H.R. Trevor-Roper

Doing easily what others find difficult is talent; doing what is impossible for talent is genius.
— Henri Amiel

how geniuses think
view their problems as gateways to success
explore significance of connection between two ideas
look at specifics and make generalizations (inductive reasoning)
develop curiosity and sense of wonder at the deep mystery of life
ideas are kept simple and beautiful
they broaden their interests
they don't reflexively dismiss conflicting information
they transform thoughts into actions, even if seemingly "obvious"
  — Michael Powell, *Mind Games*

If you haven't genius-level IQ, don't sweat it. Focus on quality thinking as much as you can, accept nothing but reality as your guide, and you'll have plenty of genius moments!

📁 3

INTEGRITY & CHARACTER

If it is not right, do not do it; if it is not true, do not say it.
— Marcus Aurelius, *Meditations*, XXII:17

Better keep yourself clean and bright; you are the window through which you see the whole world.
— George Bernard Shaw

Do good, because good is good to do.
— Stoic proverb

The courage we desire and prize is not the courage to die decently but to live manfully.
— Thomas Carlyle

The best revenge is not to be like that.
— Marcus Aurelius

"integrity"
An uncompromising adherence to a code of moral, artistic, or other values; utter sincerity, honesty, and candor; avoidance of deception, expediency, artificiality, or shallowness of any kind.

To have integrity means that all your parts are "integral" — together. You are whole, sound, and entire. Roman soldiers used to shout "*Integras!*" to declare themselves ready for battle.

"character"
A composite of good moral qualities typically derived from moral excellence and firmness blended with resolution, self-discipline, high ethics, force, and judgment.

We define character as the sum of those qualities of moral excellence that stimulates a person to do the right thing, which is manifested through right and proper actions despite internal or external pressures to the contrary.
— United States Air Force Academy

I cannot but think that Ray Stannard Baker summed up the great purpose of the home training of boys when he said once that, "The one essential purpose of education is to set an individual to going from within; to start his machinery so that he will run himself."
What we are after is a self-propelling goodness. We are trying to produce men who will do right because they like to.
— William Byron Forbush, *The Boy Problem In The Home* (1915)

What a fine phrase from 1915: "*self-propelling goodness.*" This is what we mean by "character." Somebody who does right because they *like* to, and not because others are watching. And, from 1916:

There is nothing like a clean record, the reputation of being square, absolutely reliable, to help a young man along. There is nothing comparable to truth as a man builder. Nothing else will do more toward your real advancement than the resolve, in starting out on your career, to make your word stand for something, always to tell the truth, whether it is to your immediate material interest or not. Truth and honesty make an impregnable foundation for a noble character.
— Orison Swett Marden, *Making Life a Masterpiece*, 1916

Character is what you are in the dark.
— Dwight L. Moody

The foundation of a noble character is self-mastery.
It is essential that we properly nourish our bodies, to see that they have proper food, rest and exercise, so they will be perfect machines for our spirits. But, always there is an opposing force which pulls us downward away from these high goals. Inborn in us all is the tendency to evil. We are inclined to be carnal, sensual, lazy, irresponsible, selfish, and filled with fear. To overcome these weaknesses of flesh, we must employ the virtue of self-mastery and in so doing reach a higher plateau of character.
You may have a genuine desire and willingness, but unless supported by a strong will, little will be accomplished.
The goal of life is to have self-mastery over our natural [destructive] impulses.
— Aubrey Andelin, *Man of Steel and Velvet*

If you were given a nickname descriptive of your character, would you be proud of it?

Never esteem anything as of advantage to you that will make you break your word or lose your self-respect.
— Marcus Aurelius (121-180)

A person does not genetically inherit morals; he acquires them. And, unfortunately, he presently acquires them, to a great extent, through the public school system.   To rediscover the morals, ethics, and values that once served as the foundation of Western Civilization, the majority of people in Western society must be reeducated. (p. 236)
What do I mean?   Simply that, when chaos overtakes our society, unless the general public is well educated in both morals and economics, they may very well follow some socialist demagogue down the road to collectivist enslavement.   . . .
Meaning that the idea is to begin to educate people now for a final understanding necessary to reject solutions that will lead to the loss of their remaining freedoms. (p. 241)
— Robert J. Ringer, *How You Can Find Happiness During the Collapse of Western Civilization*

It is easier to fight for one's principles than live up to them.
— Alfred Adler

Talent is nurtured in solitude, but character is formed in the stormy billows of the world.
— Chinese proverb

John C. Maxwell's 4 things about character
The meaning of earthly existing lies, not as we have grown used to thinking, in prospering, but in the development of the soul.
— Alexander Solzhenitsyn

❶ Character is more than talk
❷ Talent is a gift, but character is a choice
❸ Character brings lasting success with people
❹ You cannot rise above the limitations of your character

the 3 types of people
Character is the ability to follow through on a resolution long after its formative emotion has passed.
— Brian Tracy

In my half-century of human experience, I've come to believe that people fall into one of these categories:

people who haven't integrity at all, regardless of the circumstances
(psychopaths, pathological liars, thieves)   10%

people who maintain integrity only when it's convenient
(most people)   85%

people who maintain integrity even when things are bad
(human jewels)   5%

The human jewels place a value on their principles, not a price!

Ben Franklin's 13 Daily Virtues
industry, frugality, temperance, silence, order, resolution, sincerity, justice, moderation, cleanliness, tranquility, chastity, and humility.

Personal
The eight personal virtues relate to your attitudes toward activities and their challenges. Good personal character traits will better your chances of success in achieving your goals.

Temperance
Eat not to dullness; drink not to elevation.

Order
Let all your things have their places;
let each part of your business have its time.

Resolution
Resolve to perform what you ought;
perform without fail what you resolve.

Frugality
Make no expense but to do good to others or yourself;
i.e., waste nothing.

Moderation
Avoid extremes;
forbear resenting injuries so much as you think they deserve.

Industry
Lose no time; be always employed in something useful;
cut off all unnecessary actions.

Cleanliness
Tolerate no uncleanliness in body, clothes, or habitation.

Tranquility
Be not disturbed at trifles, or at accidents common or unavoidable.

Social
These five social virtues of Franklin concern your attitudes toward people with whom you deal. Good social character traits result in other people wanting to do business with you or to have relationships with you.

Silence
Speak not but what may benefit others or yourself;
avoid trifling conversation.

Sincerity
Use no hurtful deceit;
think innocently and justly, and, if you speak, speak accordingly.

Justice
Wrong none by injuries, or omitting the benefits that are your duty.

Chastity
Rarely use venery but for health or offspring, never to dullness,
weakness, or the injury of your own or another's peace or reputation.

Humility
Imitate Jesus and Socrates.

Read Franklin's autobiography to learn how he made it in Life. It's a classic self-study, and one which will work for you!

an example of character: "Carl" of *Slingblade*
One of my favorite movies is Billy Bob Thornton's *Slingblade*. Carl, a moderately retarded man, was released from the mental hospital back to his hometown. If you watch the movie several times, you appreciate how complete and emotionally healthy a person he really was given his child abuse, low IQ, and dirt-poor background.

Carl owned up to his mistakes.
Carl never whined about his bad lot in life.
Carl told the truth, simply and clearly.
Carl took responsibility for his life.
Carl learned to read, and endeavored to understand.
Carl improved his living situation.
Carl kindly helped others.
Carl worked hard, and gave good value for his paycheck.
Carl did not complain.
Carl avoided bad company.
Carl made friends.
Carl was generous.
Carl sought spiritual rebirth.
Carl worked at self-improvement.
Carl confronted his father about past abuse.
Carl honored his murdered brother.
Carl was verbally thankful.
Carl was polite and courteous.
Carl loved, expressed love, and was loved.
Carl was sympathetic.
Carl was a team player and good sport.
Carl had a sense of humor.
Carl was a considerate houseguest.
Carl recognized and praised quality in others.
Carl pondered tough choices before he acted.
Carl committed to action once he had decided.
Carl gave closure to his friends before he acted.
Carl sacrificed himself for those he loved, to protect them.
Carl manfully accepted the consequences of his choices.
Carl set and enforced personal boundaries.

Carl had very little in Life, but what he did have he used properly and fully. Very few people of wealth and superiority of birth can boast that.

character is more than the lack of evil

> *Untried men who live at ease will do well to remember that there is a certain sublimity even in Milton's defeated archangel, but none whatever in the spirit who kept neutral, who remained at peace, and dared side neither with hell nor with heaven.*
> — Theodore Roosevelt

As the old saying goes, "*If you don't stand for something, you'll fall for anything.*"

Virtue is not the absence of vices or the avoidance of moral dangers; virtue is a vivid and separate thing, like pain or a particular smell.
— G.K. Chesterton

The study of values might once have been a matter of primarily individual concern and deliberation as to how best lead the "good life". Today it is a matter of collective human survival. If we identify the study of values as a branch of philosophy, then the time has arrived for all women and men to become philosophers — or else.
— Dr. M. Scott Peck, Foreword to *A Question of Values*

character comes from within

A man's character is like a fence — all the whitewash in the world won't strengthen it. Before our conscience punishes us as a judge, it warns us as a friend.
— Perry Tanksley

Don't let circumstances dictate your behavior. Your values, ethics, morals, purpose, and so on should not be contingent on the circumstances in which you find yourself. A man who chooses to be happy can be happy anywhere, while the man who wishes to be morose will find reason for complaint in even the most favorable of situations. The reliable man is the same man no matter what befalls him and makes the most of whatever hand he is dealt.
— www.artofmanliness.com

character is acquired through actions

I have always thought the actions of men the best interpreters of their thoughts.
— John Locke

Good habits are not made on birthdays, or Christian character at the new year. The workshop of character is everyday life. The uneventful and commonplace hour is where the battle is lost or won.
— Maltbie D. Babcock

Bad habits are easier to form than good ones, because good habits require conscious effort.
— Sherry Argov

Sow an act and you reap a habit.
— George D. Boardman

Watch your thoughts; they become words.
Watch your words; they become actions.
Watch your actions; they become habits.
Watch your habits; they become character.
Watch your character; it becomes your destiny.
— Frank Outlaw

As I grow older, I pay less attention to what men say. I just watch what they do.
— Andrew Carnegie

Good actions ennoble us, and we are sons of our own deeds.
— M.de Cervantes

Cultivate only the habits you are willing should master you.
— author unknown

character is much more easily lost than gained

The most unfortunate thing about the world is that good habits are so much easier to give up than bad ones.
— W. Somerset Maugham

Honor is like an island, rugged and without shores; we can never re-enter it once we are on the outside.
— Nicholas Boileau

good character is often lonely and even unpopular

The Superior Man seeks within himself.
The inferior man seeks within others.
— Confucius in 'Analects' 15:20

Et si omnes, ergo non. (Even if everyone else, not I.)

I believe that being despised by the despicable is as good as being admired by the admirable.
— Kurt Hoffman, *Armed and Safe*

Virtue is its own reward.
— J. Dryden

Virtue is its own revenge.
— E.Y. Harburg

character can be dangerous, and even cost you your life

Character cannot be developed in ease and quiet. Only through experience of trial and suffering can the soul be strengthened, ambition inspired, and success achieved.
— Helen Keller

There are plenty of devices for shunning death in every kind of danger if a man sticks at nothing in word and deed. But the difficulty does not lie so much avoiding death as in avoiding dishonor, for she runs faster than death.
— Socrates

Let justice be done, though the world perish.
— Ferdinand I

It is a royal thing to do good and to be abused.
— Antisthenes

TRAINING YOUR WILL FOR SELF-MASTERY

The chains of habit are generally too small to be felt until they are too strong to be broken.
— Samuel Johnson

Character is the sum total of all our everyday choices.
— Margaret Jensen, *A Nail in a Sure Place*

You don't have to like it, you just have to do it.
— heard in every army boot camp

The Germans, perhaps, at first ill-treated the Jews because they hated them: afterwards they hated them much more because they had ill-treated them. The more cruel you are, the more you will hate: and the more you hate, the more cruel you will become — and so on in a vicious circle for ever.
Good and evil both increase at compound interest. That is why the little decisions you and I make every day are of such infinite importance. The smallest good act today is the capture of a strategic point from which, a few months later, you may be able to go on to victories you never dreamed of. An apparently trivial indulgence in lust or anger today is the loss of a ridge or railway line or bridgehead from which the enemy may launch an attack otherwise impossible.
— C.S. Lewis, *Mere Christianity*, book 3; ch. 9

Human beings naturally want to seek comfort and avoid effort, however, Life requires effort that is often inconvenient and arduous. Thus, you must train yourself to do the difficult and unpleasant. To overcome weakness, you must become strong — that's the irony. From the excellent book by Aubrey Andelin, *Man of Steel and Velvet*, are these proven steps:

do something you do not want to do, and do it regularly
It may be something unpleasant, like taking a cold shower every day or getting at a job you have been avoiding.

A good idea here is to donate your time to a worthy person or charity. Always stretch yourself, especially in regards to helping others. It is instantly good for them, and soon after good for you!

I have generally found that the man who is good at an excuse is good for nothing else.
— Benjamin Franklin

deprive yourself of something pleasant
Like not watching your favorite T.V. program, giving up your favorite desert, not snacking between meals, giving up candy, etc.

This will be especially fruitful if you give up things which cost you money and/or time, which you use for productive goals.

demand definite quotas and performance of yourself
Such as arising at 4:30 each morning, getting a certain number of jobs done at a particular time, exercising a specific amount of time each day, outlining a definite program of responsibility . . .

Life has a way of slipping through the fingers day by day, and hour by hour. Start demanding clear and measurable results from yourself. Before you go to bed, schedule the next day and wake up early to do it! As Jim Rohn says, "*Stress comes from doing less than you can.*"

Offer your wife, your son or some business associate a dollar every time they catch you violating a certain principle.
— Norman Vincent Peale

It takes less time to do a thing right than it does to explain why you did it wrong.
— Perry Tanksley

In great matters men show themselves as they wish to be seen; in small matters, as they are.
  — Nicolas Chamfort

do something difficult

Set a goal for yourself that is not out of reach, but difficult. Pursuing a difficult goal will train the will, whereas seeking an easy goal does nothing for it.

As the U.S. Marines say, "*Train hard — fight easy.*"

guard your appetites

Tell me what you eat, and I will tell you what you are.
  — Anthelme Brillat-Savarin, 1825

You cannot consume a lifetime of crap and expect to be a quality Man. Garbage in. Garbage out. This rule applies not just to computer programming (the phrase's origin), but to everything.

QUALITY CHARACTER WITH YOURSELF

seek the truth

Prove all things; hold fast that which is good.
  — 1 Thessalonians 5:21

Men occasionally stumble over the truth, but most of them pick themselves up and hurry off as if nothing happened.
  — Winston Churchill

"Truth" is just a way of accurately describing reality. Recall Dr. M. Scott Peck's "*an ongoing process of dedication to reality*".

be good company with yourself

You must first be good company for yourself before you've any good company to offer others. Much of the time you will necessarily be by yourself, even if you are a "people person." (Some people, however, cannot stand to be alone for even a day. I wonder what that says about themselves?)

The great omission in American life is solitude . . . that zone of time and space, free from the outside pressures, which is the incinerator of the spirit.
  — author unknown

accept responsibility for yourself and your actions

If you don't accept accountability, you will misdiagnose every problem you have. If you misdiagnose, you will mistreat. If you mistreat, things won't get better, plain and simple. Even if you think there can't possibly be a link between your problems and yourself, assume I'm right and keep digging for your role in the problems. It is there, I promise you.

Keep your focus where it belongs: on your own choices and behaviors in the here and now.
— Dr. Phil, *Life Strategies*

Whatever is being done, accustom yourself as much as possible to inquire, "Why is this man doing this thing?" But begin with yourself, and examine yourself first.
— Marcus Aurelius, *Meditations*, X:37

never violate your own conscience

You arrive at your own conscience for a personal standard. This is what you adhere to for the rest of your Life. Nothing is more important than that. Be true to your highest self.

be decisive

If you come to a fork in the road, take it.
— Yogi Berra

Regret for the things we did can be tempered by time; it is regret for the things we did not do that is inconsolable.
— Sydney J. Harris

Life requires decisions. What you don't make will eventually be made *for* you (and usually poorly).

learn new things continually

When the student is ready, the teacher appears.

The greatest obstacle to discovery is not ignorance — it is the illusion of knowledge.
— Daniel J. Boorstin

Pleasure is a shadow, wealth a vanity, and power a pageant; but knowledge is ecstatic in enjoyment, perennial in frame, unlimited in space and indefinite in duration.
— De Witt Clinton

The superior man is distressed by his want of ability.
— Confucius

There are some things which cannot
be learned quickly, and time, which is all we have,
must be paid heavily for their acquiring.
There are the very simplest things,
and because it takes a man's life to know them
the little new that each man gets from life
is very costly and the only heritage
he has to leave.
— Ernest Hemingway

stand up for yourself
To submit tamely and meekly to theft or to any other injury is to
invite almost certain repetition of the offense . . .
— Theodore Roosevelt

The price of freedom is the willingness to do sudden battle,
anywhere, anytime, and with utter recklessness.
— Robert A. Heinlein

A society of sheep must in time beget a government of wolves.
— Betrand de Juvenal

People expect you to stand up for yourself. Why would they stand up
for you if you do not?

resist and speak out against evil
He who passively accepts evil is as much involved in it as he who
helps to perpetrate it.
— Martin Luther King, Jr.

Wherever a Knave is not punished, an honest Man is laugh'd at.
— George Savile (1633–1695)

When the eagles are silent, the parrots begin to jabber.
— Winston Churchill

As Edmund Burke is justifiably famous for writing, "*All that is*
necessary for the triumph of evil is that good men do nothing." Evil is
a cowardly darkness which flees from a single candle. Light yourself
afire with truth and boldness!

Dark and difficult times lie ahead. Soon we must all face the
choice between what is right and what is easy.
— *The Goblet of Fire*, Professor Dumbledore

To be neutral between right and wrong is to serve wrong.
— Theodore Roosevelt

A time comes when silence is betrayal.
— Martin Luther

continually conquer your fears

As the old Indian put it, "The first step in a successful life is the conquest of fear. Once that has been achieved, everything else falls into place."
— Jeff Cooper

I cannot overemphasize the vitality of this! All fear is a form of control over you. Read my *Conquering* Chapter 4 for more on this.

keep a good humor, always

Laughter is like inner jogging.
— Norman Cousins

While some people are naturally good-natured, others are not and you may have to work on this. It's a daily choice, really.

be of buoyant temper

I'm reminded of that *Far Side* cartoon of the whistling, happy soul in Hell. One devil remarks to another, "*We're just not reaching that guy!*" To be "buoyant" means to be unsinkable. This is yet another minute-by-minute choice. Agree what weight you take on, and do not accept the rest, lest you sink.

like yourself more and more

All relationships are with yourself — and sometimes they involve other people.
— John-Roger & Peter McWilliams, *Do It!*, p. 199

If you are lonely when you are alone, you are in bad company.
— Jean-Paul Sartre

If you don't like something about yourself, change it! Why spend your Life in the uncomfortable dwelling of yourself?

Carpe diem! ("Seize the day!" or YouOnlyLiveOnce/YOLO)

It is only possible to live happily ever after on a day-to-day basis.
— Margaret Bonnano

Today is what you have, not tomorrow. Make the most of every moment, and you will look back on a Life of great fulfillment.

find your calling, and obey it

Hide not your talents.
They for use were made.
What's a sundial in the shade?
— Ben Franklin

The greatest use of life is to spend it for something that will outlast it.
— William James

Every calling is great when greatly pursued.
— Oliver Wendell Holmes

Here is the test to find whether your mission on earth is finished: If you're alive, it isn't.
— Richard Bach

The great mystery isn't that people do things badly but that they occasionally do a few things well. The only thing that is universal is incompetence. Strength is always specific!
— Peter Drucker

Concentrate on what you do well, and do it better than anybody else.
— John Schnatter, founder of Papa John's Pizza

Strong lives are motivated by dynamic purposes.
— Kenneth Hildebrand

Be honest with yourself: what would you rather be doing? What do you love *so* much that you'd do it for free? That is your "calling". The sooner you get on track with it, the better for you and everybody else.

make habits of good things

We are what we repeatedly do.
Excellence, then, is not an act, but a habit.
— Aristotle

We first make our habits, then our habits make us.
— English poet

Everyone is the son of his own works.
— Cervantes

Even if a good thing is inconvenient, not exciting, or expensive, do not forsake it for a worse thing (which is convenient, exciting, a "bargain", etc.). Aim high for quality always!

never practice a known mistake
Quality skills are nothing more fancy than this. Once you know what a mistake is, it is your goal never to revisit that mistake. When I discovered in the book *The Fateful Fork* just how bad industrial foods are for the body (and how the "bargain" price equals poor health later), I cleaned out my pantry for organic food replacements. To have first eaten up the bad foods would have practiced a known mistake.

always keep growing up
When I was a child, I spake as a child, I understood as a child, I thought as a child: but when I became a man, I put away childish things.
— 1 Corinthians 13:11

Comfort zones are most often expanded through discomfort. Whatever comes along, look for the lesson.
— John-Roger & Peter McWilliams, *Do It!*, p. 277

The world breaks everyone and afterward many are strong at the broken places.
— Hemingway

Life is an endless process of self-discovery.
— John Gardner

Prune yourself — like a tree — and you will bear more fruit.

don't do skanky things to/with your body
But Daniel purposed in his heart that he would not defile himself.
— Daniel 1:8

Your body is your "Earth suit" on this spaceship, and you must honor the miracle God gave you. Furthermore, a Christian's body is *"the temple of the Holy Spirit."* Avoid all drugs, including (if you can) alcohol (at least to excess). Try to remain a virgin until marriage, and if you're not a virgin then consider a new-found chastity. There is a very high (though often hidden) cost to pre- and extramarital sex. Save yourself for your precious maiden, who saved herself for you.

learn to be content with what you have

I have learned, in whatsoever state I am, therewith to be content.
    — Phillipians 4:11

The happiest people don't necessarily have the best of everything. They just make the best of everything.

Until you make peace with who you are, you'll never be content with what you have.
    — Doris Mortman

Don't compare your life to others. You have no idea what their journey is all about. If we all threw our problems in a pile and saw everyone else's, we'd grab ours back.
    Life isn't fair, but it's still good.
    — author unknown

Everybody is shortchanged on something: a loving family, looks, brains, money, etc. Get over it and accentuate what you *do* have.

never be content with who you currently *are*

We are all "pleomorphic" — changing over our lifetimes. Who you were and are do not have to be who you must remain. Constantly work to improve yourself. Expose your own demons to the light. From every hour banish laziness and pride. Tackle fear as the cowardly burglar it really is.

What in life would you not be able to stop doing, no matter what the consequences were?
    — John C. Maxwell

focus on the *being* versus the having

The having is fleeting and often lost. However, the being remains with you (and is foundation to the having, anyway). Focus on quality experiences, skills, and character.

Regarding the physical possessions, as much as possible, avoid: malls, stores, flea markets, catalogs, and eBay. Then:

severely limit your purchases
buy only excellent quality
pay cash
take delivery
stay on top of preventative maintenance

strive for increasing unselfishness

Our spiritual growth is in direct proportion with our growth in unselfishness. Unselfishness is a willingness to give up one's own comfort or advantage for the benefit of someone else. There must be an element of <u>sacrifice</u> in a truly unselfish act.
— Aubrey Andelin, *Man of Steel and Velvet*

The reason why rivers and seas receive the homage of a hundred mountain streams is that they keep below them. Thus they are able to reign over all the mountain streams. So the sage, wishing to be above men, putteth himself below them; he putteth himself behind them. Thus, though his place be above men, they do not feel his weight; though his place be before them, they do not count it an injury.
— Lao-tse

seek balance and perspective in all things

Frame every so-called disaster with these words:
"In five years, will this matter?"

Get rid of anything that isn't useful, beautiful, or joyful.

All that truly matters in the end is that you loved.

Whatever doesn't kill you really does make you stronger.

Over prepare, then go with the flow.

discipline yourself

In the last analysis, our only freedom is the freedom to discipline ourselves.
— Bernard Baruch

A note to the Libertarians. — We have taken freedom too far. Today's freedom: nothing but soil for the cultivation of dictators. **For what is freedom but a tyranny of conscientiousness?** *And what has become of this tyranny of conscientiousness? <u>It is gone.</u> Freedom has now become synonymous with the absence of guilt, the abdication of self-control, and a decline in moral standards. Freedom and licentiousness are now indistinquishable. Thus is freedom discredited. Thus do we make ourselves unfit for liberal institutions.* (p. 141-142)
— J.R. Nyquist, *Origins of the Fourth World War*

do your duty

Do something every day that you don't want to do. This is the golden rule for acquiring the habit of doing your duty without pain.
— Mark Twain

take on bigger and bigger burdens
This is what builds up your manhood, like weight-lifting. I call it the "Gym of Life". Never rest with what you've done, with the comfortable. Keep loading your shoulders with more!

resist temptation
God is faithful; he will not let you be tempted beyond what you can bear. But when you are tempted, he will also provide a way out so that you can stand up under it.
— 1 Corinthians 10:13

Whether you are aware of it or not, you have an area of weakness. You have an "Achilles heel". Ironically, your enemies will spot it before your friends do, and your friends will before you do. Ask around.

*I let myself be lured into long spells of senseless and sensual ease. Tired of being on the heights, I deliberately went to the depths in search for new sensation. I grew careless of the lives of others. I took pleasure where it pleased me, and passed on. I forgot that **every little action of the common day makes or unmakes character**, and that therefore what one has done in the secret chamber, one has some day to cry aloud from the housetop. I ceased to be lord over myself. I was no longer the captain of my soul, and did not know it. I allowed pleasure to dominate me. I ended in horrible disgrace.*
— Oscar Wilde, shortly before he died destitute in Paris

Let the harm done by another man stay where the harm was done.
— Marcus Aurelius, *Meditations*, VII:29

maintain a dignified and kingly composure
He errs as other men do, but errs with integrity.
— Thomas Jefferson, speaking of George Washington

In *The Black Swan*, author Nasim Nicholas Taleb tells a great example of a friend who never runs for buses or trains. There will be another one along soon enough, and catching the previous one after an undignified sprint is not worth the assault on one's regal composure. Act like a king, and you'll be treated as one. Exhibit no sweaty effort for pedestrian things.

don't give up — keep at it!
Nothing in the world can take the place of persistence. Talent will not; nothing is more common than unsuccessful men with talent. Genius will not; unrewarded genius is almost a proverb.

Education will not; the world is full of educated derelicts. Persistence and determination alone are omnipotent.
— Calvin Coolidge

The man who can drive himself further once the effort gets painful is the man who will win.
— Roger Bannister, first to run a sub-4-minute mile

Always bear in mind that your own resolution to success is more important than any other thing.
— Abraham Lincoln

The soul of a free man looks at life as a series of problem to be solved and solves them, while the soul of a slave whines, "What can I do who am but a slave?"
— George S. Clason, *The Richest Man in Babylon* (1926), p. 104

have faith in Jesus

Pride looks inside,
Worry looks around,
Sorry looks back,
Faith looks up.

The greatest act of faith is when man decides he is not God.

I am the way, the truth, and the life.
— Jesus, in John 14:6

I am the light of the world: he that followeth me shall not walk in darkness, but shall have the light of life.
— Jesus, in John 8:12

QUALITY CHARACTER WITH OTHERS

Personality has the power to open doors, but character keeps them open.
— author unknown

People take your example far more seriously than they do your advice.
— Perry Tanksley

It's never too late to do the right thing.
— Terence Gillespie

Character is actualized with other people. A desert island hermit wouldn't need character as does a husband/father/businessman.

speaking with integrity
speak the truth
Let your "Yes" mean "Yes" and your "No" mean "No." For whatever is more than these is from the evil one.
— Jesus, Matthew 5:37

Practice telling the truth — quickly, succinctly, and without apology. (Tom Selleck's "Jesse Stone" character is a good example.)

never use truth as a tool of anger or envy
Operate in love. The truth will get lost within impure emotions.

when in doubt, keep silent
One of the lessons of history is that nothing is often a good thing to do, and always a clever thing to say.
— Will Durant

Or, as the old saying goes: *Never miss a good chance to shut up.*

do not lie
Lying is an accursed vice. It is only our words which bind us together and make us human. If we realized the horror and weight of lying, we would see that it is more worthy of the stake than other crimes. Once let the tongue acquire the habit of lying and it is astonishing how impossible it is to make it give it up.
— Montaigne

The Institute of Behavior Modification has found that 97 out of 100 people tell lies — and they do it about 1000 times a year.
— Patrick Morley, *The Man In The Mirror*

The 9th Commandment (Exodus 20:16) does not say "*Thou shalt not lie.*" It says "*Thou shalt not bear false witness against thy neighbor.*" Basically, you must not harm another through a lie.

A lie is when you communicate (even by an omission) a material untruth which will tend to unethically cause a person to unknowingly act to their detriment. If somebody needs to know something in order to act in their own best interests, you've a moral duty to tell them.

The essence of lying is in deception, not in words. A lie may be told by silence, by equivocation, by the accent on a syllable, by a

glance of the eye attaching a peculiar significance to a sentence. All these kinds of lies are worse and baser by many degrees than a lie plainly worded.
— John Rushkin

All lies are acts of cowardice, uttered to flee from the consequences of truth. The foundation of every evil is a lie. No evil can stand on truth.

tell the truth, wisely

I do not mean that it's wise to always tell the truth. I mean that it's sometimes wise *not* to. If the listener has no personal right to the truth (especially if it regards something about you), then you've no obligation to speak such information. Learn how not to answer — without lying, but by silence, avoidance, and refusal. If you'd rather not answer at all, then simply say something like:

"Why are you asking?"
"Isn't that rather a personal question?"
"Do you have the right to ask that?"
"I prefer not to answer that."
"I can't speak to that."

when to withhold the truth

Omitting relevant information is one of the most frequently used forms of lying, and one of the most difficult to reconcile philosophically. The guideline I use in trying to determine whether or not something should be "omitted" (i.e., whether or not I should refrain from volunteering certain information) is to ask myself, "Will the other party draw wrong conclusions, and therefore make decisions injurious to himself, because of information that I have not divulged?"
— Robert J. Ringer, *How You Can Find Happiness During the Collapse of Western Civilization*

On withholding the truth, Dr. M. Scott Peck wrote:

So the expression of opinions, feelings, ideas and even knowledge must be suppressed from time to time in these and many other circumstances in the course of human affairs. What rules, then, can one follow if one is dedicated to the truth?
First, never speak falsehood.
Second, bear in mind that the act of withholding the truth is always potentially a lie, and that in each instance in which the truth is withheld a significant moral decision is required.

Third, the decision to withhold the truth should never be based on personal needs, such as a need for power, a need to be liked or a need to protect one's map from challenge.

Fourth, and conversely, the decision to withhold the truth must always be based entirely upon the needs of the person from whom the truth is being withheld.

Fifth, the assessment of another's needs is an act of responsibility which is so complex that it can only be executed wisely when one operates with genuine love for the other.

Sixth, the primary factor in the assessment of another's needs is the assessment of that person's capacity to utilize the truth for his or her own spiritual growth.

Finally, in assessing the capacity of another to utilize the truth for personal spiritual growth, it should be borne in mind that our tendency is generally to underestimate rather than overestimate this capacity.

— *The Road Less Traveled*

If withholding about a nonmaterial matter will not damage another, then no harm is done. **What you *are* obliged to tell people is any material fact that without which would cause them to act to their detriment.** Granted, such is judgment only you can make, and this might seem self-serving to some. The irony is that only honorable people may withhold truth or "lie".

If you're uncomfortable about all this, then the next time you are asked a question you'd rather not answer truthfully, reply, "*That feels to me like a personal question.*"

Finally, you are not required to tell a mugger about the money hidden in your shoe. Truth is never to be used to facilitate evil.

do not lie to shield the listener or to be "kind"

It may seem embarrassing or unkind to speak a difficult truth to somebody, but you should more often trust their ability to hear it for their own good.

do not lie by exaggeration

The unvarnished truth is amazing enough for anybody.
— Jeff Cooper

Once you become known as a truth stretcher, nobody can trust any part of what you say. Practice telling the truth — cleanly and concisely. This is surprisingly difficult to do, as we are all used to adding our own "spin". While a "story" or "version" of what happened can contain the truth, the truth rarely needs any such coating. "*The trouble with stretching the truth is that it's apt to snap back.*"

The moment you catch yourself adding to the bare truth, stop and ask yourself *why*. Is it to gain sympathy? Look cool? Sound brave? Create a new ally? Avoid embarrassment?

do not lie by "half-truths"

And then she understood the devilish cunning of the enemies' plan. By mixing a little truth with it they had made their lie far stronger.
— C.S. Lewis, *The Last Battle*, ch. 9

A half-truth is usually less than half of that.
— Bern Williams

Which half is true and which is not? (This includes replies not technically dishonest, but nonetheless designed to misrepresent.) After a while, you won't be able to discern. Also, you'll include less and less of the truth until you become a bald-faced liar.

do not lie when the correct answer is *"No"*

The most exhausting thing in life is being insincere.
— Anne Morrow Lindbergh

If somebody asks you to do something or go somewhere, and you really don't want to, then politely decline. Do not make up a false excuse. In fact, try not to use an excuse at all.

The only man who is really free is the one who can turn down an invitation to dinner without giving an excuse.
— Jules Renard

When tempted to explain your *"No"* say, *"My time and resources are otherwise engaged."* Don't even add a *"sorry"* if you don't mean it.

do not lie by artificial delays

Delay is the deadliest form of denial.
— C. Northcote Parkinson

If you already know that you don't want to do something or see someone, just say so. Don't lie with, *"Ask me next week."*

do not lie to save yourself

A lie will easily get you out of a scrape, and yet, strangely and beautifully, rapture possesses you when you have taken the scrape and left out the lie.
— C.E. Montague

The superior man thinks always of virtue; the common man thinks of comfort.
— Confucius

With lies you can go forward in this world, but never back.
— Russian proverb

Anything you feel compelled to lie about is usually to avoid pain for some mistake you made. Every temptation to lie is yet another crossroad within your psyche.

do not brag about yourself

The most difficult secret for a man to keep is the opinion he has of himself.
— Maurcel Pagnol

Success requires no explanations. Failure permits no alibis.
— Napoleon Hill

Don't take yourself so seriously. No one else does.

Rule: The more one talks, the less one does. The most competent and capable men are usually the quietest. If you let others toot your horn, the sound will go twice as far.

learn to take constructive criticism

The trouble with most of us is that we would rather be ruined by praise than saved by criticism.
— Norman Vincent Peale

Other people are often necessary sandpaper to take off our rough spots. This is always unpleasant, but necessary. If you are being constructively criticized, listen in silence. Do not protest or justify. hear them out fully, while not defending yourself sequentially along the way. They express grievance #1, and I try to repeat it back to them in my own paraphrasing to let them know that I understood them. Then I ask, *"OK, I heard you clearly on that. What's the next beef you have with me?"*

Not, "*is there any other beef*" (as grievances are usually stacked together), but "*what is the next one?*" Then, I listen to that one fully, without defending myself. And so forth, until they have emptied their complaint bucket. Finally, I go back and revisit them in order with whatever comments, objections, and apologies seem right to me.

I used to bristle at once, and thus defend myself along the way, but I learned that such inhibits the other's communication of heart. So now, I try to let them get it all out first. A fine last thing to mention is, "*I will carefully consider what you have said. Thank you for caring enough to help me improve myself.*"

be a good sport if you lose

> *How a person plays the game shows something of his character. How he loses shows all of it.*
> — Perry Tanksley

Say "*Good game! Thank you for bringing out my best!*" A great modern example of good sportsmanship is tennis pro Roger Federer. He knows how even to lose with style.

do not solict, hear, or repeat gossip

> *A man never discloses his own character so clearly as when he describes another's.*
> — Jean Paul Richter

Gossip is unsubstantiated talk about other people. Try not to say or hear about another anything disparaging outside his presence. As the Chinese say, "*Hear the other side.*" Here are some tips:

❶ Assume the best, not the worst about a person.
❷ Find out what's going on before you open your mouth.
   Talk to all parties involved, especially the primary one.
❸ Work to refute slander and libel.
❹ Confront the rumormongers.
❺ Apologize. (To say a thing is to own that thing.)
❻ Forgive.

actions of integrity
do not steal — not pennies, not hotel towels

> *The towels were so thick there I could hardly close my suitcase.*
> — Yogi Berra

We've all seen pennies laying around, and they seem ripe for the taking. After all, they're "only" pennies, right? Wrong. There are just two questions to ask yourself: Are those pennies your property? If not, then have you permission to take them? If No and No, then to take them is stealing.

If you'll steal pennies, you'll later steal quarters, and then dollars. Sooner than you think, stealing will be your style and you will have become a thief. Stealing is . . . *stealing.* Don't start down that ruinous path of justifying petty hotel thefts because of poor service, etc. Ask to buy their towels.

do a quality job
Build up to a standard, not down to a price.

Shoddy work is a form of stealing. A man of character doesn't do a "good-enough" job; he does quality work. He even does a better job than expected; he "goes the extra mile."

> *Do your work with your whole heart, and you will succeed — there's so little competition.*
> — Elbert Hubbard

> *My great-grandfather, an Iowan farmer whose company I enjoyed enormously, told me: focus on quality and never take on debt.*
> — Will Groves

keep your agreements
> *When a Samurai has said he will perform an action, it is as good as done. Nothing will stop him from completing what he said he will do. He does not have to "give his word". He does not have to "promise". Speaking and doing are the same action.*
> — the Samurai's *Makoto* (Complete Sincerity)

This is the first of Rick Maybury's Two Rules. Nothing will faster cement your reputation than how well you keep your agreements. You're no better than your ability to honor your own word. My mother has a great policy of "*honoring your word even to your own hurt.*" Meaning, if you made a bad bargain, then you still keep it even though it will cost you. This will teach you to make better agreements in the future, while preserving your good reputation.

> *One-half the trouble of this life can be traced to saying "yes" too quickly, and not saying "no" soon enough.*
> — Ben Franklin

Never make an unqualified promise about the future.
  — Dr. Walter F. Rittman

Although keeping agreements is a good technique for building trust with others, the real reason for keeping agreements is for building trust with ourselves. If we frequently break agreements — either with another or with ourselves — we have trained ourselves to ignore our own word. So, committing to something means nothing. (p. 279)
  Don't make commitments you don't plan to keep.
  Learn to say No.
  Make conditional agreements.
  Keep the commitments you make.
  Write commitments down.
  Renegotiate at the earliest opportunity. (p. 285)
  — John-Roger & Peter McWilliams, *Do It!*

The guide to acquiring the virtue of dependability is a simple one: Do the thing you are obligated to do, at the time it needs to be done, whether you want to do it or not.
  Dependability suggests a concern and interest in other people.
  — Aubrey Andelin, *Man of Steel and Velvet*

own your emotions, and control them
Anyone who angers you conquers you.
  — Sister Elizabeth Kenny

No one is in charge of your emotions except you. (In Japan, the first one to raise his voice loses the argument.) It takes many years to begin to master your emotions, so get started now.
  The best way I yet know of to defuse and thus control emotions is to immediately analyze the reason for the emotion. You cannot long be angry once you are looking at the *reason* for your anger. Try it!

own your actions and be responsible for them
For the Samurai, having done some "thing" or said some "thing," he knows that he owns that "thing". He is responsible for it, and for all the consequence that follow.
  — the Samurai's *Chu* (Duty and Loyalty)

The more responsible you make yourself be for your actions, the better you will act. The less responsible, the worse your actions.

be generous
It is more blessed to give than to receive.
  — Acts 20:35

The Sea of Galilee and the Dead Sea are made of the same water. It flows down, clear and cool, from the heights of Hermon and the roots of the cedars of Lebanon.   The Sea of Galilee makes beauty of it, for the Sea of Galilee has an outlet. It gets to give. It gathers in its riches that it may pour them out again to fertilize the Jordan plain.

But the Dead Sea with the same water makes horror. For the Dead Sea has no outlet. It gets to keep.
      — Harry Emerson Fosdick, *The Meaning of Service* (1920)

Money-giving is a very good criterion of a person's mental health. Generous people are rarely mentally ill people.
      — Dr. Karl A. Menniger

do not be envious of others' honest success

It is the character of very few men to honor without envy a friend who has prospered.
      — Aeschylus

Envy is a killer. Root out every first sprouting of that foul weed. When you begin to feel envious, ask yourself why you haven't yet acquired such a skill or luxury good. Spend time improving yourself rather than running down those who have earned more than you have.

At the 1971 Congressional Black Caucus, Bill Cosby observed:

And you have to stop blaming people.   Can't blame the Jew who owns the store — "We oughta go over there and take his store" — 'cause there ain't but seven of you in this place can run a store!

People who are running their own businesses don't have time to be envious of others who are . . . also running their own businesses!

be a Man of value

An honest man is one who knows that he cannot consume more than he produced.
      — Ayn Rand, *Atlas Shrugged*

Much done in life creates no real value whatever; it's just shuffling around the cake and jiggling it for some crumbs.

A little integrity is better than any career.
      — Emerson

do not encroach on other people or their stuff

This is the second of Rick Maybury's Two Rules.   Since encroachment has been sanctified by the political process, people have become used to encroaching on others and their property without even thinking about it.

be on time, and ready to start

Don't be one of those losers who is always "*a day late and a dollar short*". Punctuality is a vanishing quality, so yours will be noticed. Show respect for others, and yourself. Appear organized and in control of your Life. Be on time!

> *Unfaithfulness in keeping an appointment is an act of clear dishonesty. You may as well borrow a person's money as his time.*
> — Horace Mann

> *I have always been a quarter of an hour before my time, and it has made a man of me.*
> — Horatio, Lord Nelson

Better than punctuality is "Lombardi Time" (15 minutes early). If practice was scheduled for 9A.M. any player who showed up at 8:50 was 5 minutes late. So, start planning your day to arrive 15 minutes early, and most unexpected small delays won't make you late.

> *If you're early, you're on time. If you're on time, you're late. And if you're late, you're left behind.*

Bring a book so that your time is never wasted (which helps to avoid becoming angry with the tardy). I generally wait 15 minutes at most, and then move on. From www.artofmanliness.com:

> Being punctual strengthens and reveals your integrity.
> Being punctual shows you are dependable.
> Being punctual builds your self-confidence.
> Being punctual assures you're at your best.
> Being punctual builds and reveals your discipline.
> Being punctual shows your humility.
> Being punctual shows your respect for others.
> Being late is a form of stealing.
> Being late disturbs the experiences of other people.
> Being late strains your relationships.
> Being late hurts your professional career.
> Being late takes a toll on your life.

> *The courage of time is punctuality. When there is a hard piece of work to be done, it is pleasanter far to sit at ease for the present,*

and put off the work. "The thousand nothings of the hour" claim our attention. The coward yields to "their stupefying power," and the great task remains forever undone. The brave man brushes these conflicting claims into the background, stops his ears until the sirens' voices are silent, stamps on his feelings as though they were snakes in his path, and does the thing now which ever after he will rejoice to have done. In these crowded modern days, the only man who "finds time" for great things is the man who takes it by violence from the thousands of petty, local temporary claims, and makes it serve the ends of wisdom and justice.
— William De Witt Hyde, *The Cardinal Virtues*, 1902
www.artofmanliness.com/2012/04/14/manvotional-the-cardinal-virtues-courage

Have accurate clocks and watches, all set to atomic time. (Citizen's EcoDrive watches are solar-powered, and some are slaved to the atomic clock.) Plan your arrival backwards in stages, adding some cushion to each. Prepare for tomorrow the night before. Put stuff you need to take with you by the door the night before.

require punctuality in others
First be clear that punctuality [is] very important to you. Second, stipulate an offbeat time for the rendezvous. Never an easygoing 7:30. Rather, 7:25. Or, 7:35. If you were back in the CIA, you'd say 7:33. Nobody is ever late if told to be there by 7:33.
— William F. Buckley Jr., *Miles Gone By*

learn and practice good manners
Manners really consist of thinking about others before yourself. Well then, who will be thinking of *your* needs? Why, those around you with manners! Manners help to maintain an others-oriented society.

pay your debts, and quickly
Especially your credit cards, to avoid the interest charge. Become known as a debtor of quality who chases down his creditor with payment.

be trustworthy
The measure of a man's real character is what he would do if he knew he would never be found out.
— Thomas Macaulay

"Integrity is loyalty to those not present."
This is the best definition I've ever heard. Most people have face-to-face "integrity" but that's easy because it takes little moral

effort. The *real* test of integrity is what you will do if you are convinced you won't get *caught*. What you will do when others aren't looking. That is the only measure of integrity that really matters. Take the Ethical Competence Scale at:

www.ethicalleadership.com/EthicalLeadershipScales.html

do not be "two-faced"
I.e., everybody should know you as the same moral entity. You are not one person to Group A and another to Group B.

keep confidences
If somebody asks you to keep something private, you must do so (unless they are planning to harm somebody). Even if you become mad at them later for something, you cannot use their secret against them. Find another way to settle your anger.

if a relationship has to be a secret, you shouldn't be in it
In the movie *The Quiz Show* is a scene about a man who confessed to his wife about an affair he'd had years previously. His family were shocked that he said anything, having gotten away with it for so long. "*It was the 'getting away with it' that bothered me,*" he explained. Guilt forced him to finally speak up.

own up to your mistakes, quickly
The sooner you do, the sooner they can be fixed. Don't try to hide them under the carpet; it will just make things worse. A real Man stands up and says, "*I blew it!*"

apologize quickly, and properly
To properly apologize, you must say, "*Please forgive me.*" This acknowledges the bilateral nature of forgiveness.

A private apology for a public error is not acceptable. If you hurt somebody's feelings in public, you must apologize just as publicly and *use their name.* Generic apologies for personalized insults are cheesy.

learn to forgive, and quickly
Life is too short to waste time hating anyone. Make peace with your past so it won't screw up the present.

A primary difference between Christianity and other religions is that Christians are not only forgiven, but they are commanded *to* forgive. This is very difficult, and often the final Big Lesson you will accept. It certainly has been mine, especially with people who not only are not remorseful, but who seem to get away with theft and fraud.

No matter what a man's past may have been, his future is spotless.
— John R. Rice

I never look back, Darling — it distracts from the NOW!
— Edna Mode, from *The Incredibles*

What other people think of you is none of your business.

It's never too late to have a happy childhood. But the second one is up to you and no one else.

Forgive everyone everything.

play sports and practice good sportsmanship

Sports can help build manhood. Pick a team sport (football, baseball, etc.) and an individual sport (track, tennis, etc.) and excel at both. While you're young, also choose to develop a lower-impact sport that you will still be able to play in middle-age (which mean something like tennis, vs. football).

give credit where credit is due

You must publicly honor those who deserve it. This is practically a property right, and one you must respect.

be helpful ("*Anticipate. Participate.*")
Make yourself necessary to somebody.
— Ralph Waldo Emerson

He helps his fellow man at every opportunity. If an opportunity does not arise, he goes out of his way to find one.
— the Samurai's *Jin* (Compassion)

If you desire to help thy friend, do so in a way that will not bring thy friend's burden upon theyself. (p. 78)
— George S. Clason, *The Richest Man in Babylon* (1926)

be compassionate

Everybody is hurting somehow, and in need of help. Look for ways to be of service and comfort. This is especially good advice when you are hurting — it helps somebody else, and it takes your mind of your own pain.

be patient with others
We never know their full story, and rarely enough to judge harshly. Don't jump to conclusions. Give folks time to do the right thing. *"Patience is bitter but its fruit is sweet."*

avoid intrigue
People who live for intrigue (watch the movie *Dangerous Liaisons*) are the lowest form of humanity. Causing unannounced and inexplicable pain is a form of sport to them. Have nothing whatever to do with such gutless cruelty. *"Be honest and trustworthy in all things. Avoid the deceit and manipulation of intrigue."*

"err on the side of kindness"
This is another of my mother's personal rules, and it's maybe unique to her as I've never heard it anywhere else. In many social situations, your choice of response or behavior will be unclear. Too often your emotions will be challenged, thus offering an easy temptation to take something personally and reply harshly. People remember viciousness.

This quote long ago helped me to be more gentle with people:

Never cut with a knife that which can be cut with a spoon.

be thankful to people, publicly
You must clearly appreciate those who help you. This has to be done out loud so that all can hear. Public assistance deserves public thanks. Cultivate a smooth and flawless habit of this!

associate only with people of good character
It is better to be alone than in bad company. You have no business hanging out with losers: those who lie, steal, back-stab, wallow in drugs or alcohol, and cheat. While God loves them just as much as He loves you, that doesn't mean you must be their friend. As the Bible says, *"Bad company corrupts good morals."* (It doesn't work the other way around! You will not raise up a pack of losers by your example. They will only bring you to their low level.) Think of it this way: people of good character deserve each other!

know when to lead and when to follow

A man who wants to lead the orchestra must turn his back on the crowd.

When leadership is called for, and everybody else is looking around, they are actually looking for *you*. Step up and take charge.

Conversely, if another has already done so, and you are more confident in his abilities than your own, led him lead.

always play on an even field
do not change the rules to suit you at another's expense

"So, now you give the devil the benefit of law?"

"Yes. What would you do? Cut a great road through the law to get after the devil?"

"Yes! I'd cut down every law in England to do that!"

"Oh? And when the last law was down and the devil turned round on you, where do you hide, Roper, the laws all being flat? This country is planted thick with laws from coast to coast — man's laws, not God's laws — and if you cut them down, and you're just the man to do it, do you really think you could stand upright in the winds that would blow then? Yes, I give the devil benefit of law, for my own safety's sake."

— Robert Bolt, *A Man For All Seasons*

Even the devil deserves fair justice. So do terrorists, and child molesters, and rapists, and all other evil people. Whenever you begin to make exceptions, you will make *other* exceptions and finally the only person exempted from justice will be yourself because you've made it that way over time. If that happens, then there is no longer justice at all.

Today, the Government is very busy making exceptions to their justice system in the case of "*enemy combatants*" overseas. The Government claims that these people are so bad they cannot expect us to recognize their rights to an attorney or to a fair trial. We are told that such people can be tortured for information which can then be used against them in a court. This is a very dangerous notion, and one which has already been tried (and failed) by other countries.

America was *supposed* to be different because the Government had first to prove an accused person was guilty of a crime. Today, certain people are being punished as if they are guilty, and *without any trial.*

A man of honor regrets a discreditable act even when it has worked.

— H.L. Mencken

consistently apply fair justice in rewards and punishments
From Aubrey Andelin's *Man of Steel and Velvet* are these steps:

❶ ensure the accused understood what was expected of him
❷ discover all the relevant facts
❸ free yourself from all prejudice and partiality
❹ do not expect more of the accused than is fair
❺ make a fair judgment of the offense and its just penalty
❻ after any severe penalty, follow up with kindness and love

THE COST OF GOOD CHARACTER

He who tells the truth must have one foot in the stirrup.
— old Armenian proverb

Try not to become a man of success but rather try to become a man of value.
— Albert Einstein

If I take care of my character, my reputation will take care of itself.
— Dwight L. Moody

Waste no more time arguing what a good man should be. Be one.
— Marcus Aurelius

If there were no backlash to good character, more folks would have it. **Doing the right thing is always the right thing**, so forget all about the cost. If it is a high cost, rejoice! Nothing of value ever comes cheaply.

I have found men more kind than I expected, and less just.
— Samuel Johnson

Virtue is its own revenge.
— E.Y. Harburg

TECHNO-"MORALITY"

what about "evil"?
Curiously, the only thing which communists and libertarians can agree on is that man is "*perfectible*." That science will overcome

the vitalists who believe in such twaddle as souls and supernatural. Logic will triumph over superstition; technology over religion. In the *"pitched battle between science and mysticism"*, novelist James Halperin of *The Truth Machine* believes that science is now winning, and will win. Scientists have often believed that, and have so far always been proven wrong. I don't see the 21st century being any different, nanotechnology notwithstanding.

And what about "evil"? Don't evil men always co-opt new technology for evil purposes? In Halperin's novel, personal Truth Machines (TMs) make it impossible to be lied to without one's knowledge — so folks resign themselves to speak without falsehood. Ubiquitous licensing tests under TMs ferret out criminal intent prior action. (Apparently, the 5th Amendment had long since been repealed.) Thus, an electronic Thought Policeman eliminates the opportunity to steal, kill, and maim: *"Violence and cruelty arise from impulses such as ambition, misplaced idealism, and sadistic pleasure — but only if such impulses remain unchecked. Fortunately, the current state of technology and political science appears to offer scant breeding ground for evil."*

Oh, if it were but that easy. It's the sort of "answer" drooled over by high-tech libs, and it's invariably often wrong. I recall one *Eris Society* where Charles Murray was waxing on about how technology could enhance freedom. His idea was to put satellite transponder chips in every convicted assailant. Then, after an assault is committed the police simply review the location of all chipped convicts and easily identify the perpetrator. Elegant, right? Not really. First, the system has to work. Second, it won't catch the unconvicted criminals. Third, it does not prevent the attack. Finally, — and most importantly — it usurps courageous self-defense through high-tech wimpiness.

So, I piped up from the back of the room, *"Why not carry a gun and shoot the mugger?"* (Charles did not appreciate this.) An ideal self-defense works against convicted and unconvicted criminals, prevents their attack, and fortifies the defender. Plus, we can do it today, and it's cheap. Sounds right to me!

Universal Truth Machines may prevent being lied to, but they will not inform you who *would* have spoken the truth regardless. I wouldn't want a TM even if they existed. I prefer to seek and find honorable people by my own devices, by my own B.S. detector. And once I find such good folks, I reward their integrity by believing what they say. By my mind's default, they tell the truth until proven otherwise.

What kind of world would you prefer? One where everybody had no choice but to tell the truth because of universal and intrusive monitoring — or one where honest people who told the truth were highly prized, and liars were eventually found out and shunned?

The best test of character is what a man will do when nobody is looking. **In an age of Truth Machines, how will we be able to differentiate between a man who *could* lie but won't, vs. one who *would* but can't?** Is not the distinction important? Vital, even? A bad man prevented from acting is not the equal of a good man who would not do evil even if he could get away with it. While their resulting nonactions are the same (*i.e.*, neither commit evil), their hearts and characters are not. And aren't heart and character more important than act and deed? This is understood even in the law — criminal intent must be proven in many cases. "*Even a dog can tell the difference between being tripped over and being kicked.*"

I would rather a world where truth is told because it's the nature of the teller, rather than because the teller has no choice in Halperin's vision. Right things can be done for both right and wrong reasons. Truth machines would weed out actions done for the right reasons. Halperin proposes to make irrelevant the clean and noble heart, and we cannot even begin to contemplate what kind of bizarre and putrid world that will make.

In short, I want morality through better morals — not through better technology. Another author heartily agrees:

> The reasons, then, for dishonest acts are principally a desire for money or possessions, fear of criticism or humiliation, desire for acclaim, laziness, and enslaving habits. If we can rid ourselves of these human weaknesses, we will find it easier to more consistently apply the virtue of honesty.
>
> In the Ideal man I am attempting to describe, honesty is not enforced through outside measures nor is it practiced through fear of detection or punishment. His integrity is not weighed out each night or at every critical period of testing. **Honesty is an integral part of his being and comes automatically.** Such a man is not governed by law so much as he is governed by his own conscience. The fear of violating his own integrity would provide the greatest deterrent to any act of dishonesty. His honesty provides for him strong guidelines of behavior which can be relied upon with certainty.
>
> — Aubrey Andelin, *Man of Steel and Velvet*

📁 **4**

CONQUERING YOUR:
FEAR
DEPRESSION
LAZINESS
ANGER
IMPATIENCE
PRIDE

Make it thy business to know thyself, which is the most difficult obstacle in the world.
— Cervantes

Our business in life is not to get ahead of other people, but to get ahead of ourselves.
— Maltbie D. Babcock

The first and best victory is to conquer self.
— Plato

He that conquereth himself is greater than he that taketh a city.
— Proverbs 16:32

A man without decision of character can never be said to belong to himself . . . He belongs to whatever can make captive of him.
— John Foster-Dulles

Be thine own palace, or the world's thy jail.
— John Donne

Looking back, my life seems like one long obstacle race, with me as its chief obstacle.
— Jack Paar

Fear, Depression, Laziness, Anger, Impatience, and Pride are your primary internal enemies. Everybody has to fight them, every day, for as long as they live. You will never completely win, but you can keep them enough at bay to become a balanced and quality Man. The battle against the self is the longest and the most tiring. Only one of you will win. Your greatest strength is always, though indirectly, your greatest weakness. This will be quite obvious to everyone but you. Your life is the sum total of all your choices and actions up to right now.

CONQUERING YOUR FEAR

As soon as there is life, there is danger.
— Ralph Waldo Emerson

There can be no security where there is fear.
— Felix Frankfurter

How many cowards,
whose hearts are all as false as stairs of sand,
wear yet upon their chins the beards of Hercules
and frowning Mars;
who inward searched, have livers white as milk?
— Shakespeare, *The Merchant of Venice*

There is no security in life, only opportunity.
— General Douglas MacArthur

The core basis of fear is pride. Where fear is, there lies your allegiance. Think about it. And, to be afraid is to not fully trust God.

Fear is undignified. We cannot avoid it, but we certainly can conceal it — and avoid discussing it. As the old Indian put it, "The first step in a successful life is the conquest of fear. Once that has been achieved, everything else falls into place."
— Jeff Cooper

You will not enjoy a full and successful Life if you have significant fears. Living in fear is like driving down the highway with your foot on the brake. Your journey will neither be easy nor far — and it will have that "brakes-on" stink. Besides, what is your fear trying to *tell* you?

Fear is an instructor of great sagacity . . . . One thing he always teaches, that there is rottenness where he appears. He is a carrion crow, and though you see not well what he hovers for, there is death somewhere. Our property is timid, our laws are timid, our cultivated classes are timid. Fear for ages has boded and mowed and gibbered our government and property. That obscene bird is not there for nothing. He indicates great wrongs which must be revised.
— Emerson, "Compensation"

fear: it's all in your mind

We crucify ourselves between two thieves;
Regret for yesterday and fear of tomorrow.
— Fulton Oursler

Doubt is a thief that often makes us fear to tread where we might have won.
— Shakespeare

I'm not talking about nearly drowning or being chased by an angry grizzly. These are body-originating primal fears, and quite natural. What I am talking about here are unreasonable fears.

phobias and paranoia

To him who is in fear, everything rustles.
— Sophocles

Phobias are *irrational* fears which cause great anxiety, often shutting down the person. For example, I met a grown man who was terrified of birds. If somebody lightly touched his hair as if a bird had fluttered past, he got the shakes and nearly passed out.

face your fears and live your dreams!

Notice that you don't (can't) live your dreams first? You must face your fears *before* you can live your dreams. There is no way around it. How do you face your fears? By diving into them. The best movie scene of this was *Batman Begins* when Bruce Wayne (as part of his martial-arts training) is thrown into a cellar full of bats. He reaches a point of unimaginable terror, but the experience does not kill him, and he passes through phobia to later embrace bats as his own symbol.

A science-fiction book author writes about life on other worlds — yet this agoraphobic hermit is nervous to regularly leave the house. He writes about spaceships but doesn't drive a car. A 100 mile trip (his wife driving) is practically an African expedition for him.

Such phobias can be challenged and conquered. No, such would neither be easy nor painless, but it's vastly preferable to being saddled their whole lives with those burdens. Irrational fears are *learned* (usually when very young), and they can be unlearned. The sooner you start unlearning, the easier and further it will go.

A friend of mine, a young man who joined the FSW and moved to Wyoming, was so painfully shy that could not give a public talk. (He was embarrassed in even private conversation.) So, he took that fear head-on, joined Toastmasters, and within two years won its city-wide competition. It has been very gratifying to watch him bloom as a person and grow increasingly excited about his Life. He now coaches other young men how to overcome their fears.

> *Resolve to accept the worst, should it occur.   Now you can stop worrying.*
> — Brian Tracy, *The Great Big Book of Wisdom*

G. Gordon Liddy was terrified of rats, until he faced that fear by cooking and eating a rat. (Rather extreme, but you must sometimes fight an extreme fear with an extreme remedy.)

> *Ships are safe in port, but that's not what ships are for.*

Life is made up of risk. Get used to it. Learn to stretch yourself and take reasonable chances. Ask yourself, "*What's the worst that can happen if_____?*" If the downside isn't too steep, then go for it. You won't learn to swim while clutching your life-preserver. Many things in life are mutually exclusive. You must give up A to obtain B. Often, it is scary to first relinquish that A, but if B is worth it, then you'll have to take a chance. *Whatever* your fear, begin to envision yourself becoming fearless about the thing. Then, start taking small steps to de-terrorize yourself as you increasingly embrace what scares you. It could be water, heights, public speaking, airplanes, talking to girls, skiing, or camping in the woods.

fear is a focus, and what you *focus* on will happen

> *For the thing which I greatly feared is come upon me, and that which I was afraid of is come into me.*
> — Job 3:25

The law of mental focus applies also for things you fear and don't want. Stop focusing on fearful objects, lest "the universe" confuse them as your goals and give them to you.

worry — the stepchild of fear

Worry is the misuse of the imagination.
— Dan Zadra

The misfortunes hardest to bear are those which never come.
— James Russell Lowell

Fear is like prayer in reverse. *Anything you fear is much more likely to harm you than it would be if you did not fear it. Only fear can rob you of love and liberty.*
— Napoleon Hill, *Grow Rich with Peace of Mind*

Let us not look back in anger or forward in fear, but around in awareness.
— James Thurber

I am an old man and have know a great many troubles, but most of them never happened.
— Mark Twain

Worry is always too early or too late; it's never on time. This is reason enough alone to not give it heed.

action is the solution to fear

No one ever would have crossed the ocean if he could have gotten off the ship in the storm.
— G.K. Chesterton

If you are not afraid to face the music, you may get to lead the band.
— Edwin H. Stuart

He has not learned the lesson of life who does not every day surmount a fear. Fear always springs from ignorance. Men suffer all their life long under the foolish superstition that they can be cheated. [I]t is as impossible for a man to be cheated by anyone but himself. Do the thing you fear to do and the death of fear is certain.
— Emerson

One ought never to turn one's back on a threatened danger and try to run away from it. If you do that, you will double the danger. But if you meet it promptly and without flinching, you will reduce the danger by half. Never run away from anything. Never!!
— Winston Churchill

> *Fear isn't cowardice. Cowardice is the failure to fight fear. The weakling feels fear and quits. The man of courage feels fear and fights.*
> — Arnold H. Glasow

> *Which activity on your list do you fear most? That's your Feared Thing First (FTF). When you start your day, ask yourself, "What's my FTF today?" Start your day with that activity.*
>   *Generally, whenever you hesitate or resist doing something, there is a reason. Often, it is fear. People are simply afraid to fail. Fear blocks us from doing our highly leveraged activities . . . Fear blocks our success. Some people would rather do nothing successfully than do what really counts and risk failing. Fear is too expensive a habit. So let's learn to recognize it, face it, tackle it, and move through it. Then reward yourself.* (p. 314)
> — Robert G. Allen, *Multiple Streams of Income*

failure is not so awful as regret

> *You don't regret so much the things you did.*
> *You regret the things you didn't do.*

This is true about 80% of the time. I remember the girls I didn't ask to dance because I was too shy. I remember the trips I didn't take because I was too busy. I remember the apologies I didn't make because I was too angry. I remember the fun I didn't have because I was too serious. Try to live each day with no regrets. Ask yourself, "*If I don't do this, will I regret it later?*" If yes, then do it — no excuses!

> *Consider this: The potential of trying new things, reaching for more and suffering a setback or a rejection, is something that, ultimately, you can deal with, whereas the fear of that event is formless, elusive, and difficult to fight. Fighting fear is like trying to sack fog; you just can't get a handle on it. Giving your power away to fear is worse than suffering the consequences that you're afraid of. Choose to give yourself the chance. It's normal to be anxious and afraid, but you can't be dominated by the fear.*
> — Dr. Phil, *Life Strategies*, p. 142

> *You don't want to die wondering!*
> — a friend of a friend

> *The fear of death keeps us from living, not from dying.*
> — Paul C. Roud, *Making Miracles*

anger is also a (temporary) solution to fear

The answer to fear is anger.
— Eric Hoffer

You can only have power over people so long as you don't take everything away from them. But when you've robbed a man of everything he's no longer in your power — he's free again.
— Solzhenitsyn

Before you can get into action, you might have to get mad. This was the central theme in the movie *Network*:

"I'm as mad as hell, and I'm not going to take it any more!"

courage

The strength and power of despotism consists wholly in the fear of resistance.
— Thomas Paine

Folks, courage is not conjured up out of thin air in a sudden moment of crisis. Courage is like a muscle, steadily strengthened over time. You will have in the future only what you've earned and paid for in previous risk and anxiety. We need to be mentally resisting every day. We need to be strengthening our resolve, not our shrewd ability to remain legal for just one more day by complying with increasingly arcane and contradictory regulations. If you have no experience in disobeying tyranny when it was mild, then you certainly won't do it when tyranny becomes heavy.

Cowardice is not the lack of bravery, but bravery *misused.* I am not brave enough to be a coward. **The highest bravery is to face in the mirror, everyday, a coward's face.** Dodging bullets and clearing minefields can't compare to the daily realization that brave people are doing your thinking and taking your risks and shouldering your responsibilities for you. Here is the only way to live:

Keep calm, and carry on.
Face your fears.
Live your dreams.

CONQUERING YOUR LAZINESS

How long will you lie down, O sluggard?
When will you arise from your sleep?
— Proverbs 6:9

There's always room for improvement. It's the biggest room in the house.
— Louise Heath Leber

We pray like it is all up to God. We work like it is all up to us.
— Dwight L. Moody

Don't quit, because once you get into that mode of quitting, then you feel like it's okay.
— Jerry Rice, football wide receiver

Any one who does what he must only when he is in the mood or when it's convenient isn't going to be successful.
— John C. Maxwell, *The 21 Indispensible Qualities of a Leader*

How many people live on the reputation of the reputation they might have made!
— Oliver Wendell Holmes

Instead of tackling the most important priorities that would make successful in life, we prefer the path of least resistance and do things simply that will relieve our tension, such as shuffling papers and majoring in minors.
— Denis Waitley

Almost all our faults are more pardonable than the methods we think up to hide them.
— La Rochefoucauld

Laziness is terminally corrosive. It will neutralize the keenest talent and kill the grandest dream. Laziness is *anti*-action — a form of *death*. (An interesting spiritual theory of Dr. M. Scott Peck in *The Road Less Travelled* is that laziness is the root of all sin. Peck makes a strong argument that it was Adam's and Eve's core sin, by not asking God about the forbidden fruit after hearing Satan's claim. I think that pride is more foundational, even to laziness. Lazy people weirdly somehow believe that they have a *right* to be lazy, and that stinks of pride.)

All that said, you will accomplish very, very little as a slug. Root out laziness from your Life!

Dig the well before you are thirsty.
— Chinese proverb

He who has begun has half done. Dare to be wise: begin!
— Horace, c. 65 B.C.

A small daily task, if it be really daily, will be the labors of a spasmodic Hercules.
— Anthony Trollope

Nothing is worth more than this day.
— Goethe

Working hard will not guarantee success, but not working hard will guarantee failure. Unfortunately, success does not always come in direct proportion to the amount of effort we put forth, but failure always comes in direct proportion to our laziness.
— Patrick Morley, *7 Seasons of the Man in the Mirror*

the source of laziness

Laziness is nothing more than the habit of resting before you [deservedly] get tired.
— Jules Renard

The worst bankruptcy in the world is the man who has lost enthusiasm.
— author unknown

Barring a true medical condition such as chronic fatigue syndrome, laziness is a psychological issue.

Laziness stems from a lack of *enthusiasm*.
Lack of enthusiasm stems from no *dreams and goals*.
Lack of dreams and goals stems from a lack of *purpose*.
Discover a purpose for living.

Have you noticed that happy people are usually *active* people? In fact, how many happy *lazy* people do you know? Get urgent about your Life! You were given a total of only 29,000 days to live, and probably 20-40% of them you've already spent.

The best time to plant a tree is 25 years ago.
The second best time is today.
— a nursery in Canada

Get out of your own way; most of your excuses for underachievement are figments of your imagination.
— Brian Tracy, *The Great Big Book of Wisdom*

. . . understand that a man is worth just as much as the things about which he busies himself.
— Marcus Aurelius, *Meditations*, VII:3

Get action; do things; be sane. Don't flitter away your time; create; act; take a place wherever you are and be somebody!
— Theodore Roosevelt

I love that quirky command, "*Get action*." I'd always thought of action as something one does, vs. something one "gets". *Go get some action!*

physical lethargy feeds laziness

Today, big-guttedness represents enervation and decrepitude, decadence, softness, and lack of self-control. They say, in America, that the current generation is the fattest yet known in history.

Fatness now kills more people in the West than war, pestilence, and famine. Fatness is typical-archetypal of modern capitalist life. It dramatically exemplifies all that is wrong in us. We are soft and flabby, in mind and body — and in body politic. While we grow in physical corpulence, and its attendant diseases, there appears a parallel in civilization as a whole; that is, our tendency to indulge in thoughts the same way we have indulged our grosser appetites. **In other words, we seek out what is palatable instead of what is healthful.** We refuse the nutritious but bitter-tasting truths. We yearn instead for a high-cholesterol plate of love, peace, utopia, brotherhood, quick cures and equality for all human beings. We yearn for chocolate mousse humanitarianism. Fat has not only filled our hearts, but plugged our ears and closed our eyes. (p. 176)
— J.R. Nyquist, *Origins of the Fourth World War*

Now if you are going to win any battle you have to do one thing. You have to make the mind run the body. Never let the body tell the mind what to do. The body will always give up. It is always tired morning, noon, and night. But the body is not tired if the mind is not tired. You've always got to make the mind take over and keep going.
— Gen. George S. Patton

Persistence is to the character of man as carbon is to steel.
— Napoleon Hill

If you don't have a *daily* exercise program, start today. Not tomorrow, not on January 1, but *today*. This is one reason why rebounder exercise trampolines are so effective: you can almost immediately get a workout, and in your own home. No shoes, no prep time, and no driving anywhere. I often spend hours on the computer writing, but take 15 minutes here and there to rebound. It restores my energy at once! (I recommend a quality bungee cord model, such as the Jumpsport or Bellicon.) Pushups require no equipment and can be done anywhere. Choose *something,* and begin today.

Oh, and to make it become a habit, you have to do it about 66 days in a row. That's nearly 10 weeks of commitment before working will feel automatic.

get up *early* and work out!
Lose an hour in the morning, and you will be all day hunting for it.
— Richard Whately

Early morning has been proven the best time to work out, as it shocks your body into action. To wait later will invite a dozen excuses of why you don't have time, are too tired, etc. It can even be a short work-out, but you must do *something* soon after you've woken up — every day!

> *Steps to Reduce Your Feelings of Depression*
> *   * Initiate Cardiovascular Exercise*
> *   * Cut Your Sugar and Caffiene Intake*
> *   * Increase Protein Intake*
> *   * Decrease Daily Emotional Stress*
> *   * Increase Your B-Vitamin Intake*
> *Cardiovascular exercise should be performed at a minimum of four to five days a week for 30-45 minutes per day. A change in emotional state can usually be seen within three to six months.*

fighting petty laziness about chores
The longest distance between two points is a shortcut.
— Nancy Dornan

Accretion of daily laziness is like compound interest. It quickly adds up to a frighteningly large sum, and increasingly paralyzes action. Finish today's work today! Tomorrow has time only for tomorrow, not yesterday. Much of this laziness comes from fooling yourself that you can (if not should) put off a chore until later. Here is a way to prevent this self-deception. Ask yourself these questions:

Must this be done at *all*?
If yes, is this *today*'s business?
If yes, is it better to do it *sooner* than later?
If sooner, is it better to take care of it *now*?

There's your *answer*. There's your formula for getting *to* that answer. I came up with this late one night when the sink was full of dishes and I was tired and ready for bed. Basically, I didn't give myself a chance to say that I was too tired, that I'd do them first thing in the morning, etc. The dishes had to be done sometime, they were today's business, and it was best just to knock them out while I was already in the kitchen.

If all that doesn't work, you must ask yourself:

What would a QUALITY person do?

Ouch. If that doesn't do it, then I'm all out of ideas, you slug.

> *Sleeping another 30 minutes instead of getting up and exercising matter. Not calling your customers back at the agreed time matters. Showing up 15 minutes late matters.*
> *"Oh come on! This is little stuff. You can't be serious. This stuff doesn't matter — I have been doing stuff just like this for years and nothing bad has happened."*
> *Has anything amazing happened? When you stop letting things slide and start taking advantage of every moment, then amazing things happen. The little stuff matters the most. Everyone gets the big stuff. Very few take care of the little stuff. That is why very few end up rich, successful, happy, and healthy, with great relationships. They take care of the big things and the let little things slide. That's a surefire way to live a life of mediocrity. Not much bad — but not much amazing either.*
> — Larry Winget, *Shut Up, Stop Whining, Get A Life!*

Actually, fear is just a manifestation of entrenched laziness. Why do you hold onto your fears? Because it's easier to avoid the pain of confronting them now — and that's laziness. Why are you lazy? Because laziness pays off now (by avoiding effort). In a way, the ease and convenience of the present buys off our most vital qualities: courage and industry. The "now" is your biggest enemy, because it tries to sell death (in the form of a false gratification) to you every second of every day.

Human beings are naturally inclined to shrink from pain and from effort. If you make a daily habit of this, you will become a chronically fearful and lazy person. A loser. A loser who always whines about how "unfair" life has been, and how "lucky" others are.

Yeah, I had to get off of that merry-go-round,
Cuz I found out I was nowhere bound!
  — Starguard, "Which Way Is Up?"

Whenever you feel fear or laziness upon you, ask yourself:

Am I trying to avoid a necessary pain or effort?
Am I actually just being *lazy?*

Seek the honorable effort and the proper pain in all that you do. This requires nothing but an act of your own will. A man who has conquered his own fear and laziness has already conquered the world. He is not snared by instant gratification, nor does he try to escape the pressure of moving forward.

CONQUERING YOUR DEPRESSION

Some common causes for depression are:

an inability to relax
a lack of pleasant activities
difficulties in social behavior
troublesome thoughts

I would add a fifth cause: anger. A deep-seated and little understood anger. Anger at injustice, your unfulfilled life, loneliness, etc. Learn to ask yourself: "*Why am I angry?*"

While physical exercise will not cure the roots of depression, it will mostly keep the symptoms away. Exercise flushes out the harmful anger chemicals, and replaces them with uplifting endorphins.

CONQUERING YOUR ANGER

Anyone can become angry — that is easy. But to be angry with the right person, to the right degree, at the right time, for the right reasons, and in the right way — that is not easy.
  — Aristotle

That was written over 2,000 years ago, but it could have been last week. Also notice that Aristotle didn't assert that anger is inherently bad. (Even Jesus exhibited anger.) However, there *is* a correct time/place/manner to be angry. (*E.g.*, Jesus with the Pharisees and the temple moneychangers.) Emotion is a wonderful petrol, but a poor chauffeur. Those who fly into a rage make crash landings.

> *In your anger, do not sin. Do not let the sun go down while you are still angry, and do not give the devil a foothold.*
> — Ephesians 4:26-27

> *Whatever is begun in anger, ends in shame.*
> — Benjamin Franklin

many defeats are snatched from the jaws of victory

> *An emotional response to a situation is the single greatest barrier to power, a mistake that will cost you a lot more than any temporary satisfaction you might gain by expressing your feelings. Emotions cloud reason, and if you cannot see the situation clearly, you cannot prepare for and respond to it with any degree of control.*
> *Anger is the most destructive of emotional responses, for it clouds your vision the most. It also has a ripple effect that invariably makes situations less controllable and heightens your enemy's resolve. If you are trying to destroy an enemy who has hurt you, far better to keep him off-guard by feigning friendliness than showing your anger.* (p. xix)
> — Robert Greene, *The 48 Laws of Power*

> *Use soft words in hard arguments.*
> — H.G. Bohn

> *Speak when you are angry and you will make the best speech you will ever regret.*
> — Ambrose Bierce

> *How much more grievous are the consequences of anger than the causes of it.*
> — Marcus Aurelius

what makes us angry that we can work to minimize

According to Patrick Morley in *The Man In the Mirror*, these all stem from pride and/or impatience:

violation of rights
disappointment with station in life

blocked goals
irritations
feeling misunderstood
unrealistic expectations
pathological / psychological

3 main types of anger

They are: a low flashpoint (frequency problem), losing control (intensity problem), and holding a grudge (duration problem).

low flashpoint (frequency problem)

If this is true for you, then anger is one of your enjoyable habits. This is very weird, if you think about it.

We are never more discontented with others than when we are discontented with ourselves. The consciousness of wrongdoing makes us irritable, and our heart in its cunning, quarrels with what is outside it, in order that it may deafen the clamour within.
— Henri Frederic

The size of a man can be measured by the size of the thing that makes him angry.
— J. Kenfield Morley

learn all the facts — many angers are mistakenly placed

I can't count the many times I quickly became angry, only to find out that I had misunderstood the situation. (As the old bromide goes: Never assume, for it makes an "ass" out of "u" and "me".)

One manager I knew was a master at reining in his anger until he had the facts. If you had failed him, he first would calmly and patiently inquire if there were any misunderstandings or extenuating circumstances. He covered all possibilities, ending with something along the lines of, *"Did aliens from the mothership steal from your mind the precise instructions I gave you?"* After you had admitted that the goof was totally your fault, *then* he would rip into you. But never before.

anger is different from its expression

First, there is the matter of becoming angry or not. This is separate from the expression of such anger. Mastering your expression is important, but more mature still is mastering what angers you. This is more of a choice than you know.

The trick to deflecting would-be autonomous emotions is to *analyze* it. Thinking about something immediately takes you out of the experiencing/feeling realm, as C.S. Lewis explained:

> *The enjoyment and the contemplation of our inner activities are incompatible. You cannot hope and also think about hoping at the same moment; for in hope we look to hope's object and we interrupt this by (so to speak) turning round to look at the hope itself. Of course the two activities can and do alternate with great rapidity; but they are distinct and incompatible . . .*
> *The surest means of disarming an anger or a lust (I concluded) was to turn your attention from the girl or the insult and start examining the passion itself.*
> — *Surprised by Joy*, ch. 14

> *This is our dilemma — either to taste and not to know or to know and not to taste — or, more strictly, to lack one kind of knowledge because we are in an experience or to lack another kind because we are outside it. As thinkers we are cut off from what we think about; as tasting, touching, willing, loving, hating, we do not clearly understand. The more lucidly we think, the more we are cut off; the more deeply we enter into reality, the less we can think.*
> *"If only my toothache would stop, I could write another chapter about Pain." But once it stops, what do I know about pain?*
> — *"Myth Became Fact", World Dominion* (Oct. 1944)

Once you analyze the anger, the anger is placed on "Pause". Meanwhile, you may come to know that there wasn't real reason to be so angry in the first place, or have time to reflect and forgive. With practice, this will happen not only before you express anger, but ideally before you deeply feel anger.

losing control (intensity problem)

The late comedian Andy Kaufman was known for creating comic scenarios to foment authentic anger in others. (Sasha Baron Cohen as Borat is another.) Kaufman seemed to think that such was a legitimate style of comedy until somebody explained to him that he was adding to the anger quotient of humanity, and thus soiling our general experience of being alive. This apparently got it him, and he stopped his anger *schtick*.

if the situation is truly angering, is the anger worth it?

> *Anger is often more harmful than the injury that caused it.*
> *Use empathy in all your dealings with people.*
> — Grant G. Gard, *Don't Just Talk About It — Do It!*

> *Half your mastery of power comes from what you do not do, what
> you do not allow yourself to get dragged into. For this skill you
> must learn to judge all things by what they cost you. . . . In the
> end, life is short, opportunities are few, and you have only so
> much energy to draw on. Never waste valuable time, or mental
> piece of mind, on the affairs of others — that is too high a price to
> pay.* (p. xxi)
> — Robert Greene, *The 48 Laws of Power*

The expression of anger should be shackled to some kind of real utility.
It must pay its own way, else you're being angry for anger's sake.

holding a grudge (duration problem)

> *If we could read the secret history of our enemies, we would find
> in each person's life sorrow and suffering enough to disarm all
> hostility.*
> — Longfellow

While not least obvious of the three manifestations of anger, it may be
the most destructive. Suppressed anger, like money in a savings
account, builds up with compounded interest. The only way to purge
suppressed anger is through direct expression:

> *If anger is not expressed directly, it is not experienced directly.
> Unless a person experiences anger in the body and acknowledges
> the experience, the anger does not complete itself — does not
> discharge, subside, and go away. When anger is expressed
> indirectly, in ways that are calculated to avoid the experience of
> anger, anger gets stored up rather than dissipating.*
>
> *As difficult as it may be for our minds to accept, the direct
> expression of resentment works better than the suppression of
> anger to protect ourselves and each other from damage by anger.
> When we communicate our resentment to the person we resent,
> the anger dissipates more completely in the moment of
> expression. The anger may get cranked up to a higher pitch than
> seems reasonable in many small arguments, but the intensity of
> the experience allows the heat out where it can cool. People can
> get over being mad if they face resentment one instance at a
> time.*
>
> *The extreme alternative to this one-step-at-a-time approach
> is to be the youngest kid to make Eagle Scout in Boy Scout history,
> get good grades, always be nice, become a good Marine and then
> go up in the tower at the University of Texas and shoot to kill
> everybody in sight for two hours.*
> — Dr. Brad Blanton, *Radical Honesty: How To Transform Your
> Life by Telling the Truth*

An older friend of mine practices this well. Every few years he will approach me and say, "*I've got a bone to pick with you.*" He then calmly describes his issue, and we talk it out. I appreciate that gives me first chance to make things right — instead of bitching to others.

perfectionists are actually angry people

Another hint of hidden anger is perfectionism. People who are proud of being perfectionists and for whom hardly anything is ever good enough are angry at someone else.
— Dr. Brad Blanton, *Radical Honesty*

don't vent to others, as it's indirect and ineffective

Most people, however, won't express their resentment in person to the person at whom they are angry. Instead, they gossip, complain, criticize, fantasize about telling the person off, and let [some of] it out in other indirect ways.

Expressing resentment directly is a requirement for creating an authentic relationship between two human beings instead of an entanglement of two minds.
— Dr. Brad Blanton, *Radical Honesty*

expressed anger rarely harms *quality* relationships

However, there is a greater possibility that by not expressing your anger, you will sabotage your relationship with your boss or co-workers to the point where you may as well quit, or will end up quitting or getting fired.

We have an oversupply of cowards with lousy, dead, depressing jobs and lousy, dead, depressing family lives. We don't need any more.

When we express only our appreciation and withhold our anger, we lose our ability to be fully present with the ones we love, and, sooner or later, we become less able to appreciate them.

The purpose of expressing your anger directly instead of indirectly is to get in touch with the source of your own judgments. By the time a person decides that he doesn't like someone, he is already one step removed from his anger. When asked if we are angry, many of us manifest this being-removed-from the anger, saying, "I'm not angry, I just don't like him (her) very much," or "I just don't feel he's the kind of person that I want to be around." But these judgments are founded on one or more very specific incidents about which we were angry at one time. We may not be consciously lying, because we may not be experiencing that anger right now. The form the anger presently takes is that of judgments, evaluations, and other thoughts.
— Dr. Brad Blanton, *Radical Honesty*

do not fuel your anger into hatred

The moment I start hating a man, I become his slave. I can't enjoy my work anymore because he even controls my thoughts.
— Dr. S.I. McMillen, *None of These Diseases*

Never think about people you do not like.
— Dwight D. Eisenhower

Get rid of all bitterness, rage and anger, brawling and slander, along with every form of malice. Be kind and compassionate to one another, forgiving each other, just as in Christ God forgave you.
— Ephesians 4:31-32

My dear brothers, take note of this: Everyone should be quick to listen, slow to speak and slow to become angry, for man's anger does not bring about the righteous life that God desires.
— James 1:19-20

Love is sharing what you have, even if you're having a fit.
— Dr. Brad Blanton, *Radical Honesty*

forgiveness needs direct expression of anger

People ask me, "Why do I have to express my anger directly to another person? Isn't it possible to just forget about it or just understand the other person's situation and forgive him?" The answer is no. You cannot forgive someone else without expressing your resentment directly to her or him.

Forgiving someone with whom you are angry — actually experiencing forgiving him — only happens after you tell him what he did or said that you resent. Only when you allow yourself to experience and express anger openly will it disappear.
— Dr. Brad Blanton, *Radical Honesty*

Blanton then outlines the step-by-step method to doing this.

The process of forgiveness involves the following six minimal requirements, none of which may be skipped.

❶ *You have to tell the truth about what specific behavior you resent, to the person, face-to-face;*

❷ *You have to be verbally and vocally unrestrained with regard to volume and propriety;*

❸ *You have to pay attention to the feelings and sensations in your body and to the other person as you speak;*

❹   *You have to express any appreciations for the person that come up in the process, with the same attention to your feelings and to the other person as when you are expressing resentments;*
❺   *You have to stay with any feelings that emerge in the process, like tears or laughter, regardless of any evaluations you may have about how it makes you look;*
❻   *You have to stay with the discussion until you no longer feel resentful of the other person.*
— Dr. Brad Blanton, *Radical Honesty*

Speak in the present tense, begin with "*I resent you for* _____ " or "*I appreciate you for* _____ ", and be specific. As Blanton describes:

New appreciation for a person can only emerge in a clearing created by completing the experience of past appreciations and resentments.

When resentments are stated in the present tense, you get the chance to feel angry again and to experience the anger. When you can experience the feeling, it disappears. As I have said over and over, when you avoid the experience of anger, it persists in the form of apparently reasonable thoughts. The thoughts are poisonous and destructive. They are destructive because they distance you from the other person.

What you put out there relieves you. What you withhold will kill you. *After we release our withheld anger, we discover our appreciation.*

Being honest about anger puts you on the road back home to being alive like you were as a child instead of mind-deadend by what you have learned to lie about. . . . Revealing the withheld judgments and feelings you have hidden, out of politeness and your protection racket, is the difference between a life lived in hate and a life lived in love.

responding to the suppressed anger temptation

Some excellent advice from Morley's *The Man In The Mirror:*

keep control
A fool gives full vent to his anger, but a wise man keeps himself under control.
— Proverbs 29:11

overlook offenses
A man's wisdom gives him patience; it is to his glory to overlook an offense.
— Proverbs 19:11

avoid angry people
A hot-tempered man must pay the penalty; if you rescue him, you will have to do it again.
   — Proverbs 19:19

Do not make friends with a hot-tempered man, do not associate with one easily angered, or you may learn his ways and get yourself snared.
   — Proverbs 22:24-25

appease anger
A gentle answer turns away wrath, but a harsh word stirs up anger.
   — Proverbs 15:1

And, to cap this off with Dr. Blanton's great advice:

speak out your anger when required
Telling the truth about anger means making a present-tense statement about your experience, while angry, to the person with whom you are angry . . . lets you function better in a pragmatic way, achieving your goals and enjoying the process, instead of feeling driven by forces beyond your control. When you are willing to have an experience be as it is, prior to categorizing the experience as "good" or "bad," and you don't waste all of your energy trying to avoid or lie about the experience, you have a choice about how you can respond to that experience.
   One of the hallmarks of suppressed anger is helplessness.
   — Dr. Brad Blanton, *Radical Honesty*

CONQUERING YOUR IMPATIENCE

Everything comes gradually and at its appointed hour.
   — Ovid

Everything comes to him who hustles while he waits.
   — Thomas A. Edison

Impatience is also often a form of pride and unresolved anger. Impatience is a dead giveaway to immaturity and shallow experience. It also betokens a lack of confidence in your own abilities, for if you believed in yourself then you wouldn't have to rush things to make them happen.

A boy will borrow and pay interest in order to "have" it now, but without real ownership. A man will save and earn interest in order to truly own it later. A boy will grasp for a girl's body before he's won her heart. A man will first win a woman's heart (and her body will follow).

How can a society that exists on instant mashed potatoes, packaged cake mixes, frozen dinners, and instant cameras teach patience to its young?
— Paul Sweeney

Patience and passage of time do more than strength and fury.
— Jean De La Fontaine

Patience and fortitude conquer all things.
— Emerson

Patience is the supreme virtue of the gods, who have nothing but time.
— Robert Greene, *The 48 Laws of Power*

There aren't shortcuts to learning patience. Having other goals to divert your mind can help. Understanding how little or nothing is lost if you wait is another tip — while envisioning the benefit to waiting.

You're only as big as the things that annoy you.

Wow! This is a tough one to swallow, but it's true. That's why the wealthier one becomes, the more one shrinks as one begins to whine and pout over the tiniest of annoyances.

wait for the "Isaac" — don't settle for the "Ishmael"

A great example of impatience is the story of Abram and Sarai in the Bible (Genesis 17 and 21). They were old, yet had no son. Becoming impatient, Abram (at Sarai's behest) conceived with Sarai's maid Hagar, who bore a son named Ishmael. (Ishmael would be destined to cause a lot of trouble through his many descendents.) Only after Abram showed patience and trusted in God did Sarai finally have a son, Isaac.

Moral: Don't be impatient. Wait for the Isaac; don't settle for the Ishmael. Inferior choices abound — rarely does the best manifest itself first. Be ... patient!

impatience is merely an expression of pride

"How dare this keep me waiting!?"

Be honest; you know this is true!

CONQUERING YOUR PRIDE

Egotist: A person of low taste, more interested in himself than in me.
— Ambrose Bierce

You can always find some Eskimos ready to instruct the Congolese in how to cope with heat waves.
— Stanislaw Lec

Do not judge so that you will not be judged. For by the standard you judge you will be judged, and the measure you use will be the measure you receive. Why do you see the speck in your brother's eye, but fail to see the beam of wood in your own?
— Jesus, in Matthew 7:1-3

There is one vice of which no man in the world is free; which every one in the world loathes when he sees it in someone else; and of which hardly any people, except Christians, ever imagine that they are guilty themselves . . .
The essential vice, the utmost evil, is Pride. Unchastity, anger, greed, drunkenness, and all that, are mere fleabites in comparison; **it was through Pride that the devil became the devil:** *Pride leads to every other vice: it is the complete anti-God state of mind . . .*
As long as you are proud you cannot know God. A proud man is always looking down on things and people: and, of course, as long as you are looking down, you cannot see something that is above you . . .
— C.S. Lewis, *Mere Christianity*, bk 3, ch. 8

After you've conquered fear and laziness and anger, you'll begin to do great things. Then comes Pride. It is a weird disease. Pride makes everybody sick except the guy who has it. Pride is the last thing which you will begin to conquer. When you're young, and daily reveling in your growing knowledge, physical strength, and freedom, it's difficult not to feel a swelling sense of pride. However, pride is the first sin, which comprises all others. As C.S. Lewis described, "*it is the complete anti-God state of mind.*"

besides, nobody likely really cares, anyway . . .

As somebody once quipped, "*Vanity is the result of a delusion that someone is paying attention.*" Just as you are paying attention to yourself, others are paying attention to themselves. What you imagine was impressive probably went by without notice at all.

Hear about the terrorist that hijacked a 747 full of narcissists? He threatened to release one every hour if his demands weren't met.

the risk of overconfidence

Pride cometh before a fall, and a haughty spirit precedeth destruction.
— Proverbs 16:18

Where you are strongest you are ironically the most vulnerable to becoming overconfident, and thus blind to reason. The trouble with pride is that it rarely knows where to stop.

get off your high-horse

In a free country you have the right to be offended anytime and any place by anything, but you do not have the right to be taken seriously.
— Angus MacDonald

There is perhaps no phenomenon which contains so much destructive feeling as moral indignation, which permits envy or hate to be acted out under the guise of virtue.
— Erich Fromm

Consider how hard it is to change yourself and you'll understand what little chance you have trying to change others.
— Arnold Glasow

I beseech you . . . , think it possible that you may be mistaken.
— Oliver Cromwell

Teach thy tongue to say, "I don't know."
— Maimonides

don't be inauthentically humble

A man is never so proud as when striking an attitude of humility.
— C.S. Lewis, "Christianity and Culture", *Christian Reflections*

He that falls in love with himself will have no rivals.
— Ben Franklin

fall out of love with yourself

The pleasure of pride is like the pleasure of scratching. If there is an itch one does want to scratch; but it is much nicer to have neither the itch nor the scratch. As long as we have the itch of self-regard we shall want the pleasure of self-approval; but the happiest moments are those when we forget our precious selves

and have neither but have everything else (God, our fellow humans, animals, the garden and the sky) instead.
— C.S. Lewis, *Letters* (18 February 1954)

Problems, as a rule, solve themselves or disappear if you remove yourself as an information bottleneck and empower others.
— Timothy Ferriss, *4-Hour Work Week*

Don't talk about yourself; it will be done when you leave.
— Addison Mizner

You're never as bad or as good as you think you are. People generally have either a very low or a very high opinion of themselves. Both stem from "*Look at me!*" pride, and both are usually overblown.

For everyone who exalts himself will be humbled, but he who humbles himself will be exalted.
— Jesus, in Luke 18:14

CONQUERING YOURSELF

Contrary to a belief that is popular in both senses of the word, the life without principle is not a happy one. It is darkened by the tyranny of appetite, and unlighted by the glow of self-knowledge.
— R. Mitchell, *The Underground Grammarian*

Never affect to be other than you are — either richer or wiser. Never be ashamed to say, 'I do not know.' Men will then believe you when you say, 'I do know.'
Never be ashamed to say, whether as applied to time or money, 'I cannot afford it.' — 'I cannot afford to waste an hour in the idleness to which you invite me — I cannot afford the guinea you ask me to throw away.'
Learn to say 'No' with decision, 'Yes' with caution; 'No' with decision whenever it resists a temptation; 'Yes' with caution whenever it implies a promise. A promise once given is a bond inviolable.
A man is already of consequence in the world when it is known that we can implicitly rely upon him. I have frequently seen in life a person preferred to a long list of applicants for some important charge, which lifts him at once into station and fortune, merely because he has this reputation — that when he says he knows a thing, he knows it, and when he says he will do a thing, he does it.
— Lord Bulwer Lytton, from the Inaugural Address of the Lord Rector of the University of Glasgow, 1856

We all want progress. But progress means getting nearer to the place where you want to be. And if you have taken a wrong turning, then to go forward does not get you any nearer. If you are on the wrong road, progress means doing an about-turn and walking back to the right road; and in that case the man who turns back soonest is the most progressive man.
— C.S. Lewis, *Mere Christianity*, ch. 5

This is the very perfection of a man, to find out his own imperfections.
— Saint Augustine

No man is free who is not master of himself.
— Epictetus

The first principle is that you must not fool yourself, and you are the easiest person to fool.
— Richard P. Feyman

I used to think my brain was my most important organ. But then I thought: wait a minute, who's telling me that?
— Emo Phillips

Let us train our minds to desire what the situation demands.
— Seneca

He who rules within himself and rules his passions, desires and fears is more than a king.
— Milton

You are your own most formidable enemy. You not only sense all your weaknesses, you know how to exploit them — and without effort. And even if you master your own fear and laziness, you still have Pride to always contend with. Not only do you have an outpost in your head, you *are* the outpost! What a pervasive enemy!

A fool may be known by six things: anger without cause, speech without profit, change without progress, inquiry with object, putting trust in a stranger, and mistaking foes for friends.
— Arab proverb

There is scarcely any man sufficiently clever to appreciate all the evils he does.
— La Rochefoucauld

The superior man will watch over himself when he is alone. He examines his heart that there may be nothing wrong there, and that he may have no cause of dissastifaction with himself.
— Confucius

We should every night call ourselves to an account: what infirmity have I mastered today? What passions opposed? What temptation resisted? What virtue acquired? Our vices will abate of themselves if they be brought every day to the shrift.
— Seneca

Dr. Phil's Life Law #4:
You cannot change what you do not acknowledge.

Strategy: Get real with yourself about life and everybody in it. Be truthful about what isn't working in your life. Stop making excuses and start making results.

If you're unwilling or unable to identify and consciously acknowledge your negative behaviors, characteristics or life patterns, then you will not change them. (In fact, they will only grow worse and become more entrenched in your life.) You've got to face it to replace it.

Acknowledgment means slapping yourself in the face with the brutal reality, admitting that you are getting payoffs for what you are doing, and giving yourself a no-kidding, bottom-line truthful confrontation. You cannot afford the luxury of lies, denial or defensiveness.

do not be ruled by your emotions!

Emotions are biased — whimsical — unreliable. They lie as often as they tell the truth. They are manipulated by hormones — especially in the teen years — and they wobble from early morning, when we are rested, to the evening, when we are tired.
— Dr. James Dobson, *Life On The Edge*, p. 147

Each man kills the thing he loves.
— Oscar Wilde

reform yourself before trying to reform others

Discontent is the first necessity of progress.
— Thomas Edison

There are simple answers; there are just no easy answers.
— Ronald Reagan

1. *I'm not OK, You're OK.*
        mindset of an infant
2. *I'm not OK, You're not OK.*
        hating yourself and others
3. *I'm OK, You're not OK.*
        narcissistic anger and manipulation of others
4. *I'm OK, You're OK.*
        self-esteem and trust
    — from Thomas A. Harris, M.D., *I'm OK, You're OK*

Not only progress technologically, but progress within yourself. Before you can grow, you must become discontent with yourself have you have remained. Read Marcus Aurelius's *Meditations* and Ben Franklin's self-reform through the 13 virtues.

When the fight begins within himself, a man's worth something.
— Robert Browning

I count him braver who overcomes his desires, than him who conquers his enemies, for the hardest victory is the victory over self.
— Aristotle

For I will not presume to speak of anything except what Christ has accomplished through me.
— Romans 15:18

only 3 ways to deal with necessary change
the common way
Accept change only through the imperative of pain. (Example: you cheated on your woman, she found out, but still forgave you and kept you.) Some damage is done, but not as much as:

the worst way
Ignore and resist the pain of change. This can be done for some time, but the accruing compound interest is breathtaking and often destructive. Example: you continually cheat on your woman with her knowing it. You eventually break her heart/mind/body/soul, or she one night while you're sleeping gets even with a kitchen knife.

the best way
Anticipate and pre-empt important change *before* it painfully arrives at your door. Example: instead of even once cheating on your woman, you come to terms with your own lust and temptation.

INDIVIDUALITY
COURAGE
MANHOOD

BECOMING AN INDIVIDUAL

Weed — a plant whose virtues have not yet been discovered.
— Emerson

Whoso would be a man must be a nonconformist.
— Emerson

The best things and best people rise out of their separateness; I'm against a homogenized society because I want the cream to rise.
— Robert Frost

The masses lack the capacity to think logically. A momentary, special advantage that may be enjoyed immediately appears more important than a lasting greater gain that must be deferred.
— Ludwig von Mises

change is always sparked by a single individual

We are the opening verse of the opening page of the chapter of endless possibilities.
— Rudyard Kipling

The universe is full of magical things patiently waiting for our wits to grow sharper.
— Eden Phillpotts

The reasonable man adapts himself to the world; the unreasonable man persists in trying to adapt the world to himself. Therefore, all progress depends on the unreasonable man.
   — George Bernard Shaw, 'Maxims For Revolutionists'

Civilization is the process toward a society of privacy. The savage's whole existence is public, ruled by the laws of his tribe. Civilization is the process of setting man free from men.
   — Stephen Rinehart

Hell is — other people.
   — Jean-Paul Sartre

every Man has his own Purpose

Since you are God's idea, you are a good idea. Scan history for your replica; you won't find it. God tailor-made you. And if you aren't you, we don't get you. The world misses out. You are Halley's comet; we have one shot at seeing you shine. You play no small part, because there is no small part to be played. Live your life or it won't be lived. We need you to be you. God never called you to be anyone other than you. "If I am me, how can I mess me up?" Remember, you find your sweet spot at the intersection of success and satisfaction.
   — Max Lucado, *Cure for the Common Life*

If you don't know where you're going, any road will get you there.
   — Thomas Carlyle

We base our entire lives on whether others like us instead of whether we like ourselves. Instead of self-esteem, it's other's-esteem.
   — Larry Winget, *Shut Up, Stop Whining, Get A Life!*

Two-thirds of Americans work in the wrong career for themselves, and half of them "hate" their job. Most suicides occur on Sunday nights, and most heart attacks occur on Monday mornings. All because people never took the time to deeply know their own Purpose. Here me very carefully on this point: if you do not early on study yourself deeply to learn your own purpose, you're not likely to later stumble on it by accident.

Admit to yourself that if you had to choose one or the other, the perfect intimate relationship or achieving your highest purpose in life, you would choose to succeed at your purpose. Just this self-knowledge often relieves much pressure a man feels to

---

prioritize *his relationship when, in fact, it is not his highest priority.*

Your mission is your priority. **Unless you know your mission and have aligned your life to it, your core will feel empty.** *Your presence in the world will be weakened, as will your presence with your intimate partner.*

Without a conscious life-purpose a man is totally lost, drifting, adapting to events rather than creating events. *Without knowing his life-purpose a man lives a weakened, impotent existence, perhaps eventually becoming even sexually impotent, or prone to mechanical and disinterested sex.*

The core of your life is your purpose. Everything in your life, from your diet to your career, must be aligned with your purpose if you are to act with coherence and integrity in the world. If you know your purpose, your deepest desire, then the secret of success is to discipline your life so that you support your deepest purpose and minimize distractions and detours.

But if you don't know your deepest core, then you can't align your life to it. *Everything in your life is disassociated from your core. You go to work, but since it's not connected to your deepest purpose, it is just a job, a way to earn money. You go through your daily round with your family and friends,* **but each moment is just another long string of moments, going nowhere, not inherently profound.**

The superior man is not seeking for fulfillment through work and woman, because he is already full. For him, work and intimacy are opportunities to give his gifts, and be vanished in the bliss of the giving.

A man must be prepared to give 100% to his purpose, fulfill his karma or dissolve it, and then let go of that specific form of living. He must be capable of not knowing what to do with his living, entering a period of unknowingness and waiting for a vision or a new form of purpose to emerge.

As you open yourself to living at your edge, your deepest purpose will slowly begin to make itself known. In the meantime, you will experience layer after layer of purposes, each one getting closer and closer to the fullness of your deepest purpose. It is as if your deepest purpose is at the center of your being, and it is surrounded by layers of concentric circles, each circle being a lesser purpose. Your life consists of penetrating each circle, from the outside toward the center.

Each purpose, each mission, is meant to be fully lived to the point where it becomes empty, boring, and useless. Then it should be discarded. This is a sign of growth, but you may mistake it for a sign of failure.

— David Deida, *The Way of the Superior Man*

Moral: To achieve something new, you must do someone new.

Nothing, except your own lack of insight, compels you to remain as you are.
— Huang-Po

A sculptor removes everything from the stone that isn't the statue. You must remove everything in and around you that isn't you. Then, you'll be left with just you. What in your life is in conflict with your nature, dreams, and goals? Why carry that stuff around any more?

discovering your true self

This you must always bear in mind: what is the nature of the whole, and what is my nature, and how this is related to that, . . .
— Marcus Aurelius, *Meditations*

Know Yourself — in talents and capacity, in judgment and inclination. You cannot master yourself unless you know yourself. There are mirrors for the face but none for the mind. Let careful thought about yourself serve as a substitute. When the outer image is forgotten, keep the inner one to improve and perfect. Learn the force of your intellect and capacity for affairs, test the force of your courage in order to apply it, and keep your foundations secure and your head clear for everything.
— Balthasar Gracian, *The Art of Worldly Wisdom*

[If you picked up the wrong bag at the airport], what would you do in such a case? You could make do with what you have. Cram your body into the tight clothes, deck out in other-gender jewelry, and head out for your appointments. But would you?
No one wants to live out of someone else's bag.
Then why do we? Odds are, someone has urged a force fit into clothes not packed for you.
— Max Lucado, *Cure for the Common Life*

When the ego-self is out of the way, you can go anywhere and do anything with total victory. This is because you have an entirely new definition of success, unknown to those still drugged by delusion. The deluded man thinks that success consists of ego-gratification, therefore, he fears whatever clashes with his egotistical demands. He has borrowed confidence of a man who has borrowed his feelings from exterior conditions which are subject to change. How will he feel when he loses them?
— Vernon Howard, *Pathways to Perfect Living*

Not that I urge buying this book (too uneven and inefficient; a biography masquerading as a self-help title), but John T. Reed's *Succeeding* has some good tips here: Reject Little Old Me-sim.

Substitute "All they can say is no-ism" instead. Ask yourself, "*If God said I could be anything I want, what would I choose?*" You have to work hard at learning who you are and thus in which niche you will thrive, and this takes time, usually until your mid-20s. Try as many things as you can as early as possible (the only way to learn about yourself). Shadow different careers for 2-3 weeks as an intern. Do your reconnaissance and rehearsal for tests, matches, etc. The corporate world has only so many "holes" — you might not fit there.

From HBS he learned: Write a synopsis of your life story and scrutinize it for recurring themes. Analyze who was important to you, your transitions, moves, jobs. What did you like? Analyze "roads not taken" and how you felt in retrospect. This will help you learn purpose.

> *The oak indwells the acorn. Want direction for the future? Then read your life backward.*
>
> *Simply quarry . . . your uniqueness. Da Vinci painted one Mona Lisa. Beethoven composed one Fifth Symphony. And God made one version of you. He custom designed you for a one-of-a-kind assignment. Mine like a gold digger the unique-to-you nuggets from your life.*
>
> *When God gives an assignment, he also gives the skill. Study your skills, then, to reveal your assignment.*
>
> *Look back over your life. What have you consistently done well? What have you loved to do? Stand at the intersection of your affections and successes and find your uniqueness.*
>
> *We exist to exhibit God, to display his glory. We serve as canvases for his brush stroke, papers for his pen, soil for his seeds, glimpses of his image. ("God has given gifts to each of you from his great variety of spiritual gifts. Manage them well . . . Then God will be given the glory." 1 Peter 4:10-11 NLT)*
>
> — Max Lucado, *Cure for the Common Life*

Reed's p. 47 "Things you cannot change" include height, personality, relatives, IQ, uncorrectable physical features, irreparable physical handicaps, talent (the ability to do something almost effortlessly), general body type, leadership ability/charisma, age, race, and ancestors.

On the next page is a list of things you *can* change, and it's extensive: weight, friends, career, knowledge, correctable physical features and handicaps, blood pressure, muscle memory, stamina, bad habits, physical fitness, hair style/color, grooming, the way you dress, diet, exercise, medical care habits, sleep habits, where you live and work, whether you are self-employed, spouse, where your money is invested, marriage, goals, hobbies, whether you make an honest living, and savings habits. His takeaway quote is spot on:

With regard to the things on this list of things you can change, you ought to be squared away on all of them. To put it another way, none of these things should be hampering your ability to achieve your goals. If one or more of them is, fix it.

Succeeding isn't easy. It's stupid to unnecessarily make it harder.

everyone has gifts — what are yours?

*Changing your temperament is probably impossible, and you don't have to change yourself to change your life. What you love is as unique to you as your fingerprints. Nothing you love is there without a reason. You need to know that because **nothing will make you happy but doing what you love.** When you love to do something, that means you have a gift for it. Every time. And when you're gifted at something, you have to do it. That love is the surefire indicator of hidden gifts, and it is the only way to find them. Skills don't count. They're just abilities that were useful enough to be developed. You will need to find out what motivates you, so you'll treat yourself right.*

Whatever you need, you're going to get. That's how you'd treat anyone else if you sincerely wanted them to succeed, and that's how you're going to treat yourself.

— Barbara Sher, *Live the Life You Love*

A gift is an inborn ability that seems to come naturally and effortlessly, and you wonder why everyone else cannot also do it. Existing gifts can be developed, but you cannot create giftedness in yourself where none exists. (*I.e.*, you *cannot* become anything you want to be! You have a set of gifts, and that is your range.) They come in many forms: social, leadership, artistic, critical thinking, athletic, mathematical, financial, salesmanship, musical, physical prowess, counseling, etc. From the book *Unique Ability*, classify all these gifts as: strong, relatively strong, relatively weak, and weak.

Once you've discovered your core gifts, you must develop them until they are impossible to overlook. *Then,* your gifts will make you money. For example, see if you can discern the ideal job for a person with the below personality types and capabilities:

A strong disposition to pay attention to the outside world rather than what is going on inside his own head.

A strong tolerance for highly repetitive work.

A perfectionist streak, or at least a need for accuracy.

A strong tolerance for frustration due to others' mistakes.

The ability to handle multiple external stimuli at once.

Reliable spatial visualization capability.

A stellar short-term memory.

Better than average hearing ability.

This is a very unique mix, pointing to an Aircraft Traffic Controller.

In Matthew 25:14-15 Jesus tells the parable of the talents, where a wealthy man before going on a trip divided up his fortune to be managed by his three servants. A "talent" in the Greek currency meant 10,000 denari, and a denari was worth about a day's wages. Now, if you work about 260 days/year, it would take you nearly 40 years to work 10,000 days. That is a working lifetime. So, one talent means a lifetime of earnings. Your talent — if discovered, properly developed, and fully exploited — will support you throughout your entire life. In that parable, only two servants invested their master's wealth; the third, as Lucado remarked, "*hugged the trunk* [and] *failed to benefit the master with his talent. Sin, at its ugly essence, confiscates heaven's gifts for selfish gain.*"

> *Make a careful exploration of who you are and the work you have been given, and then sink yourself into that.*
> — Galatians 6:4

other men can help you find your way

> *A man's capacity to receive another man's direct criticism is a measure of his capacity to receive masculine energy. If he doesn't have a good relationship to masculine energy (e.g., his father), then he will act like a woman and be hurt and defensive rather than make use of other men's criticism.*
> *Choose men who themselves are living at their edge, facing their fears and living just beyond them. Men of this kind can love you without protecting you from the necessary confrontation with reality that your life involves.*
> — David Deida, *The Way of the Superior Man*

always be true to yourself

> *You better not compromise yourself — it's all you've got.*
> — Janis Joplin

> *No one can live on a level inconsistent with the way he sees himself.*
> — John C. Maxwell, *The 21 Indispensable Qualities of a Leader*

You have an individuality. It is your most precious possession. Cherish it and develop it to the fullest. It is your only claim to importance. There's genius in all of us if we'll look for it and believe in ourselves enough.
— Grant G. Gard, *Don't Just Talk About It — Do It!*

What I must do is all that concerns me, not what the people think. . . . It is easy in the world to live after the world's opinion; it is easy in solitude to live after your own; but the great man is he who in the midst of the crowd keeps with perfect sweetness the independence of solitude.
— Emerson

If a man does not keep pace with his companions, perhaps it is because he hears a different drummer. Let him step to the music which he hears, however measured or far away.
— Thoreau

Your ego as you reflect it to the world has been built for many years out of childhood influences, later influences and a great many other factors. Your ego is as individual as your fingerprints, and what is "healthy" to you will not be healthy for another man.
— Napoleon Hill, *Grow Rich with Peace of Mind*

The world is in a constant conspiracy against the brave. It's the age-old struggle — the roar of the crowd on one side and the voice of your conscience on the other.
— Douglas MacArthur

living Life *your* way

Everything popular is wrong.
— Oscar Wilde

You don't have to accept the "accepted" society, you can invent your own, and therefore avoid, to a large degree, the pitfalls of the accepted society system.
— Michael W. Dean, *A User's Manual For the Human Experience*

Everything can be taken from a man but one thing: the last of the human freedoms — to choose one's attitude in any given set of circumstances, to choose one's own way.
— Viktor Frankl

The world is before you, and you need not take it or leave it as it was when you came in.
— James Baldwin

Rabbi Zusya said that on that day of judgment, God would not ask him why he had not been Moses, but why he had not been Zusya.
        — Walter Kaufmann

It doesn't matter how badly you paint, so long as you don't paint badly like other people.
        — George Moore

You will always gravitate to that which you secretly most love. Men do not attain that which they want but that which they yearn. You will become . . . "as small as your controlling desire, as great as your dominant aspiration."
        — James Allen

What is the remedy? . . . Is it not the chief disgrace in the world, not to be a unit; — not to be reckoned one character; — not to yield that particular fruit which each man was created to bear, but to be reckoned in the gross, in the hundred, or the thousand. Not so, brothers and friends — please God, ours shall be not be so.
        — Emerson (1837)

Two roads diverged in a wood, and I
— I took the one less traveled by,
And that has made all the difference.
        — Robert Frost, "The Road Not Taken"

The world clamors for conformity and regularity. A plant not growing where desired is called a "weed". Insist on being different and you'll pay a "traitor's" price. It's nothing personal but it took me years to realize that. To survive, the black sheep must be made of steel wool. A great man is not great because he does great things. A great man is great because he takes on the neglected tasks of many other men who have failed to answer their own calling. Don't wait for your ship to come in; swim out to it. If you have a gift, take it further than where you found it. Everyone lives their own length of life, but rarely their fullest width or depth. It is your attitude about yourself that others will adopt. And why wouldn't they? Aren't you the World's Expert on You?

Think of what the best version of yourself would be. When picturing the best version of yourself, stop and ask, "Are the words I use in alignment with the best I can possibly be?" If not, then change the way you are talking.
        — Larry Winget, *Shut Up, Stop Whining, Get A Life!*

Why should you be a "somebody"? So that you can join others in the madhouse? Earn your own living, live you own life, and be a decent person. This is being somebody in the right way.

There is a way to be successful every day. It is to determine that each worry or tension will reveal some new esoteric secret to you.   Then, no event can be called a failure, for you are succeeding inwardly, which is the only place that counts.

If you want to know what you value in life, notice what you get in life. They will be the same, for we always get what we truly value. Everyone on earth may support a lie, but your own nature won't. To change what you get, change what you value.

Internal freedom must come before external liberty, for, in fact, all freedom is internal. When your mind is liberated from a sense of being insulted or ignored, no one can insult you. A free mind has no self-reference, for there is no false self to be insulted or ignored.

— Vernon Howard, *Pathways to Perfect Living*

Compare not yourself to others. You must take responsibility for doing the creative best you can with your own life.
    — Galatians 6:4-5

If it is to be, it is up to me.
    — E. Wilford Edmar

To those of you under 22: after high-school and college there is basically no pressure to be "cool". Adults are too busy making their way in the real world to care about being popular at the expense of meaningful goals. Get through your teenage years knowing this in advance, and it will help you ignore any taunts from the so-called "jocks" (who will never have any professional sports career, anyway).

You say the little efforts that I make
will do no good: they never will prevail
to tip the hovering scale
where Justice hangs in balance.
    I don't think
I ever thought they would.
But I am prejudiced beyond debate
in favor of my right to choose which side
shall feel the stubborn ounces
of my weight.
        — Bonaro W. Overstreet, "Stubborn Ounces"

Be who you are and say what you feel because those who mind don't matter and those who matter don't mind.
    — Dr. Suess

As Balthasar Gracian wisely counseled, *"You should aim to be independent of any one vote, of any one fashion, of any one century."*

10 Commandments of Entrepreneurs, Artists, Free-Thinkers
From Michael Powell's *Mind Games* are some great tips:

❶   *Be prepared to make mistakes and ignore social disapproval.*
❷   *Tolerate being "different".*
❸   *Face your mistakes and angering stuff head on.*
❹   *Resist grasping for the first solution; tolerate the anxiety of uncertainty to discover the best results.*
❺   *Develop an accurate perception of reality, rather than twisting it to suit your own laziness, narcissism, or need for comfort.*
❻   *Stop wasting time on "inner growth" — get out there and party — meet new people every day.*
❼   *Keep in touch with old friends. Take nothing for granted.*
❽   *Distrust "fixing" your beliefs. Admit when you're wrong.*
❾   *Enjoy the contradictions in life — tidy living is for lifestyle magazines.*
❿   *Be yourself; don't be misguided by another's "personal vision".*

don't forget about God
You cannot be anything you want to be. But you can be everything God wants you to be.   . . . God never prefabs or mass-produces people.   "Don't live carelessly, unthinkingly.   Make sure you understand what the Master wants." Ephesians 5:17 MSG
Lonely? God is with you.
Depleted? He funds the overdrawn.
Weary of an ordinary existence: Your spiritual adventure awaits.
The cure for the common life begins and ends with God.
When you're full of yourself, God can't fill you.
Moses had a staff.
David had a sling.
Samson had a jawbone.
Rahab had a string.
Mary had some ointment.
Aaron had a rod.
Dorcas had a needle.
All were used by God.
What do you have?
    — Max Lucado, *Cure for the Common Life*

Throw yourself into the work of the Master, confident that nothing you do for Him is a waste of time or effort.
    — 1 Cor. 15:58 MSG

If you try to keep your life for yourself, you will lose it. But if you give up your life for me, you will find true life.
— Jesus, from Matthew 16:25 NLT

look for quality "barriers to entry", and go through them

A friend of mine likes to attend horse races, though he does not bet. Walking past the paddock (which required a pass to enter) he inquired about the fee. $3. He paid, entered, and was astonished at the dramatically higher level of people inside. Better dressed, well-spoken, entrepreneurs, doctors, etc. For just $3! I remarked that he didn't pay $3 to get *in*, but that folks inside had paid $3 to keep the unwashed hordes *out*. ($3 was a sufficient barrier to entry for oafs who proudly wear sweatpants and *Who Farted? — I did!* T-shirts.)

Two very large public events occur every August: the Sturgis, South Dakota Harley rally, and the EAA AirVenture Fly-in at Oshkosh, Wisconsin. Every year at Sturgis there are numerous DUIs, fights, arrests, injurious accidents, and several deaths. However, at Oshkosh, there are very few arrests and often no injuries or deaths — even after 10 days of thousands of aircraft coming and going on only three runways, often with a separation of less than 30 seconds.

Life consists of many strata "barriers to entry". Becoming a private pilot takes considerable dedication, study, and daring. Not to mention about $10,000. To maintain flying skills costs about $100/hour for an average rental Cessna. To fly just 100 hours/year for skills currency and growth is a $10,000 expense. It's no wonder that only 1 American in 300 is a pilot. The "barrier to entry" to become a biker (although more than a car driver) is far less than a pilot.

At Oshkosh AirVenture, it is absolutely routine to leave your iPad on a public charger, and come back for it an hour later. This, amongst literally thousands of strangers milling about. Nobody will take it. Why? Because they know that . . . it . . . is . . . *not* . . . *theirs*. Pretty simple.

The most astonishing I learned about the general aviation (GA) culture when I became a private pilot was the universal level of trust amongst airmen. You can fly to a faraway airport, land for lunch, and the Fixed Base Operator (FBO) almost always has a courtesy car on hand to lend you. For free, if just for a couple of hours. (Just replace the fuel you used.) The keys will usually be hanging on a hook for you. Snacks and drinks are in the fridge, with an honor system cash box. Why this trust? Because you pushed through a very significant barrier to entry to have become a pilot; you are assumed to be a better class of person. And you very probably are. Almost as much as the flying itself

I have enjoyed being treated automatically as a responsible, competent, and honest person. There are very few bozos to deal with.

It's like living on Planet Adult.

Elsewhere, on Planet Hooligan, people are assumed to be irresponsible and incapable of running their own lives. (This must be true, as they don't seem to chafe much about being treated that way.) They are not even trusted enough to routinely board a commercial airliner without weapons and evil intent, so they must be bombarded with terraherzian energy (known to damage DNA) and then groped by surly blue-gloved strangers who seem to actually suspect that toddlers and white-haired grannies pose a threat to airline safety.

Moral: seek out notable barriers to entry, as they are there for good reason. Pay the money or get the training you need to break through, as there are high-quality people on the other side.

COURAGE

Courage is the first of human qualities because it is the quality which guarantees all others.
  — Sir Winston Churchill

Courage is grace under pressure.
  — Ernest Hemingway

Often the test of courage is not to die but to live.
  — Conte Vittorio Alfieri

Brave men can live well anywhere.
A coward dreads all things.
  — Norse mythology proverb

As Aristotle so wisely put it in his *Eudemian Ethics*, courage is the proper balance between fear and recklessness. Another element of courage is to not forsake the future for the present:

> *I am aware that orderliness and punctuality are not usually regarded as forms of courage. But the essential element of all courage is in them — **the power to face a disagreeable present in the interest of desirable permanent ends**. They are far more important in modern life than the courage to face bears or bullets. They underlie the more spectacular forms of courage. The man who cannot reduce to order the things that are lying passively about him, and endure the petty pains incidental to doing hard things before the sheer lapse of time forces him to action, is not*

*the man who will be calm and composed when angry mobs are howling about him, or who will go steadily on his way when greed and corruption, hypocrisy and hate, are arrayed to resist him. For whether in the quiet of a study and the routine of an office, or in the turmoil of a riot or a strike, **true courage is the ready and steadfast acceptance of whatever pains are incidental to securing the personal and public ends that are at stake.***
— William De Witt Hyde, *The Cardinal Virtues*, 1902
www.artofmanliness.com/2012/04/14/manvotional-the-cardinal-virtues-courage

(I hadn't considered that one's time horizon is a factor in courage, but Hyde makes an excellent observation.) There are many variants of courage (physical/martial social, financial, moral, etc.), and very few people possess them all. That is, nearly everybody is afraid of something. A battle-hardened vet may be scared to speak out in public, while combat terrifies the moral orator. Perhaps neither would dare challenge the IRS. Basically, there are two main types of courage: physical and moral.

physical/martial courage (valor)

Valor is a martial courage, *i.e.*, bravery under great physical danger. This is required of soldiers in combat, a man defending himself in a street attack, or a fireman entering a burning building. Prior training helps immensely. To be capable of valor, you must have stretched yourself through some hard training involving denial, pain, discomfort, and fear. You routinely live at your edge, and thus know how to handle your fears. Train hard; fight easy!

moral courage (intellectual, social, financial, political)

Courage is not limited to the battlefield or the Indianapolis 500 or bravely catching a thief in your house. The real tests of courage are much deeper and much quieter. They are the inner tests, like remaining faithful when nobody's looking, like enduring pain when the room is empty, like standing alone when you're misunderstood.
— Charles R. Swidoll

Valor would cease to be a virtue if there were no injustice.
— Agesilaus

What is interesting is that many men have shown great valor in their fields, yet *moral* courage — risking unpopularity, censure, or money for a just cause — seems far too uncommon, as Henry Hazlitt explains in his superb 1922 essay:

Moral courage is the rarest of all the rare things of this earth. The war has shown that millions have physical courage. Millions were willing to face rifle and cannon, bombardment, poison gas, liquid fire, and the bayonet; to trust themselves to flying machines thousands of feet in air, under the fire of anti-aircraft guns of enemy planes; to go into submarines, perhaps to meet a horrible death. But how many had the courage merely to make themselves unpopular? The bitter truth must be told: the many enlisted or submitted to the draft on both sides of the conflict not because they were convinced that they were helping to save the world, not because they had any real hatred for the enemy, not to uphold the right, but simply that they hadn't the moral courage to face the stigma of "slacker" or "conscientious objector." . . .

Fear of death? No; the soldiers faced death bravely. But they feared unpopularity, they dreaded the suspicion of their fellows. What was needed in war is needed no less urgently in peace. How many persons in public or even in private life have the courage to say the thing that people do not like to hear?

— Henry Hazlitt (1922), www.mises.org/books/willpower.pdf

To sin by silence when they should protest makes cowards of us all.
— Edmund Burke

The late William F. Buckley, Jr. also touched on this theme in his 1961 essay "Why Don't We Complain?":

. . . we are all increasingly anxious in America to be unobtrusive; we are reluctant to make our voices heard, hesitant about claiming our rights; we are afraid that our cause is unjust, or that if it is not unjust, it is ambiguous, or if not even that, then too trivial to justify the horrors of a confrontation with Authority; we will sit in an oven or endure a racking headache before undertaking a head-on, I'm-here-to-tell-you complaint. That tendency to passive compliance, to a heedless endurance, is something to keep one's eyes on — in sharp focus.

Buckley opined that increasing technology has sapped our ability to personally look after our own needs — our *"direct responsibility for our material environment"*. We are thus *"conditioned to adopt a position of helplessness"*. Good point. This is why I like to do as much for myself as possible, and always have basic tools nearby for the task. It is a rare occasion for me to actually need a plumber or mechanic. Moderate self-sufficiency can indeed bolster one's moral courage. Men who *can* do something will tend to act, vs. merely sulk.

As Justice Clarence Thomas remarked, *"the term 'non-judgmental' is simply a matter of moral cowardice"*. Moral courage means not letting the opinions of others (and their consequences) dissuade you from what you believe is right. Everyone — and I do mean *everyone* — will be confronted with at least one important issue in his Life where the only right thing to say is: "*This is wrong. I won't do it.*" The relevant phrase in Latin is worth learning: *Et si omnes, ergo non.* ("Even if everyone else, not I.")

> *Doesn't matter what the press says. Doesn't matter what the politicians or the mobs say. Doesn't matter if the whole country decides that something wrong is something right. This nation was founded on one principle above all else: The requirement that we stand up for what we believe, no matter the odds or the consequences. When the mob and the press and the whole world tell you to move, your job is to plant yourself like a tree beside the river of truth, and tell the whole world — "No. You move."*
> — Mark Twain

Finally, it takes courage to stand up to overreaching government:

> *Government exists to protect my rights, not to order my life. And I damn sure don't exist to serve government.*
>
> *You are not a tool of the state. You are not to be used as political cannon fodder for the elevation of a politician or political movement. You belong to you, certainly not to the government. Reclaim your ownership of yourself, and let these politicians know that you recognize and reject their war on the individual.*
> — Neal Boortz, *Somebody's Gotta Say It*

life requires courage

> *Those who are guided by their fears are not men but rabbits. The hyenas of the world count upon cowardice for their success. Once we admit that we are afraid, we have lost the war without firing a shot.*
> — Jeff Cooper

> *No good tactical plan grows from a timid mindset.*
> — USMC Captain Nathaniel, Fick *One Bullet Away*

> *Liberty extends in many directions. Those who fear slavery are the ones who have made themselves slaves, for they have conditioned themselves to it and they know how defenseless they have become. Cast out fear of loss of liberty and drive ahead.*
> — Napoleon Hill, *Grow Rich with Peace of Mind*

Fortes Fortuna Juvat. (Fortune favors the brave.)

courage is the control of fear, not the lack of fear

Courage is doing what you're afraid to do.
There can be no courage unless you're scared.
I'll fight like a wildcat!
— WWI fighter pilot ace Eddie Rickenbacker

Take therefore no thought for tomorrow; for tomorrow shall take thought for the things of itself. Sufficient unto the day is the end thereof.
— Matthew 6:34

Our fears are always more numerous than our dangers.
— Seneca

Courage is fear that has said its prayers.
— Karl Barth, Swiss theologian

Keep your fears to yourself, but share your courage with others.
— Robert Louis Stevenson

courage is an organ, with automatic function

Fearful people are centered in the head. Courage depends upon the body's ability to act appropriately from a nonthinking state of mind. It is doing before thinking, a time when the body acts before the acquired personality has time to intervene.
— Helen Palmer, *The Enneagram*, p. 267

As I've remarked many times in speeches and in other books, courage is like a muscle which must be exercised regularly. Daily, even.

new and good things require initial courage

The desire for safety stands against every great and noble enterprise.
— Tacitus

Fear not that your life will come to an end but that it will never have a beginning.
— John Henry Newman, British theologian

anyone can develop courage

Courage is the product of self-confidence and habit.
— Gen. George S. Patton

Make us to choose the harder right instead of the easier wrong, and never to be content with a half-truth when the whole can be won. Endow us with courage that . . . knows no fear when truth and right are in jeopardy.
  — West Point prayer for moral courage

If the Lion in the *Wizard of Oz* can develop courage, so can you!

a conscience is maintained by courage
To know what is right and not to do it is the worst cowardice.
  — Confucius

Nothing is easier than saying words. Nothing is harder than living them day after day.
  — Arthur Gordon

Apathy is the glove into which evil slips its hand.
  — Bodie Thoene

The advice "choose your battles" implies that you do indeed choose some! Why do certain people go on a moral crusade?

. . . because they dread living with a corrupted self more than they dread isolation from others.
  — C. Fred Alford, *Whistleblowers, Broken Lives and Organizational Power*

courage is often very simply exercised
"I would prefer not to." He offers no emotion, no enlargement on any refusal; he prefers not to explain himself.
  The simple exercise of free will, without any hysterics, denunciations, or bombast, throws consternation into social machinery — free will contradicts the management principle. Refusing to allow yourself to be regarded as a "human resource" is more revolutionary than any revolution on record.
  — www.johntaylorgatto.com, *The Bartleby Project*

You must do the thing you think you cannot do.
  — Eleanor Roosevelt

John C. Maxwell's 3 steps
  ❶ face the music (stretch yourself, just to grow courage)
  ❷ talk to that person (stop avoiding the confrontation)
  ❸ take a giant step (and thus avoid having giant regrets)

have the courage to be *great*
The price of greatness is responsibility.
— Winston Churchill

Great is relative to yourself. Not everyone can be Theodore Roosevelt or Julius Caesar. Strive for the best *you* can become, and that is your "greatness". Change college majors, change your career, leave a bad relationship, ask out that girl of your dreams, take a stand for what you know is right. Seek the potential greatness in yourself, and do not be satisfied with anything less. Have the courage to be the biggest self possible, as you daily overcome fear and laziness.

no majority is courageous
Cowardice in a race, as in an individual, is the unpardonable sin.
— Theodore Roosevelt

Whenever you find yourself on the side of the majority, it is time to pause and reflect.
— Mark Twain

It is better to have a right destroyed than to abandon it because of fear.
— Phillip Mann

People deserve what they tolerate.
— Fred Reed, www.fredoneverything.net

What great cause would have been fought and won under the banner, "I stand for consensus"?
— Prime Minister Margaret Thatcher

Those who cannot cope, the weaklings and cowards, bitterly resent those who do not share their weaknesses, and there are plenty of them as we see continuously in the news, and they know that demanding new gun laws is a most soul-satisfying way to punish what they consider right-wing wrongheadedness on every social and political issue from defense spending to capital punishment.
— William J. Hellmer

Resolved: That the timid are not philosophically qualified to comment on the activities of the courageous.
— Jeff Cooper

Lies and ignorance and laziness are herd animals which must band together for protection. On their own, they'd be picked off by a solitary example of truth, knowledge, or action. They must operate in the *Nacht und Nebel* (night and fog) of things, splintering responsibility in so many shards that no one can be held accountable. Those huddled in the majority are cowards.

Cowardice asks . . . is it safe?
Expediency asks . . . is it political?
Vanity asks . . . is it popular?
Conscience asks . . . is it *right?*

The reason why a crowd cannot have courage is because a crowd does not have a conscience. It *cannot* have one. A crowd's driving force is *emotion,* caused by the relinquishing of individual conscience for some primal passion of anger, hatred, tribalism, or envy.

it is up to the *individual* to exercise courage
He means well, but he means well feebly.
— Theodore Roosevelt

Courage is contagious. When a brave man takes a stand, the spines of others are stiffened.
— Billy Graham

Don't look to the crowd for courage, for the crowd only has a numerical bravado. Individually, they are weak — and they know it. Individually, you must be strong, and once you are you'll never need any crowd. Never grow a wishbone where your backbone ought to be.

I can't stop it, but I don't have to suffer it.
— Fred Reed

And there comes a time when one must take a position that is neither safe, nor political, nor popular — but one must take it simply because it is right.
— Martin Luther King, Jr.

Leadership is the expression of courage that compels people to do the right thing.
— Jim Mellado

One man with courage makes the majority.
— Andrew Jackson

The black sheep must be made of steel wool. Get started!

All the significant battles are waged within self.
— Sheldon Kopp, psychotherapist

become a Hero

It is said the one machine can do the work of fifty ordinary men.
No machine, however, can do the work of one extraordinary man.
— Tehyi Hsieh

Hero is a word that's been diluted and overused into oblivion. For example, surprised victims of disaster are not really "heroes", but victims. (Those who exhibit bravery to save others are the heroes.) Let's bring back the heroism in heroes.

Forty years after his infamous Stanford Prison Experiment, Zimbardo has taken up the task of finding out what causes individuals to move from cowardly inaction, to heroic action. After analyzing the deeds of heroes both big and small, Zimbardo along with his research partner, Dr. Franco, argue that heroic individuals have a robust heroic imagination.

According to Zimbardo and Franco, the heroic imagination is "the capacity to imagine facing physically or socially risky situations, to struggle with the hypothetical problems these situations generate, and to consider one's actions and the consequences." It's the ability to see oneself as a hero and capable of heroic action before the need for heroic action arises.

— Developing the Heroic Imagination: The 5 Traits of Heroes
  www.artofmanliness.com/2010/03/14/developing-the-heroic-imagi
  nation-the-5-traits-of-heroes

This essay describes five traits to strengthen your heroic imagination:

❶ Maintain constant vigilance for situations that require heroic action.
❷ Learn not to fear conflict because you took a stand.
❸ Imagine alternative future scenarios beyond the present moment.
❹ Resist the urge to rationalize and justify inaction.
❺ Trust that people will appreciate heroic (often unpopular) actions.

I would agree with all except ❺. In my experience, such expressed appreciation (even later) is so rare that I would never factor in the chance of it as part of your motivation. Do right because you should, and forget about any potential adulation for it.

Heroism is never futile, for it is a thing of the soul, demonstrating that man is more than just another animal. This is a truth that

needs emphasis in the dingy modern era, when the race's most basic values are under attack. Honor is, at last, all we can take with us.
      — Jeff Cooper, *Another Country*

MANHOOD & MASCULINITY

The notion of character had changed. Once it was thought manly, and womanly, to bear up without complaint under adversity; today, whimpering is believed to be a manifestation of moral authenticity. The national slogan might be, "Dare to Snivel." Weakness has become strength and strength, weakness.

. . . Schools routinely eject boy children for any display of independence, masculine competitiveness, or taste for adventure. We now ban tag as violent. Instead we must be sensitive, soft, and remorselessly good. We no longer even know what sex we are. Male models are shaven-chested and oiled, male radio voices an octave higher than in the last generation. Women wear shoulder pads.

. . . The ash drifts deeper over Pompeii, the inner savages grow bolder in the thickening murk, and the best yield to epicene forcelessness and drab androgyny. Culturally, though not commercially, America is, I think, on the way out.

The curtain falls, as eventually it must on everything. Meanwhile, here is a circus worthy of the admission, a fabulous suicide, more astonishing than the implosion of the Soviet Union. We see a new kink in the historical rope: a dominant culture, the inventor of the modern world, once supreme militarily, in the sciences, commercially, boisterously confident even thirty-five years ago, suddenly and piously drinking hemlock.
      — Fred Reed, *Nekkid in Austin*, Foreword

What is a good man but a bad man's teacher?
What is a bad man but a good man's job?
If you don't understand this, you will get lost,
However intelligent you are.
It is the great secret.
      — Lao-tzu

Within the (formerly) expected timeline of a young man's life, by the age of 23 he had a college degree and his first year's job experience within his career path. However, today's 28 y/o has but two years yet of college to finish and then his first year on the job, so it will take three years to arrive at where he should have been five years ago! Thus, at 31 he is eight years behind the curve — and that's 8 years of his 13 years of adulthood. Three-fifths of his young adulthood squandered because he never took the time to grow up and discover his own Manly Purpose. Again, as I've written elsewhere: there is no shortcut to this! Aimlessness is silly, and without Purpose a male will find himself repeatedly back to "Square One".

Social media has extended youth culture into a complete self-supported insular "culture" where children never have to become adults. Boys get to remain boys, even well into their 30s. It is embarrassing that they are not ashamed of this. (Note "Pajama Boy" on the back cover. He apparently wasn't aware of his own childishness until the howl of derision from his insipid ad shilling for ObamaCare. Little Ethan then deleted all his social media accounts in shame.)

physical traits

You cannot change how tall you are, but you can change how tall you stand.
— John T. Reed

Men vary widely in their build, muscle tone, pitch of voice, facial hair, etc. If he has an inner attitude of manliness, it will show through his bearing and confidence even if he is not physically commanding. I've seen many pip-squeaks of stature who were clearly Men who tolerated no disrespect.

masculine character

As Aubrey Adelin of *Man of Steel and Velvet* explains, being a man — being "macho" — doesn't have to mean coarseness.

Traits which are strongly masculine include aggressiveness, drive, decisiveness, firmness, determination, resoluteness, unyielding steadfastness, courage, fearlessness, independence, and competence and efficiency in the masculine world.

masculine ability

It is exemplified in the leadership ability needed to guide the family or succeed in some phase of work. Or a man typifies such ability by possessing the knowledge to build his own shelter, grow a garden, or otherwise protect his family from want.

how to develop masculinity

by serving as his family's guide, protector, and provider
by building society through leadership
by developing the masculine traits of character
by increasing masculine skill and ability

by developing his physical capacity
by accentuating his differences from women
by setting challenging goals

living like a man

A man must love his father and yet be free of his father's expectations and criticisms in order to be a free man.
— David Deida, *The Way of the Superior Man*

If you have them, do not ignore powerful urgings to become your own man.
— John T. Reed

As our civilization urbanizes, and as more and more of our young people never set foot off the pavement, much less clean a fish, we can no longer take for granted that our youth naturally and automatically understand the traditions which gave us this country, and which must be maintained if we wish to keep it.
— Jeff Cooper, *To Ride, Shoot Straight and Speak the Truth*

The knight is a man of blood and iron, a man familiar with the sight of smashed faces and the ragged stumps of lopped-off limbs; he is also a demure, almost a maidenlike, guest in hall, a gentle, modest, unobtrusive man. He is not a compromise or happy mean between ferocity and meekness; he is fierce to the nth and meek to the nth . . . .
Will the ethos [of a classless society] *be a synthesis of what was best in all the classes or a mere "pool" with the sediment of all and the virtues of none?*
— C.S. Lewis, "Notes on the Way" (17 August 1940)

Optimism means expecting the best, but confidence means knowing how to handle the worst. Never make a move if you are merely optimistic.
— The Zurich Axioms

Having never climbed the mountain of discipline one is unable to climb anything at all.
— J.R. Nyquist, *Origins of the Fourth World War*, p. 121

The stronger you become, the lighter things seem. This is true not only with physical weight, but psychic weight as well. Remain weak, and even small things will seem heavy. Become, as author Aubrey Adelin urges, a "man of steel and velvet". Whining never solved anything except to separate the men from the boys. Avoid the spectacle of this:

Seven-eighths lawyer and one-eighth man.
— Theodore Roosevelt, of Senator Elihu Root

what makes a Real Man?

It looks as if whimpering is replacing doing. Used to be, a stripling kid might have all manner of doubts about his manhood. So he'd join the Army and become a paratrooper. He'd leap out of airplanes and run 70 miles with a 1200 pound pack, uphill, in a snowstorm. . . .

Today the kid would be sneered at, by people frightened of a dark night in suburbia, because he had something to prove. That's exactly what he had. And he proved it. It works. Afterwards he doesn't have to worry about what he's made of. He knows.
— Fred Reed, *Nekkid in Austin*

Sans peur et sans reproche.
(Without fear and without fault.)
— a phrase coined to describe Chevalier Bayard (1473–1532)

The way a man penetrates the world should be the same way he penetrates his woman; not merely for personal gain or pleasure, but to magnify love, openness, and depth.

. . . Yet, many men settle for enjoying a little bit of freedom and love while incompletely giving their gifts. They enjoy the freedom to buy a nice car, to have loving sex fairly often, and to sleep late on Sunday. . . . But for many men, it is still not enough.

Many men are willing to poke their woman and bloom her in a mediocre way, sharing a few orgasms and a few emotional moments of bonding before going over tomorrow's schedule. Many men are willing to poke the world and bloom it in a mediocre way, making a few bucks and contributing enough betterment so they don't feel like their life is a total waste.

If you are going to tryst with women and world at all, better to go all the way and ravish them from the depths of your true core, blooming them open with the wide gifts of your unrelenting heart. Otherwise, if you sheepishly penetrate them to gratify your own needs, your woman and the world will feel your lack of dedication, depth, and truth. Rather than yielding in love to your loving, they will distract you, suck your energy, and draw you into endless complications, so that your life and relationship become an almost constant search for release from constraint.

Make your life an ongoing process of being who you are, at your deepest, most easeful levels of being. Everything other than this process is secondary.
— David Deida, *The Way of the Superior Man*

From Patrick Morley's *7 Seasons of the Man in the Mirror* are these core values.

a Real Man is a man of courage

In his 1973 address to the U.S. Naval Academy, sci-fi author and WWI navy vet Robert Heinlein told this astounding story of courage:

> In my home town sixty years ago when I was a child, my mother and father used to take me and my brothers and sisters out to Swope Park on Sunday afternoons. It was a wonderful place for kids, with picnic grounds and lakes and a zoo. But a railroad line cut straight through it.
>
> One Sunday afternoon a young married couple were crossing these tracks. She apparently did not watch her step, for she managed to catch her foot in the frog of a switch to a siding and could not pull it free. Her husband stopped to help her. But try as they might they could not get her foot loose. While they were working at it, a tramp showed up, walking the ties. He joined the husband in trying to pull the young woman's foot loose. No luck.
>
> Out of sight around the curve a train whistled. Perhaps there would have been time to run and flag it down, perhaps not. In any case both men went right ahead trying to pull her free . . . and the train hit them. The wife was killed, the husband was mortally injured and died later, the tramp was killed — and testimony showed that neither man made the slightest effort to save himself. The husband's behavior was heroic . . . but what we expect of a husband toward his wife: his right, and his proud privilege, to die for his woman. But what of this nameless stranger? Up to the very last second he could have jumped clear. He did not. He was still trying to save this woman he had never seen before in his life, right up to the very instant the train killed him. And that's all we'll ever know about him.
>
> THIS is how a man dies. This is how a MAN . . . lives!

a Real Man is a man of wisdom

He knows when to act, and when to think things over. He keeps matters in proper perspective. He seeks advice when necessary.

a Real Man is a man of commitments

He is committed to God, to his family, and to high principles.

a Real Man is a man of balance

He earns his daily paycheck, yet has energy left over at quitting time for his family. He knows when to be kind and when to be stern. He understands that *being* is more important than *having*.

a Real Man is a secure leader

Insecure leaders are dangerous — to themselves, their followers, and the organizations they lead — because a leadership position amplifies personal flaws.
Insecure leaders have several common traits:
❶ *They don't provide security for others.*
❷ *They take more from people than they give.*
❸ *They continually limit their best people.*
❹ *They continually limit the organization.*
— John C. Maxwell, *The 21 Indispensable Qualities of a Leader*

a prime example of wholesome "bad-assery"

On 5 March 1904, while in office, President Theodore Roosevelt wrote:

> *I am wrestling with two Japanese wrestlers three times a week. I am not the age or the build, one would think, to be whirled lightly over an opponent's head and batted down on a mattress without damage; but they are so skilled that I have not been hurt at all. My throat is a little sore, because once when one of them had a strangle hold I also got hold of his windpipe and thought I could perhaps choke him off before he could choke me. However, he got ahead!*

Seven years later, while campaigning for President as the Progressive Party candidate, T.R. was shot in the chest with a .38 caliber revolver. Instead of rushing off to the hospital, he insisted on first giving a 45 minute speech!

> *Friends, I shall have to ask you to be as quiet as possible. I do not know whether you fully understand that I have been shot, but it takes more than that to kill a Bull Moose. But, fortunately I had my manuscript, so you see I was going to make a long speech! And, friends, the hole in it is where the bullet went through, and it probably saved the bullet from going into my heart. The bullet is in me now so that I cannot make a very long speech. But I will try my best . . .*
> *First of all, I want to say this about myself. I have altogether too many important things to think of to pay any heed or to feel any concern over my own death . . . I want you to understand that I am ahead of the game anyway. No man has had a happier life than I have had, a happier life in every way . . . I am not speaking for myself at all — I give you my word, I do not care a rap about being shot, not a rap. I have had a good many experiences in my time, and this is only one of them.*

"*And this is only one of them.*" Except for Andrew Jackson (and possibly George Washington), no President was ever such a bad-ass. T.R. had a Real Man's attitude:

> *There were all kinds of things of which I was afraid at first, ranging from grizzly bears to "mean" horses and gunfighters; but by acting as if I was not afraid I gradually ceased to be afraid. Most men can have the same experience if they choose.*

What is a "bad-ass"? It's a man who owns his fears courageously in order to live right at his edge.

> *Your fear is the sharpest definition of your self. You should know it. You should feel it virtually constantly. Fear needs to become your friend, so that you are no longer uncomfortable with it.* **Rather, primary fear shows you that you are at your edge.** *Staying with the fear, staying at your edge, allows real transformation to occur. . . .* **Own your fear, and lean just beyond it.** *In every aspect of your life. Starting now.*
>
> *The more a man is playing his real edge, the more valuable he is as good company for other men, the more he can be trusted to be authentic and fully present. Where a man's edge is located is less important than whether he is actually living his edge in truth, rather than being lazy or deluded.*
>
> *Some men fear the feeling of fear and therefore don't even approach their edge. They choose a job they know they can do well and easily, and don't even approach the fullest giving of their gift. Their lives are relatively secure and comfortable, but dead. The lack the aliveness, the depth, and the inspirational energy that is the sign of a man living at his edge. If you are this kind of man who is hanging back, working hard perhaps, but not at your real edge, other men will not be able to trust you can and will help them live at their edge and give their fullest gift.*
>
> *A free man is free to acknowledge his fears, without hiding them, or hiding from them. Live with your lips pressed against your fears, kissing your fears, neither pulling back nor aggressively violating them.*
>
> *In any given moment, a man's growth is optimized if he leans just beyond his edge, his capacity, his fear. He should not be too lazy, happily stagnating in the zone of security and comfort. Nor should he push far beyond his edge, stressing himself unnecessarily, unable to metabolize his experience. He should lean just slightly beyond the edge of fear and discomfort. Constantly. In everything he does.*
> — David Deida, *The Way of the Superior Man*

$\Box$ **6**

GETTING ALONG
(BETTER WITH PEOPLE)

No matter what you're after — money, love, ego food, or health — you need people. And it's easier for you to get what you want when people open their minds to you, give you their confidence, and believe in you.

In fact, if everyone you knew, everyone you met, simply believed everything you said, you could have just about anything you want.

Whatever progress you make . . . ., depends largely on those who have confidence or belief in you. (p. 147, 180)
— William J. Reilly, *How to Get What You Want Out of Life*

The most important single ingredient in the formula of success is knowing how to get along with people.
— Theodore Roosevelt

WHAT MOTIVATES PEOPLE?

Even the most destructive behaviors have a payoff. If you did not perceive the behavior in question to generate some value to you, you would not do it. If you want to stop behaving in a certain way, you've got to stop "paying yourself off" for doing it.

Find and control the payoffs, because you can't stop a behavior until you recognize what you are gaining from it. Payoffs can be as simple as money gained by going to work, to psychological payoffs of acceptance, approval, praise, love or companionship. It is possible that you are feeding off unhealthy, addictive and imprisoning payoffs, such as self-punishment or distorted self-importance.

Be alert to the possibility that your behavior is controlled by fear of rejection. It's easier not to change. Try something new or

put yourself on the line. Also consider if your need for immediate gratification creates an appetite for a small payoff now rather than a large payoff later.
— from Dr. Phil's Life Law #3, www.drphil.com/articles/article/44

What people say, what people do, and what people say they do are entirely different things.
— Margaret Mead

People are simple, really. MICE motivates people to action. MICE stands for Money, Ideology, Coercion, and Ego. People get paid to do it, or they believe in it, or they're forced to do it, or they feel good about themselves while doing it, or some combination thereof.

Author John C. Maxwell offers this very simple advice:

They like to feel special, so sincerely compliment them.
They want a better tomorrow, so show them hope.
They desire navigation, so navigate for them.
They are selfish, so speak to their needs first.
They get low emotionally, so encourage them.
They want success, so help them win.

If you deal with every customer in the same way, you will only close 25-30% of your contacts, because you will only close one personality type. But if you learn how to effectively work with all four personality types, you can conceivably close 100% of your contacts.
— Rod Nichols, marketing expert

BALANCE OUT YOUR PERSONALITY

I believe that more than half of our individual personality is guided or even determined by our genetics. For example, people who are fussy adults were likely fussy as babies. While upbringing and Life experiences certainly play an important role to shape personality, we seem to be born with a certain profile. With recognition and effort, you can balance out your own personality to the pleasure and benefit of all.

Some traits are inherently not very healthy, but tolerable in mild or occasional doses. However, they will quickly become toxic if even slightly overdeveloped:

Nonconforming   ➔   Antisocial

Shy	➜	Avoidant
Retiring	➜	Schizoid
Eccentric	➜	Schizotypal
Suspicious	➜	Paranoid
Capricious	➜	Borderline
Pessimistic	➜	Melancholic
Skeptical	➜	Negativistic
Aggrieved	➜	Masochistic

Even good traits will sour if taken too far:

Conscientious	➜	Compulsive
Cooperative	➜	Dependent
Sociable	➜	Histrionic
Confident	➜	Narcissistic
Assertive	➜	Sadistic
Exuberant	➜	Hypomanic

If our personalities were generally "issued" to us, can we really change ourselves? Yes, and to a surprising degree. Remember, what we do, we become. If you are not naturally the assertive type, and are tired of being a doormat — begin to stand up for yourself and say *No*. Or, if you're not naturally giving and helpful, start giving and helping. Over time you will improve yourself as you achieve a healthier balance in your personality. Nobody is ever perfect, but anyone can improve.

For every personality there's a tactic he's best suited to, and for every tactic, there's someone out there with the right personality for it. Diversity of tactics in the big picture is probably more important than finding the one right tactic. It's wise to choose your battles, but you don't usually get to choose what battles are available to choose from.
— kylben, from the FSW forum

Enneagram Personality Types

This is a very helpful tool for understanding yourself and others. We all have a dominant ego-archetypal type, several in the middle, and some very weak. Everybody has a main type which we utilize most and/or prefer, along with three sub-variants (social, sexual, self-preservation).

Type 1   Perfectionism ("The Perfectionist")
  "I must be perfect and good to be happy."
  Conscientious/Compulsive, Skeptical/Negativistic
  Characteristic role: **The Reformer**
                         The rational, idealistic type
  Ego Fixation: Resentment
  Holy Idea: Perfection
  Basic Fear: Being corrupt, evil, or defective
  Basic Desire: To be good, to have integrity
  Temptation: To be hypercritical of others
  Vice/Passion: Anger

Type 2   Helpfulness ("The Giver")
  "I must be helpful and caring to be happy."
  Sociable/Histrionic
  Characteristic role: **The Helper**
                         The caring, nurturing type
  Ego Fixation: Flattery
  Holy Idea: Freedom
  Basic Fear: Being unworthy of being loved
  Basic Desire: To be loved unconditionally
  Temptation: To manipulate for positive responses
  Vice/Passion: Pride (specifically, Vainglory)

Type 3   Image Focus ("The Performer")
  "I must be impressive and attractive to be happy."
  Exuberant/Hypomanic
  Characteristic role: **The Achiever and Motivator**
                         The adaptable, success-oriented type
  Ego fixation: Vanity
  Holy idea: Hope
  Basic Fear: Being worthless
  Basic Desire: To be valuable
  Temptation: To please everybody
  Vice/Passion: Deceit

Type 4   Hypersensitivity ("The Tragic Romantic")
"I must avoid painful feelings to be happy."
Capricious/Borderline, Aggrieved/Masochistic

Characteristic role:	**The Individualist and Artist**
	The intuitive, reserved type
Ego fixation:	Melancholy
Holy idea:	Origin
Basic Fear:	Being commonplace
Basic Desire:	To be unique and authentic
Temptation:	To beat themselves up and withdraw
Vice/Passion:	Envy

Type 5   Detachment ("The Observer")
"I must be knowledgable and independent to be happy."
Shy/Avoidant, Retiring/Schizoid

Characteristic role:	**The Investigator and Thinker**
	The perceptive, cerebral type
Ego Fixation:	Stinginess
Holy Idea:	Omniscience
Basic Fear:	Being useless, helpless, or incapable
Basic Desire:	To be capable and competent
Temptation:	To keep the world at bay
Vice/Passion:	Avarice

Type 6   Anxiety ("The Devil's Advocate")
"I must be secure and safe to be happy."
Suspicious/Paranoid, Pessimistic/Melancholic

Characteristic role:	**The Loyalist and Skeptic**
	The committed, security-oriented type
Ego fixation:	Cowardice
Holy idea:	Faith
Basic Fear:	No support system in a perilous world
Basic Desire:	To feel safe
Temptation:	To question the intentions of everyone
Vice/Passion:	Fear

Type 7   Adventurousness ("The Narcissist")
"I must be high and entertained to be happy."
Confident/Narcissistic, Nonconforming/Antisocial,
Eccentric/Schizotypal

Characteristic role:	**The Enthusiast and Generalist**
	The enthusiastic, productive type
Ego fixation:	Planning
Holy idea:	Work
Basic Fear:	Boredom
Basic Desire:	To experience as much as possible
Temptation:	Moving too fast
Vice/Passion:	Gluttony

Type 8   Aggressiveness ("The Boss")
"I must be strong and in control to be happy."
Assertive/Sadistic

Characteristic role:	**The Challenger and Leader**
	The powerful, aggressive type
Ego fixation:	Vengeance
Holy idea:	Truth
Basic Fear:	Being harmed or controlled by others
Basic Desire:	self-protection, determine own life
Temptation:	To be too self-sufficient
Vice/Passion:	Lust

Type 9   Calmness ("The Mediator")
"I must be peaceful and easy to get along with to be happy."
Cooperative/Dependent

Characteristic role:	**The Peacemaker**
	The easygoing, accommodating type.
Ego fixation:	Indolence, self-forgetting
Holy idea:	Love
Basic Fear:	Loss and separation; of annihilation
Basic Desire:	Maintain inner stability, peace of mind
Temptation:	To go along to get along
Vice/Passion:	Indifference

Everyone has some of each trait and all nine are psychologically connected. Some traits mix well together and enhance personality, while other mixes are ruinous. (As you mature, you take on the best qualities of the other eight.)

A good example of somebody who suffered a ruinous mix, being a cross between Type 1 (Perfectionist), Type 6 (Paranoid), and Type 7 (Narcissist). I can say this fairly (because he's been dead for over 40 years) and accurately (because one of his best friends wrote a very loving biography). Ernest Hemingway's paranoia eventually prevailed, and after several foiled desperate attempts at suicide, he ended his self-inflicted misery with a shotgun in the kitchen.

To more deeply understand these types, I like to use the directional scale matrix of Karen Horney's "Three Trends" (Moving Towards, Against, Away from), in two dimensions of "Surface Direction" and "Deep Direction".

www.similarminds.com
www.9types.com
http://en.wikipedia.org/wiki/Enneagram_of_Personality

Myers-Briggs Type Indicator (MBTI)

All of us are generally one of the sixteen MBTI personality types, based on combinations of eight characteristics (extrovert/introvert, intuitive/feeling, sensing/thinking, judging/perceiving). I highly recommend that you take a free online test, as the results will give you some valuable insights into what makes you tick.

www.similarminds.com   www.jungtype.com

ETIQUETTE & COURTESY

Acquire the Reputation of Courtesy; for it is enough to make you liked. Politeness is the main ingredient of culture, — a kind of witchery that wins the regard of all as surely as discourtesy gains their disfavour and opposition; if this latter springs from pride, it is abominable; if from bad breeding, it is despicable. Better too much courtesy than too little, provided it be not the same for all, which degenerates into injustice. Between opponents it is especially due as a proof of valour. It costs little and helps much: every one is honoured who gives honour. Politeness and honour have this advantage, that they remain with him who displays them to others.
    — Balthasar Gracian, *The Art of Worldly Wisdom*

cultivate and practice good manners
Good manners are made up of petty sacrifices.
  — Emerson

Civility costs nothing, and buys everything.
  — Lady Mary Wortley Montague, 1756

Courtesy is the "oil" to human relations. I know of no cheaper way to enhance your reputation than with good manners. Quality behavior costs you nothing, but gains you amazing favor and consideration. In an increasingly rude world, good manners really stand out.

However, the lack of good manners tells people that you don't care about them. For example, in my Free State Wyoming we saw a fellow relocate to Wyoming with his family. An energetic and ambitious guy, but he was all demands and elbows. Many of his ideas we liked, but he was so brusque and dismissive that he quickly became roundly despised. What he could have accomplished with and through the FSW had he shown decent manners and regard for others!

social etiquette
at somebody's home
Arrive in triumph!
  — my father, as we stopped to pick up some flowers for my step-mom

When arriving at your hosts, always have a gift (flowers, or a bottle of wine). Offer to help with any dinner preparations. Compliment your host on their home. Don't expect hotel service.

After using the bathroom, rinse the tub, wipe the sink, make sure the toilet is ready for the next person (bowl clear, rim wiped, seat down, toilet paper on the spindle — I try to do this even in airplane lavatories). For odors, turn on the fan, light a match, or use some air-freshner.

When visiting a single woman or the elderly, I like to ask if there is any kind of *"strong back/weak mind"* chore that I may do for them, such as moving something heavy. This always gets a nice response, and often reminds them of something that they *do* need help with. If I am an overnight guest, I like to ask if there is any sort of handyman job that I can take care for them, such as tightening a door hinge or fixing an appliance. (With a good multi-tool, many such tasks can be done.)

in somebody's car
On a road-trip in another's car, I like to clean the windshield while he's dispensing fuel, and buy some water or snacks. Be a

cheerful companion with some good stories or jokes. If the driver wants silence, oblige him. Offer to share the driving.

eating etiquette

There are good books on all the details, but the below will generally cover the basics for you.

help the nearest lady with her chair

seat and unseat yourself from the right side of the chair

put your napkin in your lap upon sitting down

with utensils, start from the outside and work your way in

use your utensils, not your fingers

soup is spooned away from you, not towards you

put butter first on the bread plate, and then on the bread

a fork is not a spoon; keep the tines pointed down

maintain good posture, and keep your elbows off the table

do not drink alcohol to excess (1-2 drinks OK; 3+ are too many)

avoid uncomfortable topics (religion, politics, gory things)

do not use profanity, even if others do

take part in conversation, learn names, don't hog the topics

if you spill or drop something, simply apologize and move on

never reach across somebody; ask them to please pass it

excuse yourself quietly and politely if you must leave the table

be polite and respectful to the waiters, but not overly familiar

when finished eating, utensils go on your plate, side by side

when calculating your portion of the group bill, total up your items and then add 30% (which will cover the 10% tax and 20% tip)

some thoughts on borrowing

Be very, very careful about borrowing things or money from others, as such is a situation ripe for disappointment. Return things promptly, cleaned up, and in good working order — preferably in better shape than how you received them.

LIVING WELL WITH OTHERS

Hypocrisy lies not in what you say to a person but what you think of him.
— Frank Rooney

Be virtuous and you will be happy; but you will be lonesome, sometimes.
— Edgar W. Nye

Civilization is just a slow process of learning to be kind.
— Charles L. Lucas

You have a reputation. You may not have wanted a reputation and you probably didn't expect to have one, but it still exists. You may be known as the office joker, the guy with bad breath, or the office slut — and sadly, it doesn't matter if it's true. It's your reputation. I suggest you try to create a reputation before one is assigned to you. And my suggestion is that you be known as the person who gets things done.
— Larry Winget, *Shut Up, Stop Whining, Get A Life!*

dress well!

Fashionable men and women don't just put on fashionable clothes . . . the truly fashionable are beyond fashion.
— Cecil Beaton

Being an entrepreneur and author, I don't have to daily mix with people at a job, and I don't have to impress others with my apparel. So, over the years, I had let my wardrobe standard slip considerably. This was a mistake, as it caused people to misjudge my nature and circumstances, which was especially important once I got into my 40s. Men that age are expected to have attained wealth and power, and I was not dressing that way. While I wasn't slovenly, I wasn't matching my expected station in life, either.

What people say behind your back is your standing in the community.
— Edgar Watson Howe

That really hit home for me years ago when I drove out to L.A. to visit a Hollywood actor friend of mine. We ended up at a local breakfast eatery one morning, and joined in a table full of nationally known comics and actors. I look rumpled, and was treated with polite disdain. (Only that I was a published author gave me *any* kind of cred with that group. Steve Landesberg from *Taxi* chatted with me about my book *You & The Police!* and was very nice.) Comic Johnny Dark was dressed perfectly in a gray/black scheme, and looked great (though without overdoing it). A lesson I never forgot.

It is remarkable what a change from jeans and T-shirt to chinos and a button-down long-sleeve shirt will make in how others treat you. Add a nice navy blue blazer to that, and you can go anywhere and meet anyone without embarrassment. (If the girl of your dreams happens to cross your path unexpectedly, you won't look like a *schnook* for your first impression.) Shortly thereafter I decided to spiff up one Friday night, and went out wearing my nice worsted wool suit with an Italian silk tie. I walked into my regular fern bar, and heads snapped toward me as if I were a movie-star. Lesson learned!

the coat and tie

Now, if a coat and tie are in order, you must *not* fail there. I was at a very swank company Christmas party in Manhattan, and a new associate from the California office showed up in a suit but no tie (claiming he had forgotten it). He really had no excuse since he must have passed several shops selling ties. He was a cocky kid, and the table enjoyed pulling him down a notch or two over this. The issue really wasn't about the tie, but that this guy *just didn't "get it"*. There are many "doesn't get it" clues — and regarding this kid, the lack of tie at a formal company dinner was sufficient. The CEO and host (perfectly attired and groomed) looked at him as if he were sort kind of odd bug. That kid will really have to hustle to even partially undo the poor impression he needlessly made that night.

A simple, though high quality, wardrobe is essential. A decent sport coat will go for under $300, a nice suit $500. Fine leather shoes (always nicely polished) are a must, and can be had for under $200. (Must American men wear sport shoes everywhere?) Start with black belt and shoes, as they're the most versatile. Ties should be silk, simple and elegant. (Never wear a tie with more personality than you.)

Wear a watch, and stop using your iPhone for the time. An ideal watch should keep good time always, never need a battery or rewinding, be rugged and at least 50m/166' water-resistant for everyday use, and be stylish. Citizen's **Eco Drive** watches are solid choices. From $200 on you can find any style you need: dress, sport, or everyday. (There are many models which will do all three.) Pilots and scuba-divers also have their choices.

So, for less than $1,000 you can immediately ramp up your image. Even half that, if spent wisely, will go a very long way. (If money is very tight, you can find real bargains in never-worn shirts at thrift stores and garage sales. I once found a new $500 suit as a $49 closeout in a men's clothing store which was relocating. $45 for the tailoring, and I have a modern suit of Italian fabric that looks smart.)

stay well-groomed always

Keep your hair nicely trimmed, your face shaved, and your nails groomed. Bath every day (use some kind of loofah or shower gloves to remove the old skin — washcloths are poor at this), and use a scent-free deodorant. Your teeth and gums must be clean and glowing.

Start *today* with a better wardrobe. People will begin to ask if you got promoted. They will then gossip about your recent success.

If you ever relocate to another city, it is imperative to land there looking your best. Why not create the best impression of this new guy?

Last tip: don't *overdress,* as it seems weird and makes others uncomfortable. (I recall the housepainting party story in *Zodiac* where the weirdo wore a suit and tie!) Sometimes a coat and tie is necessary; sometimes it's just too much. Know the difference.

let your smile be easy and authentic

There are two types of smiles: the canned and the authentic. The canned smile flexes merely your zygomatic major, but a real smile includes the tightening of your *orbicularis oculi, pars orbitalis* (the muscle that encircles the eye). As French neurologist Guillaume Duchenne wrote, this smile "*does not obey the will. Its absence unmasks the false friend*". Have you ever seen an apparently smiling (or even laughing face) that did not include smiling eyes? It's almost like the person's eyes are a pair of shutters through which the suspicious or conniving soul peeks. You've "*unmasked the false friend*" of that smile.

> *We think of the face as the residue of emotion . . . [but] the process works in the opposite direction as well. Emotion can also start on the face. The face is not a secondary billboard for our internal feelings. It is an equal partner in the emotional process.*
> — *Blink*, p. 208

Learn to relax, laugh, and smile often with sincerity. However, don't overdo it else you'll come across like a John Edwards con-man.

be reflexively kind to others

> *Kindness can become its own reward. We are made kind by being kind.*
> — Eric Hoffer

As this wonderful piece of advice goes, "*Be kinder than necessary, for everyone you meet is fighting some sort of battle.*" That's something that I would have paid good money to hear a long time ago, preventing years of generally being such a hard-ass with people. When in doubt, err on the side of kindness. This is my mother's motto. While I know she's right, I more often err on the side of personally-imposed justice.

> *People may forget what you said; people may forget what you did — but people will never forget how you made them feel.*
> — Maya Angelou

it's about others, not yourself

> *To be interesting, be interested.*
> — Mrs. Charles Northam Lee

> *Do not listen to Yourself. It is no use pleasing yourself if you do not please others, and as a rule general contempt is the punishment for self-satisfaction. The attention you pay to yourself you probably owe to others.*
> — Balthasar Gracian, *The Art of Worldly Wisdom*

Check your conversation for excessive "*I, me, mine, myself*" references. Show an obvious and authentic interest in the other person. Listen without judging, and reply without always giving advice. Be clear, and clarify to not inadvertently offend.

> *All ambiguous behavior will be interpreted negatively.*
> — Harvard Business School professor Tom DeLong

remembering names from Michael Powell of *Mind Games*
pay attention to their name when introduced
use it or lose it (at least 3x within the first 5 minutes)
association game (e.g., with a famous person)
ask "*I remember you well, but your name has slipped my mind.*"
or "*Please remind me of your name.*"

learn to cultivate more silence from yourself
> *The less you talk, the more you're listened to.*
> — Abigail Van Buren

> *Never tell all that you know, or do all that you can, or believe all that you hear.*
> — Portuguese proverb

I found out early in life that you never have to explain something you haven't said.
  — Calvin Coolidge

If I had kept my mouth shut, I wouldn't be here.
  — sign under a mounted fish

A good example is the best sermon.
  — Herbert J. Taylor

listening skills from Michael Powell of *Mind Games*
listen with your face
face the speaker with your body; maintain good eye contact
stop all other activity, including talking
pay attention to nonverbal cues (body language, tone of voice)
don't argue mentally or judge; keep open mind and empathize
try to form a mental picture of what the speaker is saying
try to feel what the speaker is feeling
ask questions to encourage discussion, explanation, ideas
prove respect for the speaker's opinions, even if disagreeable

be choosey with people
Only act with Honorable Men.
You can trust them and they you. Their honour is the best surety of their behaviour even in misunderstandings, for they always act having regard to what they are. Hence 'tis better to have a dispute with honourable people than to have a victory over dishonourable ones. You cannot treat with the ruined, for they have no hostages for rectitude. With them there is no true friendship, and their agreements are not binding, however stringent they may appear, because they have no feeling of honour. Never have to do with such men, for if honour does not restrain a man, virtue will not, since honour is the throne of rectitude.
  — Balthasar Gracian, *The Art of Worldly Wisdom*

Never contend with a Man who has nothing to Lose.
. . . for thereby you enter into an unequal conflict. The other enters without anxiety; having lost everything, including shame, he has no further loss to fear. He therefore resorts to all kinds of insolence. One should never expose a valuable reputation to so terrible a risk, lest what has cost years to gain may be lost in a moment, since a single slight may wipe out much sweat. A man of honour and responsibility has a reputation, because he has much to lose. He balances his own and the other's reputation.
  — Balthasar Gracian, *The Art of Worldly Wisdom*

forgiving others

*Waste not the remainder of your life in thoughts about others,
except when you are concerned with some unselfish purpose.*
— Marcus Aurelius, *Meditations*

He who cannot forgive breaks the bridge over which he must pass.
— George Herbert

Forgiveness is not an occasional act; it is a permanent attitude.
— Martin Luther King

The only normal people are the ones you don't know very well.
— Joe Ancis

Forgiveness is the most important and underrated thing in dealing
with others. (It is one aspect that makes Christianity utter unique.)
Face it right now: people — *all* people, including your best friends and
your wife — are going to let you down, and you must be prepared to
forgive them. He who forgives, ends the quarrel.

*A retentive memory may be a good thing, but the ability to forget
is the true token of success.*
  *Successful people forget.   They know the past is irrevocable.
They're running a race.   They can't afford to look behind.   Their
eye is on the finish line.   Magnamanious people forget.   They're
too big to let little things disturb them.   They forget easily.   If
anyone does them wrong, they consider the source and keep cool.
It's only the small people who cherish revenge.*
— Elbert Hubbard

*Forgiveness is a perfectly selfish act.   It sets you free from the
past.*
— Brian Tracy, *The Great Big Book of Wisdom*

you're not perfect to others, either!

*You must start reacting to all forms of blame in an entirely new
way.   You must not defend yourself, or more accurately, you must
not defend what you call yourself, for you are not who you think
you are.*
  *So, whenever accused, do not resist the accusation, but let it
fall upon a non-defensive mind.   Whether or not you were actually
at fault is entirely beside the point; your only task is not to
defend your mental position — but let the accusation destroy
something faulty in you.   There is something faulty and harmful or
else the accusation would not have caused grief in the first place.*
— Vernon Howard, *Pathways to Perfect Living*

I am obliged to exercise unlimited forgiveness because, if I did not forgive, I should thus act as if I were not guilty, in the same way as the other has been guilty with regard to me.
— Dr. Albert Schweitzer

The best words for resolving a disagreement are, "I could be wrong; I often am." It's true.
— Brian Tracy, *The Great Big Book of Wisdom*

The trouble with most of us is that we would rather be ruined by praise then saved by criticism.
— Norman Vincent Peale

He who slings mud generally loses ground.
— Adlai Stenvenson

To speak ill of others is a dishonest way of praising ourselves . . . let us be above such transparent egotism.
— Will Durant

however, do not suffer always in silence

Many people cannot easily express disapproval. They instead keep the hurt inside, festering into real anger. If you have a *real* grievance, let it be heard. Speak up! Speak out!

But, think before you speak. Then, think some more. We have twice as many ears than mouths for a reason. Once you speak, you have spoken. As trial attorneys like to say, "*You can't unring a bell.*" Even though the judge may command the jury to "disregard that last remark," the bell has already been rung.

but it's not fair!

Some people are always grumbling because roses have thorns. I am thankful that thorns have roses.
— Alphonse Karr

Blessed are those who can give without remembering and take without forgetting.
— Elizabeth Bibesco

You've been wronged without cause, and it isn't fair, I agree. But so what? You've also been *blessed* without cause, too, haven't you? Have you been more thankful for your blessings than bitter about your injuries? We get more — *much* more — good in this life than bad, so we should reflect that in our joy attitude. Keep this proper perspective, and consider that blessings have been "unfairly" bestowed upon you.

Another way to analyze these situations is to replace the word "unfair" with "unreasonable" and argue your case that way. However, if the situation *is* reasonable from the *other's* perspective, then perhaps you are whining more than you realize and should just get over the perception that it isn't "fair".

"*Give, as it has been given to you.*" Notice the comma. It's not "give as it has been given to you." The comma speaks volumes. You don't give in equal measure to your receiving. You give because you've been given to *at all*. Life is not perfect double entry bookkeeping, and in the long run things will probably at least even out. Quit trying to settle old accounts and injuries.

unforgiveness doesn't help, anyway

When you are offended with any man's shameless conduct, immediately ask yourself, "Is it possible that there should be no shameless men in the world?" It is not possible. Do not, therefore, require what is impossible. For this man is one of those shameless men who must be in the world.
— Marcus Aurelius, *Meditations*, IX:42

Resentment is like taking poison and waiting for the other person to die.
— Malachy McCourt

Besides, the world really doesn't care about what wrongs *you* have suffered. (Do you care more about the wrongs *they* have suffered?)

Suppose men kill you, cut you into pieces, curse you. What then can these things do to prevent your mind from remaining pure, wise, sober, just? For instance, if a man should stand by a limpid pure spring, and curse it, the spring does not stop sending up pure water; and if he should cast dirt and filth into it, it will speedily disperse them and wash them out, and will not be at all polluted. How then shall your possess a perpetual fountain? By imbuing yourself hourly with freedom, benevolence, simplicity, and modesty.
— Marcus Aurelius, *Meditations*, VIII:51

All the time you spend trying to get back what's been took from you, more's goin' out the door. After a while you just have to try to get a tourniquet on it.
— movie *No Country for Old Men*

you must forgive even without being asked to

While it can still be difficult to forgive a remorseful person, it often seems impossible to forgive a stubborn and haughty evildoer. But yet you must. You must forgive him because God commands it, and because it's required for your own well-being.

> *If you forgive men when they sin against you, your heavenly Father will also forgive you. But if you do not forgive men their sins, your Father will not forgive your sins.*
> — Jesus, from Matthew 6:14-15

> *Forgiveness is not about another person who has transgressed against you; it is about you. Forgiveness is about doing whatever it takes to* **preserve the power to create your own emotional state.** *It is a gift to yourself and it frees you. You don't have to have the other person's cooperation, and they do not have to be sorry or admit the error of their ways. Do it for yourself.*
> — from Dr. Phil's Life Law #9, www.drphil.com/articles/article/44

If you find yourself firmly bitter, at least ask God for the *will* to forgive. (Or the will to have the will!) However you get started, do so, and do it sooner than later. (Maybe you need to forgive yourself before you can forgive others?)

> *The weak cannot forgive.*
> *Forgiveness is the attribute of the strong.*
> — Mahatma Ghandi

"*Living in the past is like dining in a cemetery.*" (Wilde)

Unforgiveness chains you to the past. It prevents joy in the present and blocks plans for the future. "*To forgive sets a prisoner free, to discover that the prisoner was you.*"

> *Get busy living, or get busy dying.*
> — *The Shawshank Redemption*

asking forgiveness (different from an apology)

When (not if) you blow it with somebody, own up to it at once. If you offended in public, apologize in public (not in private, which is wussy). And while you may have your reason *why* you acted out of anger, spite, rudeness, etc. — you must apologize unabashedly for the regrettable deed without trying to qualify your actions.

Never ruin an apology with an excuse.
— Kimberly Johnson

One final point: giving an apology is not as full and powerful as asking *forgiveness*. An apology is mostly just an admission of guilt, and it doesn't sufficiently engender forgiveness. However, to explicitly say, "*I blew it, and I'm very sorry. Please forgive me.*" leaves nothing unsaid and puts the matter totally at the feet of the offended.

learn to take — and then solicit — correction

Larry Winget observes, "*There are two kinds of criticism: the kind you give and the kind you get.*" Learn to get as well as you give.

Education must be largely self-initiated, a tapestry woven out of broad experience, constant introspection, ability to concentrate on one's purpose in spite of distractions, a combination of curiosity, patience, and intense watchfulness, and it requires substantial trial and error risk-taking, along with a considerable ability to take feedback form the environment — to learn from mistakes. I once heard someone in my own family, who I once loved very much, say, "I don't take criticism very well," as if were a boast, and I knew at that instant there was no way at all for her to grow in mind or character with that self-destructive attitude.
— John Taylor Gatto, *Weapons of Mass Instruction*, p. 62

Rebuke a wise man, and he will love you. Give instruction to a wise man, and he will be still wiser.
— Proverbs 9:8-9

Ask several people who know you well to name your three greatest talents and your three greatest weaknesses. Don't defend yourself when you hear their answers; gather the information and then reflect on it.
— John C. Maxwell, *The 21 Indispensible Qualities of a Leader*

Listen to the whispers and you won't have to hear the screams.
— Cherokee saying

The best reformers are those who commence on themselves.
— Perry Tanksley

Only your real friends will tell you when your face is dirty.
— Sicilian proverb

do not criticize, unless done in love

Don't flatter yourself that friendship authorizes you to say disagreeable things to our intimates. The nearer you come into relation with a person, the more necessary do tact and courtesy become.
— Oliver Wendell Holmes

It is not the critic who counts; not the man who points out how the strong man stumbles, or where the doer of deeds could have done them better. The credit belongs to the man who is actually in the arena, whose face is marred by dust and sweat and blood; who strives valiantly; who errs, who comes short again and again, because there is no effort without error and shortcoming; but who does actually strive to do the deeds; who knows great enthusiasms, the great devotions; who spends himself in a worthy cause; who at the best knows in the end the triumph of high achievement, and who at the worst, if he fails, at least fails while daring greatly, so that his place shall never be with those cold and timid souls who neither know neither victory nor defeat.
— Theodore Roosevelt

Anything that irritates us about others can lead us to an understanding of ourselves.
— Carl Jung

Never criticize another out of anger or envy. Such is harmful, and your motivations will be obvious. Always operate from love.

"Never cut with a knife that which can be cut with a spoon." For me, this is one of most powerful quotes I'd ever read. I had the bad habit of, not merely cutting with a knife, but slashing with a sword. The sword got palpable feedback, the spoon usually wouldn't.

If you are able, correct by teaching those who do wrong; but if you cannot, remember that charity is given you for this purpose. And the gods too extend charity to such persons, helping them attain health, wealth, reputation — so kind they are. And it is in your power also. Who hinders you?
— Marcus Aurelius, *Meditations*, IX:11

know when and how to say *No*

It is not enough for a careful man not to interfere with others, he must see that they do not interfere with him. One is not obliged to belong so much to all as not to belong at all to oneself.
— Balthasar Gracian, *The Art of Worldly Wisdom*

No is the most powerful word of any language. It will save you from trouble, despair, and grief. Some great tips from www.artofmanliness.com/category/relationships-family/

Don't make the no personal.
Let them know you (if true) wish you could say yes.
Show them that you thought it over before saying no.
Offer a "consolation prize".
Show them that your "no" is really in their best interest.
Say no by helping the person say no to himself.
Let them know what it would take to get a "yes".
Expose holes in their request.
Last resort: *Just say No.*

ask *before* you offer advice

Even good advice is likely to be taken badly. The counselor has to be on guard; like a zoologist giving antibiotics to a sick polar bear, he is lucky to avoid having his limbs torn off.
— Bill Bonner, www.lewrockwell.com/bonner/bonner327.html

Men must be taught as if you taught them not,
And things unknown proposed as things forgot.
— author unknown

Am I therefore become your enemy, because I tell you the truth?
— Galatians 4:16

cultivate your generosity

The deepest principle in human nature is the craving to be appreciated.
— Professor William James

What we have done for ourselves alone dies with us; what we have done for others and the world remains and is immortal.
— Alfred Pike

I have tried to keep thing in my hands and lost them all, but what I have given into God's hands I still possess.
— Martin Luther

You give but little when you give of your possessions. It is when you give of yourself that you truly give.
— Kahil Gibran

Any good that you can do, do it now. Do not delay it or forestall it, for you will not pass this way again.
    — Brian Tracy, *The Great Big Book of Wisdom*

be appreciative

I once attended a funeral for a man who had broken with his brother. They hadn't spoken for over 20 years. The surviving brother flew in from California, utterly shattered from remorse, regret and guilt. He literally bought out the local florists, but of course it didn't assuage his feelings. Appreciate the living while they're here, and let them *know* that you do. Better a single rose for the living than an entire flower shop for the dead.

FRIENDS

Friendship is born at that moment when one person says to another, "What! You too? I thought I was the only one."

Every friendship is a sort of secession, even a rebellion. It may be a rebellion of serious thinkers against accepted claptrap or of faddists against accepted good sense; of real artists against popular ugliness or of charlatans against civilized taste; of good men against the badness of society...

Whatever it is, it will be unwelcome to Top People. In each knot of friends, there is a section which fortifies its members against the public opinion of the community in general. Each is therefore a pocket of potential resistance. Men who have real friends are less easy to manage or "get at"; harder for bad authorities to corrupt. Hence, if our masters, by force or by propaganda about "togetherness" or by unobtrusively making privacy impossible, ever succeed in producing a world in which all are companions and none are friends, they will have removed certain dangers, and will also have taken from us what is almost our strongest safeguard against complete servitude.
    — C.S. Lewis; *The Four Loves*

Have Friends. 'Tis a second existence. Every friend is good and wise for his friend: among them all everything turns to good. Every one is as others wish him; that they may wish him well, he must win their hearts and so their tongues. There is no magic like a good turn, and the way to gain friendly feelings is to do friendly acts. The most and best of us depend on others; we have to live either among friends or among enemies. Seek some one every day to be a well-wisher if not a friend; by and by after trial some of these will become intimate.

> *There is no desert like living without friends. Friendship multiplies the good of life and divides the evil.*
> — Balthasar Gracian, *The Art of Worldly Wisdom*

> *A friend is . . . a second self.*
> — Cicero

acquaintances, friends (basic, good, best)

Not all people are equal in your life. That's a Good Thing.

the ratio of acquaintances and friends

Let's say you know 1,000 people. 80% of them will be acquaintances only — the other 20% some variant of friend. Don't take this breakdown too precisely, but the approximation is useful:

acquaintances	80%	800
basic friends	18%	180
good friends	1.5%	15
best friends	0.4%	4
spouse		only 1

strangers

Of the 7 billion people on the Earth, nearly all of them are (and will remain) strangers. There is not the opportunity and time to even acquaint yourself with so many people.

acquaintances

> *Acquaintance: A person whom we know well enough to borrow from but not well enough to lend to.*
> — Ambrose Bierce

Most people whom Americans seem to call friends are actually just acquaintances. By calling a guy you had a few drinks with a "friend" is to cheapen the entire notion of friendship. He's more than a stranger, but not yet a friend. Don't overestimate the relationship to be more than it is: you're merely acquainted (and thinly, at that). And stop trusting people so readily! No wonder your "friends let you down"; they were really only acquaintances.

basic friends

A basic friend is somebody who will bail you out of jail. I would *generally* require at least a year of spending time with an acquaintance before raising them up to friendship status. Certainly you will encounter exceptions to this, but they must be exceptional.

good friends

A good friend would help you "move a body". A good friend will inconvenience themselves considerably to comport with your personality and quirks. You should have about 10-15 basic friends to every good friend — that's how rare a good friend should be to you. To progress from basic to good friend should take at least 1-2 years.

best friends

A best friend would help you *cause* that body! A best friend would sign over a blank check to you. A best friend would take the rap for you if that could save your bacon. Unless they would do any of the above, you have fewer best friends than you realize. What you probably have are some *very good* friends, but not yet a "best friend".

I think it should take at least 5 years of good friendship before somebody is elevated to "best friend". If you end up with even 3 best friends concurrently, you are a wealthy soul.

spouse

Never marry any woman who is not already one of your best friends, if not your very best friend. If you're *already* married, making a best friend of your spouse should be your Number One earthly priority. Most men are morons, slaving at a job and thinking that their wives get all turned on by the Good Provider thing. Yes, husbands *should* support their families — but families need *more* than that. Men, take *time* to be *with* your wife and children. Share *yourself,* not just your paycheck. Or, you can hear *Cats and the Cradle* over the radio, and cry enroute to the office in your Mercedes, suddenly realizing how empty your life became, and why your wife is sleeping with the tennis coach or why your children never come to visit. Guys, catch a clue. I've an entire chapter about marriage and wives.

living well with friends

You can make more friends in two months by becoming interested in other people than you can in two years by trying to get other people interested in you.
— Norman Vincent Peale

Friendship is like money, easier made than kept.
— Samuel Butler

But of all plagues, good Heaven, thy wrath can send,
Save me, oh, save me, from the candid friend.
    — George Canning

If the cause be good, the most violent attack of its enemies will
not injure it so much as an injudicious defense of it by its friends.
    — Charles Caleb Colton

Politeness is the art of selecting among one's real thoughts.
    — Madame de Stael

Have no friends not equal to yourself.
    — Confucius

Very few established institutions, governments and constitutions
are ever destroyed by their enemies until they have been
corrupted and weakened by their friends.
    — Walter Lippmann

Don't let a little dispute injure a great friendship.
    — anonymous

Better a good enemy than a bad friend.
    — Plato

It is more shameful to distrust one's friends than to be deceived by
them.
    — author unknown

don't expect quality friendship from lousy people

The quality of your friendship will sink to the level of the lesser person. (Same thing in romance.) Choose top-notch people!

do you want what they have?

Before you get more than slightly involved with somebody (friendship, dating, business, etc.) consider the totality of their life and then ask yourself, *"Do I want what they have?"* Meaning, would you choose their lifestyle, their morality, or their personality for yourself? If not, then don't go there.

There are 7 billion people on the planet. You can afford to be choosy. Go for human diamonds, not rhinestones.

Make no friendships with an angry man.
    — Proverbs 22:24

cut your friends some slack

As somebody once said, "*To make a friend, close an eye. To keep a friend, close an ear as well.*" Nobody's perfect. The more you know somebody, the more you realize this (and vice versa) as you get behind the masks. Love overlooks imperfections.

We like somebody because. We love someone although.
— Henri De Montherlant

Oh, the comfort, the inexpressible comfort of feeling safe with a person; having neither to weigh thoughts nor measure words, but to pour them all out, just as they are, chaff and grain together, knowing that a faithful hand will take and sift them, keep what is worth keeping, and then, with the breath of kindness, blow the rest away.
— George Eliot

The only way to have a friend is to be one.
— Emerson

a life-long friend is one you haven't lent money to

Before lending money to a friend, decide which you value more. The borrower is a slave to the lender. Don't change the relationship of your friend by lending him money. C.S. Lewis had some great advice when somebody asked for a loan, say, of $100. "*I'd rather not lend money, but you can have $10 now if that will help.*"

keeping in touch with friends

Not being a big fan of the phone, and often living so far in the country that cell service was spotty or nonexistent, I had unintentionally allowed many old friendships to wither from my lack of contact. (Email, by the way, is no substitute. Never underestimate the power of a human voice — especially yours.) To keep an acquaintanceship alive, you must *call* them at least 2-4 times/year. However, to keep a basic friendship alive, at least 6-12 times/year. (Note: this is bare subsistence-level, and will not enhance any growth in the relationship. Growth requires being with them in person.)

what is are your friends' "love languages"?

The book *The 5 Love Languages* is not only important for your mate, but for people in general. Find out "love language" of your friends. (This applies to children and even housepets.)

Surprise them with a random **gift** to demonstrate that you understand and were thinking of their needs and wants.

Acts of service are also important. (As Jeff Cooper explained, the finest words one can hear are "*It's already been taken care of.*")

Send a card with hand-penned **words of affirmation**. (An FSWer once emailed me out of the blue a very touching note of appreciation. This sentence alone made my week: "*Your writings have been quite influential to me. They have filled voids that I didn't know I had and aided in directing me down more righteous paths. So, I thank you, I support you and I encourage you to continue onward.*")

Spending time with people is another love language. (Men often appreciate that their lady will come hang out with them as they work on the car.) It may seem a bit pointless, but not to them.

Lastly, **physical touch** is very important to many people. Do not be too shy about hugs and kisses for them.

insist on the first (and private) chance to make it right

A true friend should first come to you with any grievance, before complaining about you to others. Insist on this protocol, as it will head off many opportunities for bitterness.

the power of showing up in person

There is a galactic difference between a hospital visit vs. sending a get-well card, and everybody understands this. Don't be time stingy.

some thought on favors

Reciprocity is the key to all relationships. Everybody "keeps track" if only informally and subconsciously. If the "account" gets too far out of whack, people naturally feel used. What can get accounts out of balance is that favors are often unequal in value given vs. received. For example, letting a friend park your boat on your country acreage costs you absolutely nothing (especially if you don't see it daily), yet it saves him paying for storage. What's a proper payback for that? Money doesn't seem right, as he could have just paid a storage yard. In my mind, a gift or some act of service seems right.

Now, if a favor costs you time and/or money, then some sort of equitable reciprocity is fair. If asking a favor of somebody, I've learned to also inquire, "*What would you like in exchange for this?*" or "*So, what can I do for you?*" Being upfront from the beginning is best. It avoids all needless misunderstandings, and you don't come across as a user. Here is what I hope is a helpful guide:

BENEFITS YOU—>	TIME	MONEY	ENHANCEMENT
C **TIME**	act of service	gift	lunch/dinner
O			
S **MONEY**	$	$	gift
T			
S **HOSPITALITY**	gift, reciprocity	gift, reciprocity	gift, reciprocity
H **NOTHING**			
I (directly)	reciprocal favor	reciprocal favor, gift	reciprocal favor
M			

I differentiate favors that *save* somebody money, and favors which actually *make* (create) somebody money. Sometimes this is a blurry line, but if I'm putting in considerable time into a favor that actually *makes* a friend money that he wouldn't have made without my help, then I feel entitled to a reasonable piece of that action. Otherwise, I could be making at least that much per hour working for myself.

Not everyone sees this my way, and generally it's because they are not entrepreneurs. For example, one girlfriend had a business deal go sour through the other party's breach of contract. At stake was $5,000 in earnest money. I spotted a murky legal point in her favor (based on a semi-coloned "*or*" — requiring a very logical and fair judge to see). As I researched the matter I learned that nobody had ever argued that particular point before, yet I grew increasingly convinced of its validity and chance of success. Convincing her to go to court, I spent at least 8 hours ironing out her case and anticipating every possible rebuttal and snag. She was thoroughly prepared, and in a very satisfying victory she won all the earnest money. Had she done this for me, I'd have given her 10%/$500 in thanks without hesitation, as even a "finder's fee" (requiring no work) was worth that. Never having owned a business, she felt differently, saying that she thought that I was doing all the work as her boyfriend. That was true, but only to the extent that I saved her the $1,000+ an attorney would have charged her. I don't make money for others for free, and still had to explain the distinction between saving her money vs. making her money. (Both of us egocentrically expected the other to see it our own way, which is why discussion beforehand is vital.)

In another incident, I personally intervened with an evil consignment shop which was trying to steal her items throughout two years of lies and evasion, and got the nasty shop owner to cough up a check. For that, I expected nothing as I was only *retrieving* property already hers (vs. creating wealth with many hours of unique work). These may seem too subtle of distinctions to some, which shows how differently people can view the same thing. Discuss things first!

FAMILY

living well with your parents

Let me speak candidly to those of you who have been most angry at your parents. Given the brevity of life and the temporary nature of all human relationships, can you find it within your heart to forgive them?

[To his wife:] Our parents will not always be with us. I see now the incredible brevity of life that will someday take them from us. We MUST keep that in mind as we live out our daily lives. I want to respond to both sets of parents in such a way that we will have NO regrets after they are gone. This is what I believe the Lord wants of us.

— Dr. James Dobson, p. 135-136

This is sound advice that I had to recall and practice with my own father, a very "emotionally inaccessible" man who caused his young wife and little boy a lot of grief long ago. The more I came to know him, the more I understood why he was such a wound-up guy. He's mellowed with age, and is very sweet to his granddaughter. My past with him is what it is, and all we've got that is malleable is our present. So, I've chosen to forgive him, and try to build from here.

ON TRUSTING PEOPLE

For example, fully 90% of all FBI arrests are directly due to the *"helpful cooperation"* of neighbors and relatives. Keep your mouth shut. Stop being so chatty and trusting.

"Trust only if you can, and then only if you have to."

It's the *second* part of this maxim which will protect you, as trusting is easier than qualifying the absolute *necessity* of trusting particularly. Let me express my aphorism another way: If you believe a person trustworthy on an issue, but can *wait* to find out, then wait. From my own experience, I cannot recall a *single* incident where I *should* have trusted, but did not, or waited too long. I can, however, think of dozens of times where I trusted too early (and sometimes *far* too early).

Trust only at the last minute, so to speak. Why trust too early? There's no advantage, and much potential risk. This is true because of immutable human nature: **People are *verbs*.** People are rarely stable nouns; they're verbs. They change without notice. They will suddenly let you down, inexplicably. Expect it. Fewer than 5 in 100 you'll ever meet are solid, dependable, and trustworthy souls.

The other 95% exhibit merely varying *degrees* of reliability, and some of them *seem* totally trustworthy for quite a while, until a real crunch arrives. Take your time to trust.

putting friendships to the test

I am retrospectively a big believer in this. Something is reliable only if it's been *proven* to be reliable. If you haven't yet tested your friendships in important (though not utterly crucial) matters, then you don't know how strong they really are.

I once knew a couple my age for many years who seemed to be high-quality people. We had spent lots of time together and knew each other well. Then, one day, I needed an urgent favor. It was a big favor to me, but a small one to them (which required no risk or expense and only 5 minutes of inconvenience). They hemmed and hawed and finally declined. (I went to another friend, who immediately and cheerfully agreed.) A few days later, they told me that they'd been *"stupid"* and were profoundly sorry, and now would gladly help. I replied that, while I appreciated their change of heart, tests of friendship often come in sudden moments and that I could never trust them as I once had. (To their credit, they took it well.)

> *The untrusting can be neither deceived nor convinced; neither betrayed nor befriended.*
> — Kenneth W. Royce

A very good friend of mine was the inspiration for this quote. He actually brags on occasion about how he trusts nobody. The flip side is that his friendships are necessarily limited — even ours. Although I've never betrayed a confidence in our 20 years of friendship, he still peers through that lens of suspicion.

Any human relationship is a gamble by nature. While you don't risk the whole stack of chips on your first bet, you should be gradually increasing your bets during a winning session.

UNPLEASANT PEOPLE

> *A gossip is one who talks to you about others; a bore is one who talks to you about himself; and a brilliant conversationalist is one who talks to you about yourself.*
> — Lisa Kirk

As it will be in the future,
it was at the birth of Man
There are only four things certain
since Social Progress began.
That the Dog returns to his Vomit
and the Sow returns to her Mire
— Rudyard Kipling, "Gods of the Copybook Headings"

Are you irritated with one whose arm-pits smell? Are you angry
with one whose mouth has a foul odor? What good will your anger
do you? He has this mouth, he has these arm-pits. Such
emanations must come from such things. . . . stir up his rational
faculty; show him his fault, admonish him. For if he listens, you
will cure him, and have no need of anger — you are not a ranter or
a whore.
The house is smoky; I leave it. Why do you call this trouble?
— Marcus Aurelius, *Meditations*

dealing with the envious

The way of the world is to praise dead saints and to persecute
living ones.
— Nathaniel Howe

When another blames or hates you, or when men say injurious
things about you, approach their poor souls, penetrate within, and
see what kind of men they are. You will discover that there is no
reason to take trouble that these men may have a good opinion of
you.
— Marcus Aurelius, *Meditations*, IX:27

Most people enjoy the inferiorities of their best friends.
— Perry Tanksley

At some point, people may begin to become envious of your talents,
your popularity, and your success. Expect this. You will be rumored as
"lucky" or the beneficiary of an inheritance — anything but the
appropriate results of good planning, hard work, delay of gratification,
and perserverance. To minimize this, avoid being flashy or
ostentatious with money. Be helpful and generous when such is called
for (and sometimes when it isn't). Be polite with all, and even cordial
with your enemies (which will go far in not antagonizing them).

If you want enemies, excel your friends; but if you want friends,
let your friends excel you.
— La Rouchefoucauld

dealing with complainers

If any man can convince and show me that I do not think or act right, I will gladly change, for I seek truth, by which no man was ever injured.   But he is injured who abides in his error and ignorance.

I do my duty. Other things do not trouble me, for they are either things without life, or things without reason, or things that have wandered and know not the way.
— Marcus Aurelius, *Meditations*, VI:21-22

Sure, there are proper occasions for complaint, but when people have no balanced perspective and just enjoy complaining, it's time to move on. Nothing satisfies them, and nothing ever will. Their negativity is corrosive.

dealing with gossipers

How much trouble he avoids who does not look to see what his neighbor says or does or thinks, but only what he does himself, that it may be just and good.
— Marcus Aurelius, *Meditations*

Have nothing to do with worldly fables fit only for old women.
— 1 Timothy 4:7

If you uncover rumors, directly confront the gossiper and sternly inquire why they did not first take their issues to you personally. And, never forget that those who gossip about others are also gossiping about *you*. To a gossiper, nobody is special. They are black belts in the ancient art of *Sum Flung Dung*. Avoid, avoid, avoid.

dealing with bullies

Let us try to persuade men to behave reasonably. But for yourself, act even against their will, when the law of justice directs you that way. If, however, anyone forcibly obstructs you, resign yourself to contentment and tranquility; at the same time, make use of his obstruction to exercise some other virtue.
— Marcus Aurelius, *Meditations*, VI:50

You either teach people to treat you with dignity and respect, or you don't. This means you are partly responsible for the mistreatment that you get at the hands of someone else. You shape others' behavior when you teach them what they can get away with and what they cannot.

If the people in your life treat you in an undesirable way, figure out what you are doing to reinforce, elicit or allow that treatment. Identify the payoffs you may be giving someone in

response to any negative behavior. **For example, when people are aggressive, bossy or controlling — and then get their way — you have rewarded them for unacceptable behavior.**
— from Dr. Phil's Life Law #8, www.drphil.com/articles/article/44

Never accept even the first attempt to be bullied. Call them on it at once, and publicly. Michael Powell author of *Mind Games* offers these great tips on becoming more assertive:

keep calm, as anger is a sign of weakness, not strength
mirror your words with your body language
don't apologize for a refusal; make your refusal unequivocable
acknowledge that you've the right to change your mind
be clear with yourself about what you want
don't be afraid to be different
conflict is a natural part of life
be prepared to compromise, but not be exploited
take your time to learn all the necessary facts before deciding

dealing with idiots, morons, clowns, critics, and pests

If you argue with a fool, a bystander may not be able to tell the difference.
— Chinese proverb

A cucumber is bitter — throw it away. There are briars in the path — turn aside from them. This is enough. Do not add, "And why were such things put into the world?"
— Marcus Aurelius, *Meditations*, VIII:50

Bad company corrupts good character.
— 1 Corinthians 15:33

All have sinned and fallen short of the glory of God.
— Romans 3:23

Life is full of these people (and they seem to spawn on the Internet). Identify them quickly so that you can cut them loose quickly. They are time and energy sinks. You may be tempted to get in the ring with them (believe me, I know!), but it's like wrestling a pig: there's no winning, you only get dirty — and the pig *likes* it. The only way to beat them is to evade, avoid, and ignore them. (That will also give you time and space to increase your powers of forgiveness!)

dealing with the weird

People are weird. This sums it up. There's just no understanding some people. They're simply weird. Recognizing this is the best you'll do. Avoid those whom you don't understand.

dealing with enemies

Judge a man by the reputation of his enemies.
— Arabian Proverb

Cherish your enemies — they teach you the most valuable lessons.
— Ho Chi Minh

You have enemies? Good. That means you've stood up for something, sometime in your life.
— Winston Churchill

Never do an enemy a minor injury.
— Machiavelli

The shaft of the arrow had been feathered with one of the eagle's own plumes. We often give our enemies the means of our own destruction.
— Aesop (620-560 BC), Greek slave and fable author

The wise man profits more from his enemies, than a fool from his friends.
— Baltasar Gracian

If you find yourself trapped, cornered, and on the defensive in some situation, try a simple experiment: Do something that cannot be easily explained or interpreted. Choose a simple action, but carry it out in a way that unsettles your opponent, a way with many possible interpretations, making your intentions obscure.
— Robert Greene, *The 48 Laws of Power*

One of the great arts of living is that you hear truth in the mouth of your enemies, that you let your critics be the unpaid guardians of your soul. It takes patience and a whole lot of self-control.
— Stephen Manfield, *Mansfield's Book of Manly Men*

Ancient Chinese wisdom declares that here are only three things to do with an enemy:

> if he is weak and unreasonable — ignore him
> if he is strong and unreasonable — destroy him
> if he is reasonable — make amends, forgive, show respect

Incidentally, the best way to destroy an enemy — to take away all his power over you — is to forgive him! (An enemy can use your bitterness by occupying your heart, but what can he do against *forgiveness?*) Meanwhile, learn from him, but keep an eye on him.

The best manner of avenging ourselves is by not resembling him who has injured us.
— Jane Porter

If we could read the secret history of our enemies, we should find in each man's life sorrow and suffering enough to disarm all hostility.
— Longfellow

By the way, to have no friends reflects poorly on one's self, but a far more damning indictment is to have no enemies. There are just some things decent humanity should be diametrically opposed to.

TIPS FROM DALE CARNEGIE

His 1936 classic *How To Win Friends and Influence People* still remains a "must read" today. People don't change, and thus good advice about people never goes out of style.

9 Ways to Change People Without Giving Offense or Arousing Resentment

❶ Begin with praise and honest appreciation.
❷ Call attention to people's mistakes indirectly.
❸ Talk about your own mistakes before criticizing others.
❹ As questions instead of giving direct orders.
❺ Let the other man save his face.
❻ Praise every improvement, no mattler how slight.
   Be *"hearty in your approbation and lavish in your praise."*
❼ Give the other person a fine reputation to live up to.
❽ Use encouragement. Make the fault seem easy to correct.
❾ Make the other person happy about doing your suggestion.

12 Ways: Win Them to Your Way of Thinking

❶ The only way to get the best of an argument is to avoid it.
❷ Show respect for the other's opinions. Never say he's wrong.
❸ If you are wrong, admit it quickly and emphatically.

❹ Begin in a friendly way.
❺ Get him saying "*Yes, yes*" immediately.
❻ Let him do a great deal of the talking.
❼ Let him feel that the idea is his idea.
❽ Honestly try to see things from his point of view.
❾ Be sympathetic to his ideas and desires.
❿ Appeal to the nobler motives.
11 Dramtize your ideas.
12 Throw down a challenge.

6 Ways to Make People Like You

❶ Become genuinely interested in other people.
❷ Smile.
❸ Remember that their name is the sweetest sound.
❹ Listen. Encourage others to talk about themselves.
❺ Talk in terms of the other's interest.
❻ Make them fee important — and do it sincerely.

10 WAYS TO LOVE

Listen without interrupting.	Proverbs 1:8
Speak without accusing.	James 1:19
Give without sparing.	Proverbs 21:26
Pray without ceasing.	Colossians 1:9
Answer without arguing.	Proverbs 17:1
Share without pretending.	Ephesians 4:15
Enjoy without complaint.	Philippians 2;14
Trust without waivering.	Colossians 3:13
Forgive without punishing.	Colossians 3:13
Promise without forgetting.	Proverbs 13:12

THE SOCIOPATH

It ain't what ya don't know that hurts ya. What really puts a hurtin'
on ya is what ya knows for sure, that just ain't so.
— Uncle Remus

A sociopath (or "psychopath") is an intraspecies predator:

> *Imagine — if you can — not having a conscience, none at all, no*
> *feelings of guilt or remorse no matter what you do, no limiting*
> *sense of concern for the well-being of strangers, friends, or even*
> *family members. Imagine no struggles with shame, not a single*
> *one in your whole life, no matter what kind of selfish, lazy,*
> *harmful, or immoral action you had taken. And pretend that the*
> *concept of responsibility is unknown to you, except as a burden*
> *others seem to accept without question, like gullible fools. Now*
> *add to this strange fantasy the ability to conceal from other*
> *people that your psychological makeup is radically different from*
> *your theirs. Since everyone simply assumes that conscience is*
> *universal among human beings, hiding the fact that you are*
> *conscience-free is nearly effortless. You are not held back from*
> *any of your desires by guilt or shame, and you are never*
> *confronted by others for your cold-bloodedness. The ice water in*
> *your veins is so bizarre, so completely outside of their personal*
> *experience, that they seldom even guess at your condition.*
> *In other words, you are completely free of internal restraints,*
> *and your unhampered liberty to do just as you please, with no*
> *pangs of conscience, is conveniently invisible to the world. You*
> *can do anything at all, and still your strange advantage over the*
> *majority of people, who are kept in line by their consciences, will*
> *most likely remain undiscovered.* (p.2)
> — Martha Stout, Ph.D., *The Sociopath Next Door*

A sociopath is somebody who, through a combination of heritable
condition, genetic predisposition and upbringing, has no sense of
interconnectedness (bonding) with living beings and thus no
foundation for an active conscience (like the 96% rest of us who do
have one). Studies indicate that sociopathy involves an altered
processing of emotional stimuli at the level of the cerebral cortex, and
they cannot process emotional experience, such as love and caring.

> *For those of us who have been successfully socialized, imagining*
> *the world as the psychopath experiences it is close to impossible.*
> — Dr. Robert D. Hare, *Without Conscience: The Disturbing World of*
> *the Psychopaths Among Us*, p. 78

sociopathy is a *noncorrectable* disfigurement of character

It cannot be cured by therapy. Sociopaths are wired wrong, and not only do they not know it, their disorder (in contrast to narcissism) causes them no anxiety:

> Sociopathy stands alone as a "disease" that causes no dis-ease for the person who has it, no subjective discomfort. Sociopaths are often quite satisfied with their lives, and perhaps for this very reason there is no effective treatment. (Stout, p.12)

> Psychopaths don't feel they have psychological or emotional problems, and they see no reason to change their behavior to conform to societal standards with which they do not agree.
> To elaborate, psychopaths are generally well satisfied with themselves and with their inner landscape, bleak as it may seem to outside observers. They see nothing wrong with themselves, experience little personal distress, and find their behavior rational, rewarding, and satisfying; they never look back with regret or forward with concern. They perceive themselves as superior beings in a hostile, dog-eat-dog world in which others in order to obtain their 'rights,' and their social interactions are planned to outmaneuver the malevolence they see in others. Given these attitudes, it is not surprising that the purpose of most psychotherapeutic approaches is lost on sociopaths. (Hare, p.195)

Morals, ethics, etc. are foreign concepts never having been internalized as personal boundaries:

> About one in twenty-five individuals are sociopathic . . . . It is not that this group fails to grasp the difference between good and bad; it is that the distinction fails to limit their behavior. (Stout)

These "people" are fairly rare, yet still common enough at 4% of adults. (It is generally believed by experts that 3% of men and 1% of women are sociopaths.) In the case of a former best friend, I was shocked to learn that he was a full-blown sociopath (*e.g.*, a pathological liar, serial thief, and shameless war vet fraud). Covetous of anybody with actual experience and reputation exceeding his own, "Jack" tried to destroy what he couldn't have. What drives them is power over other people, and they achieve this through very clever manipulation. Sociopaths cannot be even occasionally trusted.

sociopaths and morality

Dr. M. Scott Peck's seminal book *The People of The Lie* contains the best definition of evil I've yet read. To paraphrase:

❏ The evil hide their motives with lies.

❏ Evil people want to appear to be good.

❏ When confronted by evil, the wisest and most secure adult will usually experience confusion.

❏ Evil seeks to discourage self-thinking (fosters dependency).

❏ We must have an ongoing dedication to reality at all cost.

Guiltlessness was in fact the first personality disorder to be recognized by psychiatry, and terms that have been used at times the past century include *manie sans d'lire*, psychopathic inferiority, moral insanity, and moral imbecility.

According to the current bible of psychiatric labels, the *Diagnostic and Statistical Manual of Mental Disorders IV* of the APA, the clinical diagnosis of "antisocial personality disorder" should be considered when an individual possesses at least three of the following seven characteristics:

❶ failure to conform to social norms
❷ deceitfulness, manipulativeness
❸ impulsivity, failure to plan ahead
❹ irritability, aggressiveness
❺ reckless disregard for the safety or self of others
❻ consistent irresponsibility
❼ lack of remorse after having hurt or stolen from others

They understand the difference between right and wrong, but are not emotionally constrained by it. This is outlandish to moral people. Just so you aren't tempted to believe that I'm exaggerating things, read an illuminating forum exchange between three sociopaths. (Typos/misspellings are theirs.)

> *It sickens me the whole way criminals are treated in this country. Nobody is able to grasp the idea that there's no objective evil in the world, and that evil actions are caused by imbalance...*
> — sociopath A

If there is no objective evil, then there can be no objective good, either. Sociopaths truly believe that morality is just a construct, used to hinder them. They believe that nobody is actually moral, and those who claim to be are just hypocrites. The sociopath sees himself the superior being because he does not voluntarily restrain himself to such shackles. Now read the ghoulish responses that post received:

> *my cravings . . . involve extreme violence and inflicting as much*
> *physical and psychological suffering as possible. i haven't acted*
> *on them, so they're just really detailed thoughts/dreams for me*
> *also.*
>
> *personally, i feel society should be punished as thoroughly*
> *and frequently as possible. no amount of tears would ever be*
> *enough. people should live in a permanent state of terror. they*
> *have marginalized people like me . . .*
> — sociopath B

> *I get a sort of sadistic glee anytime I circumvent the*
> *conventions or do something deemed 'immoral', and the more I*
> *do such a thing, the better.*
> — sociopath A

Society tries to punish the sociopath with its fake morals, hence the
sociopath is justified in fighting back as a scumbag. At this point,
sociopath C can't resist joining in:

> *I don't get the point of whining about how society is. I, off course,*
> *would like to live far away from humans, from thier laws, morals*
> *and money. But since it ain't easy, I prefer seeing this society as*
> *a big playground. I assure you that because people are*
> *hedonist, delusional, "good", idiot and happy . . . they are*
> *much more "enjoyable". By this I'm talking about the*
> *manipulation and all those games you would probably "enjoy".*
> — sociopath C

Notice their use of quotation marks for "good" and "bad"? Again,
morality does not exist; there's no objective evil. They honestly believe
this, and trying to explain morality to them is like describing colors to
a blind man. So, to recap their demented ethos:

> the sociopath is not bound by rules which penalize him
> anything goes to achieve selfish desires
> whoever gets manipulated and burned is at fault for weakness

In 2008 the University of Chicago tested sociopaths with fMRI scans
and discovered that their brains light up with pleasure at the suffering
of others. Their empathy pathways showed no abnormality, which
suggests that sociopaths are empathic . . . but in a *sadistic* sense. (They
enjoy hurting because it confirms they are achieving power.)

Coleridge called Shakespeare's Iago a "*motiveless malignancy.*"
This is why sociopaths are so hard for most people to understand . . . at
first. They are completely counterintuitive to basic human decency.
Being evil for the sheer sake of evil is a foreign idea us. However, once

you've "wrapped your mind" around their nature (and it's a predictable one, too), sociopaths are easy to understand. They'll do what they can get away with.

the sociopath's characteristic exploitiveness

It is a high level of exploitiveness that most singularly exposes the sociopath.
— Steve Becker, LCSW

I also believe this. Sociopaths are all about manipulation and exploitation. I recall an anecdote of "Jack" regarding a family photo. His three brothers all had goofy faces, while he was only smug. Just before the shutter clicked, he suggested they all should "*look like retards*". They went along with it — he didn't. Even at just 10 years old, he was already an accomplished manipulator of his family.

mimicry of appropriate emotions and morality

The psychopath is like a color-blind person who sees the world in shades of gray but who has learned how to function in a colored world. He has learned that the light signal for 'stop' is at the top of the traffic signal. **When the color-blind person tells you he stopped at the red light, he really means he stopped at the top light.** *He has difficulty in discussing the color of things but may have learned all sorts of ways to compensate for this problem, and in some cases even those who know him well may not know that he cannot see colors.* (p.129)

Like a tourist using high-school French to ask directions in Paris, psychopaths have trouble putting into words emotional ideas because they are vague and poorly understood. In this sense, emotion is like a second language to the psychopath. (Hare, p.136)

This emotional mimicry can often come across as forced or fake. Recall from the movie *Bladerunner* the detailed test given to suspected androids to pierce through their artificial emotional landscape. A superior "Replicant" required over 100 questions, the last being *"The entrée consisted of boiled dog."* Accomplished sociopaths are like that. Sometimes it takes months or even years to unmask them, and even when you do many of your mutual friends won't easily believe it.

do sociopaths feel love or hate?

Apparently not. fMRI scans show that sociopaths respond to the linguistic brain section but not to the feeling section.

do sociopaths feel fear?
Not really, as this has been linked to dysfunctions of the amygdala. High risk situations do not much affect sociopaths, as they focus on the reward and not the likely consequences.

do sociopaths feel guilt?
Generally not, and if they somehow do it is blocked out by disassociation and compartmentalization. (*I.e.*, their victims somehow deserved being hurt.) They also are very good at focusing on their source of reward while ignoring punishment.

a sociopath *always* lies, and *how* he does it
Lies are the foundation of all evil. Avoid liars, period. If somebody is a known liar, then who knows what nasty business he'll embark on next? To feel powerful and superior to normal decent folk, the sociopath must manipulate them as his puppeteer. He feels something like a sexual thrill from this:

> . . . this is power, especially when the people you manipulate are superior to you in some way. Most invigorating of all is to bring down people who are smarter or more accomplished than you, or perhaps classier, more attractive or popular or morally admirable. **This is not only good fun; it is existential vengeance.** (p.4)

No manipulation is possible without lying. Lies are core to all sociopaths. They will lie just for the thrill of being believed.

how the sociopath succeeds in lying, and lying BIG
> The size of the lie is a definite factor in causing it to be believed, because the vast masses of a nation are, in the depths of their hearts, more easily deceived than they are consciously and intentionally bad.
>
> The primitive simplicity of their minds renders them more easy victims of a big lie than a small one, because they themselves often tell little lies **but would be ashamed to tell big ones. Such a form of lying would never enter their heads.** They would never credit others with the possibility of such great impudence as the complete reversal of facts.
>
> Even explanations would long leave them in doubt and hesitation, and any trifling reason would dispose them to accept a thing as true. **Something therefore always remains and sticks from the most imprudent of lies,** a fact which all bodies and individuals concerned in the art of lying in this world know only too well, and therefore they stop at nothing to achieve this end.
> — Adolph Hitler, *Mein Kampf*

Everybody is subject to something called "egocentrism" where you believe that other people are basically like you. If you are honest, a sociopath will know it and use it against you.

In my case, "Jack" had set up such an outlandish theft scam on me, that it didn't seem like a scam. Couldn't be a scam because friends don't scam friends. (My egocentrism working against me.) However, it was such a huge and ridiculous story that it quickly unraveled after my first suspicion. The hard part was not disproving his tale, but trying to understand *why* he had done it (and in such a risky manner). My classic mistake was trying to understand it from a morally sane perspective. Only by later learning about sociopathy did any (and all) of it make sense. All the classic clues had been there over the three years of "friendship", had I known what to look for.

a sociopath's *always* lies, and always without shame

Normal people are embarrassed when caught in a lie. This is wholly untrue with a sociopath. Since they cannot feel shame (though sometimes humiliation), catching them in a lie will not garner you an apology. Rather, he usually will attack your lack of trust in him. If not that, then he will oddly and smoothly move on to the next lie.

It doesn't matter to him if he's caught in a lie — only that the lie no longer works with *you*. He'll just go to another lie. It's very weird when you experience it, and you'll begin to wonder if you're dealing with an alien. (In a way, you *are*.)

the sociopath's algorithm of reversal

To lie believably, the sociopath understands that nothing lies like the truth. His trick, however, is tell to co-opt the flattering truth about others as his own. For example, sociopath "Jack" claimed many skills and experiences of others never his own:

> 800+ hours of fighter jet combat, with dozens of aerial kills
> shot down, yet (dramatically) escaped as a POW
> a subsequent career in "Special Forces"
> Arabic translator for a U.S. Ambassador, and then the FBI
> the saving of life with his EMT skills
> a B.S. degree in Aeronautical Engineering
> the heroic shooting of a charging elephant in Africa

What he projected from himself on others included:

> drunkenness, lying, thievery
> racist and anti-Semetic remarks
> horribly bad credit with looming home foreclosure

In both reversals "Jack" was able to initially sound very credible because he had the basic facts straight — he just changed the names. When word got out, he just moved on to other lies.

their too-pat and incredible life story
From several sociopaths I've known, one thing they all had in common was the early insistence to program others with their fanciful story. (I call it "setting the stage".) They do this to weed out the suspicious and identify the trusting, and it's very effective for that. Beware the overly impressive set-stage life history.

the indispensable pity ploy
What I like better than anything else is when people feel sorry for me. The thing I really want more than anything else out of life is people's pity.
— a convicted swindler, quoted by Dr. Martha Stout

Pity? Why would a sociopath want *pity*? Because it deactivates your B.S. detector. **You cannot pity somebody and simultaneously be *suspicious* of them.** If you learn anything about sociopaths, learn that. "Jack" was notorious about the pity ploy. Whenever he was late, he'd claim a massive plumbing leak on a jobsite. His most blatant pity ploy (none of it true, of course) was emailed to me by a friend:

Some months ago "Jack" called me and told me that he had been diagnosed with stomach cancer. He went on to describe in intricate detail the radiation treatment he was getting and how this was creating a great financial strain on him because he was also paying for all of his girlfriend's medical bills. Of course this information was told to me with the usual caveat of swearing not to tell another soul that he had cancer, especially his girlfriend.

protecting yourself from a possible sociopath
How can we recognize them? Fortunately, they cannot perfectly emulate healthy human beings:

When deciding whom to trust, bear in mind that the combination of consistently bad or egregiously inadequate behavior with frequent plays for your pity is as close to a warning mark on a conscienceless person's forehead as you will ever be given. [Though rarely violent, such a person is] probably not someone you should closely befriend, take on as your business partner, ask to take care of your children, or marry. (p.109)
— Dr. Martha Stout, *The Sociopath Next Door*

Stout recommends ceasing all contact after experiencing a total of just three: lies, no-shows, or irresponsible acts. This is excellent advice which will drastically limit the damage:

> *When considering a new relationship of any kind, practice the Rule of Threes regarding the claims and promises a person makes, and the responsibilities he or she has. Make the Rule of Threes your personal policy.*
>
> *One lie, one broken promise, or a single neglected responsibility may be a misunderstanding instead. Two may involve a serious mistake. But three lies says you're dealing with a liar, and deceit is the linchpin of conscienceless behavior. Cut your losses and get out as soon as you can. Leaving, though it may be hard, will be easier now than later, and less costly.*
>
> *Do not give your money, your work, your secrets, or your affection to a three-timer. Your valuable gifts will be wasted.*

I'd recommend that you *quietly* keep count, and not confront the suspect along the way. Once you've reached your three, simply cease all contact without any explanation. This will deny the sociopath a valuable feedback loop, and force him to thereafter wonder.

some tips for discerning the sociopath

The major red flags are grandiosity, shameless lies, unreliability, lack of empathy, and a flair for manipulation. Here some multiple signs of sociopaths which I gleaned from books, and from bitterly earned personal experience:

❏ grossly inflated view of their self-worth and importance, a truly astounding egocentricity and sense of entitlement

❏ unusually magnetic charm or charisma, excellent at impression management

❏ polished acting skills, immediately presentable

❏ often try to overwhelm others with flattery, feigned concern, kindness, or generosity

❏ make excellent use of social/professional roles and titles to dissuade dissent, scrutiny, or confrontation

❏ uncanny ability to spot decent and trusting people, the fertile soil of a sociopathic weed

❑ will find and exploit others' psychological weaknesses

❑ require our regular pity (especially with claims of being over-worked, cheated, or victimized) to keep our blinders on regarding their behavior (*i.e.*, one cannot pity a person and simultaneously suspect them of deceit)

❑ tell grandiose/unlikely-yet-convincing stories, usually putting themselves in the best light (this is common with new acquaintances). Known for "too incredible to believe" tales about themselves of luck, courage, stamina, wit, quick-thinking, etc. These stories have very little depth if you scratch the surface (disproven in 5 minutes on the Net).

❑ are deceitful to an incredible extreme ("*I lie like I breathe, one as much as the other.*"). They will baldly lie and deny with great colorfulness and detail, even when the truth is obvious to all and/or when lying serves no clear benefit.

❑ their lies, while convincing on the surface, often contain contradictory or logically inconsistent statements (which unfortunately escape initial detection because truthful people have no conception of such casual, regular, and thoughtless deceit)

❑ quite prone to regular and seemingly mindless or risky thievery, especially in the case of "covetous psychopaths" (who will steal mostly for the denying vs. the having)

❑ when challenged/confronted, will either deny everything, rationalize their behavior, or counter "*Why would I do something like that? What would be the reason?*"

❑ are notorious for not answering the question posed at them, or being evasive and unresponsive. They are masters at circumventing discussion of their own behavior.

❑ masters of misdirection; shifting focus/blame on accusers

❑ known for "*if you throw enough shit, some of it will stick*"

❑ minimize or deny consequences of their actions to others ("*They have insurance, and probably made money on the loss!*")

❏ frequently successful in talking their way out of trouble, even during confrontations with the criminal justice system

❏ seldom embarrassed at their own financial, legal, or personal problems — they haven't basic humanity to even be ashamed

❏ smooth lack of concern if found out (BIG red flag to sociopathy!), because shame or guilt is not only an emotion, but one linked to conscience. ("*The psychopath's indifference to being identified as a liar is truly extraordinary; it causes the listener to wonder about the speaker's sanity. More often, though, the listener is taken in.*" Hare, p.48)

❏ known for their impulsiveness to achieve immediate satisfaction, pleasure, or relief

❏ known for "consistent irresponsibility" extending to every part of their lives. They do not honor formal or implied commitments to people, organizations, or principles.

❏ usually with horrendously bad credit histories

❏ often late (and usually with unassailable and/or dramatic excuses). They don't care about other people's schedules, and resent having to conform to social rules of punctuality.

❏ often fail to conform to social norms, and often recklessly so

❏ inability to tolerate routine, as they are easily bored

❏ exhibit a profound general lack of empathy (the ability to "walk in another's shoes" by constructing a mental and emotional facsimile of others)

❏ cannot genuinely bond with others, and their relationships are invariably loveless, one-sided, and short-term

❏ see children as an inconvenience, and will scar their own

❏ described as "deceitful" and "manipulative" and "spooky"

❏ "*tend to see any social exchange as a 'feeding' opportunity, a contest, or a test of wills, in which there can be only one winner. Their motives are to manipulate and take, ruthlessly and without remorse.*" (Hare, p.145)

❏ able to tailor stories about the same event or person to others, and under the guise of "confidence" so that those deceived do not readily speak with each other and piece things together

❏ are masters at social compartmentalization, keeping victims mutually unaware of each other, or even mutually antagonistic by slyly pitting them against each other — all the while considering the psychopath as their "friend"

❏ just as they often try to evoke pity for themselves, they create or further poor impressions of others in a sort of pre-emptive self-protection for when others eventually discover the psychopath friend to be a liar, thief, and manipulator.

❏ see life as one big chess board, with people as pieces to move about. ("*Whoever is weak is also a sucker; that is, someone who demands to be exploited.*")

❏ sometimes able to fool elaborate psychological tests, such as the MMPI, and appear normal

❏ exhibit shallow "paint-by-the-numbers" emotions (they know the words, but not the music, of emotional life)

❏ usually lack physiological responses associated with fear or anxiety, and are known for preternatural calm and composure during intense situations (*e.g.*, police stops with a dead body in the trunk)

❏ have a greater need for stimulation (in order to feel alive at all), and thus assume greater risks / dangers

❏ incapable of actual remorse, and rarely even try to fake it

❏ do not know that they are evil (it's an alien concept to them), and thus feel fine about themselves.

❏ avoid other sociopaths (because they cannot be easily fooled), and the last thing an egocentric, selfish, demanding, callous person wants is someone just like himself

❐ are often suspected by police officers (*"I never did like that guy!"*) who deal with sociopaths every day

❐ once finally outted, are known to blithely move on to new people (*i.e.*, chess pieces), hobbies, and places

❐ generally immune to psychotherapy because they see nothing wrong with themselves — no problem need be addressed.

Over time, we can recognize their lives for their careening emptiness and hollowness (and often by their remarkably dead eyes), marked by innumerable deceits and irresponsibilities. While they cannot be cured or fixed, knowing who they are by the trail of human wreckage is sufficient warning for the curious, who then wisely shun such "people."

the sociopath's M.O.

Imagine the ocean is full of dolphins. And [the main character] *Profit is a new kind of shark that looks just like a dolphin. He could maneuver among the dolphins and the dolphins would say 'Welcome!' in dolphin talk. And then, one night, he'd start eating them.*
— PROFIT co-creator John McNamara

PROFIT follows the corporate skullduggery of junior V.P. Jim Profit, a full-blown sociopath. In his labyrinthine predation, he breaks up marriages, sets up a senior exec for a felony arrest and prison term, and even compromises the psychiatrist of his archenemy (a woman head of corporate security who sees Profit for what he is) to get inside her head during hypnosis. (And all that is post-childhood, after he set afire his father.) Teaming up with Profit is his also-sociopathic stepmother, as if one perfect sociopath weren't enough. The actor who played this sociopath thought it all rather cute:

I don't see him as an amoral or immoral individual. I think he had a superior set of moral values that enabled him to act with relative impunity.
— Adrian Pasdar, "Jim Profit"

The (deservedly) cancelled series PROFIT is a fine educational tool for discerning sociopathy, especially for those who don't grasp how sociopaths operate — and who won't believe your descriptions, either. (They could read *Othello* for the sociopath Iago, but that's probably expecting too much these days.) The sociopath's M.O. is very competently dramatized in this series (with helpful voice-overs), offering many key lessons:

   ❶   sociopaths scheme further ahead than moral people anticipate

   ❷   they A / V record their victims much more often than vice versa

   ❸   if victims tip off their plans for justice, sociopaths make it backfire

   ❹   sociopaths see sudden adversity as a challenge; they thrive on it

   ❺   they always act behind the scenes, which is difficult to discern

   ❻   they are masters of manipulation through compartmentalization

   ❼   most people are clueless (or in denial) about local sociopaths

   ❽   those who warning others are often ignored as Cassandras

dealing with a confirmed sociopath

What is so damnably frustrating to moral folks is that sociopaths seem to be coated in Teflon, rarely caught and punished for any significant percentage of their abuses. They can apparently talk and connive their way out of any scrape. This will remain true until moral folks begin to network together and expose their local sociopaths.

Reverse-engineering the sociopathic M.O. learned from PROFIT, here are some tips on how to protect yourself:

   ❶ record every conversation you have with known sociopaths

   ❷ get co-victims talking to each other and "comparing notes"

   ❸ NEVER tip your hand how you plan to expose the sociopath

   ❹ avoid appearing "obsessed" about warning others and / or getting justice — it will greatly weaken your cause

   ❺ create situations for others to discern being manipulated

   ❻ form alliances, and foment action by others — *i.e.*, don't do it all alone

   ❼ trust only those who've also been hurt by the same sociopath

   ❽ take your time in gathering evidence from all angles, anticipating his oiliness

   ❾ honestly evaluate your own weaknesses and how they've been exploited

   ❿ don't drop one ball at a time; drop several at once

Sociopaths swim throughout the human sea, and the sooner you begin to recognize their hidden shark-fin, the less damage they can do. But, it's up to you to act, because:

> All that is necessary for the triumph of evil is that good men do nothing.
> — Edmund Burke

optical illusions: sociopath autostereograms

Go to the below link for an essay I wrote for the excellent website www.lovefraud.com which informs about sociopaths.

www.lovefraud.com/blog/2007/05/20/optical-illusions-autostereograms-and-sociopaths/

sociopaths elsewhere (the "*kunlangeta*")

That is what the Yupi Eskimo call a man who repeatedly lies, cheats, steals, and sexually takes advantage of women. When anthropologist Jane Murphy inquired what was done about these *kunlangeta*, one Eskimo man replied, "*Somebody would have pushed him off the ice when nobody else was looking.*"

That so, it seems highly unlikely that their *kunlangeta* ever amount to our 3% of men in society!

final thoughts on sociopaths

> He remembers also that every rational being is his kinsman, and that to care for all men is natural to man; and that a man should not care for the opinion of everybody but of those only who live according to nature. *As for those who live not so*, he bears always in mind what kind of men they are both at home and abroad, both by night and by day, and what they are, and with what companions they live their evil life.
> — Marcus Aurelius, *Meditations*

I expounded for these past 10+pages because sociopaths are the *one* class of people which you absolutely *cannot* trust. Good character development requires these three things: the ability to love, impulse control, and moral reasoning. Sociopaths have *none* of them. (The rest of us have at least one!)

Most normal folks you *can* trust with certain information, or during particular moments, and they respond naturally over time and friendship. You understand their self-interest and ethical bounds. As long as you do not mistake a sociopath for a person of character, you are generally safe from those whom you rightfully consider your friends.

7

COMMUNICATING

Words are, of course, the most powerful drug used by mankind.
  — Rudyard Kipling (1865-1936), *Times London*, 15 Feb. 1923

A man is never master of an idea until he can express it clearly.
  — Lew Starett

Words are used to express meaning; when you understand the meaning, you can forget about the words.
  — Chuang-tzu

Unless you want to exist in a cave or deserted island, how well you do in Life depends largely on how effectively you can communicate. It is vital to be able to communicate to those above and beneath you. Through the power of words, you can please, amuse, arouse, anger, and alienate others. Words are not only powerful, they are never *not* powerful.

USING WORDS CORRECTLY

If we do not know what we mean by what we say, we will never be able to know what we think.
  — Jeff Cooper

As Cooper was keen to point out, professional does not mean expert, and to decimate is not to devastate.

There are those who maintain that the English language is "evolving". Perhaps, but I see it rather as degenerating. Any author who thinks he can improve upon the usage of Theodore Roosevelt or Winston Churchill has much to prove. As I see it, the essence of good English is clarity. This does not depend upon

vocabulary, but rather upon perceptivity. The versatility of the English language permits a truly artistic flow of thought. If you use it right, you make your meaning absolutely clear. . . . The only way one can achieve full competence in English is by reading good English, and lots of it. In the age of television this become increasingly unlikely.
— Jeff Cooper

SPEAKING

The power of the spoken voice (any spoken voice) is awesome. It conveys the essence of the speaker: authority or weakness, truth or lie, knowledge or ignorance, doer or *poseur*.

develop your own pleasant speaking voice

Get rid of: extreme accents, high-throatedness, stammers, stutters, slurring, monotone delivery, bad grammar, excessive slowness or rapidity, unpleasant accent, and poor cadence. These things are deadly to a listener's ear.

Most men could speak with a deeper voice, and should. A deep voice conveys calm confidence and manliness.

Speak from your diaphragm, not your throat. Relax and breathe out your words from the gut. When you're doing it right, you'll feel your chest resonate (and not your head). Practice reading poetry into a digital voice recorder and hearing yourself played back.

the art of conversation

It was impossible to get a conversation going; everybody was talking too much.
— Yogi Berra

The opposite of talking is not listening.
The opposite of talking is waiting.
— Fran Lebowitz

Real conversation is not verbal ping-pong; it is an expansive process of great listening. It meanders a bit with ebb and flow, has few foregone conclusions, and always ventures into unexplored territory.

listening

The most important thing in communication is to hear what isn't being said.
— Peter Drucker

do not be too glib and open

Tell one your thoughts, but beware of two.
All know what is known to three.
   — Norse mythology proverb

A fool uttereth all his mind.
   — Proverbs 29:11

Silence is often misinterpreted, but never misquoted. Aside from the privacy aspect, the more open you are about yourself, the less people will respect you. Keep a bit of reserve and mystery about you. *"People who know the very least seem to know the loudest."*

Better to remain silent and be thought a fool than to speak and remove all doubt.
   — Abraham Lincoln

Let thy speech be better than silence, or be silent.
   — Dionysius the Elder

prefer silence or a question to a lie

You're not obliged to answer every question put to you. Know when to withhold the truth — not by lying, but with a counter-question or by silence. Here are some effective lines:

"Is that really relevant?"
"Why do you want to know?"
"Let's not have this conversation right now."

15 Rules of Good Communication with women

From Dr. Guy Grenier's fine book *10 Conversations You Must Have Before You Get Married*:

productive communication strategies
❶ focus on feelings, not facts
❷ stick to what you know ("I" versus "you" language)
❸ paraphrase and explain what you just heard
❹ keep the discussion on topic
❺ take turns: one speaks, one listens
❻ pick a good time to talk
❼ use good body language

destructive communication strategies
❶ using absolutes (*i.e.*, never, always, must, should, etc.)
❷ yelling
❸ insults
❹ mind-reading

anger-control stategies
❶ keep anger on the clock (the 30-minute rule)
❷ take a time-out (the 24-hour rule)

Never forget, you can tell a guy to "go to hell" tomorrow. You don't give up the right, so just keep you mouth shut today, and see if you feel the same way tomorrow.
   — Tom Murphy, via Warren Buffett

long-term relationship maintenance strategies
❶ connect with your partner for at least 20 minutes per day
❷ ask her *"How are we doing?"* once a month . . . forever

giving a speech
There are two kinds of speeches: prepared and unprepared. Until you've learned how to give a prepared speech, an impromptu one will probably be out of your league. Toastmasters is your answer.

getting over your fear of public speaking
Thorough knowledge of your subject goes the furthest in chasing away the jitters. Then, make sure you have an exact opening planned out. Once you've spoken for a couple of minutes, you'll find your groove and relax.

the prepared speech
A good five-minute speech requires one month's advance notice. A fifteen-minute speech requires a week's notice. A one-hour speech requires no advance notice.
   — *Rules of Thumb 2*, compiled by Tom Parker

the unprepared speech
It's just like the prepared speech, but the preparation is done on the spur of the moment. After lots of practice with prepared speeches, this will come naturally. The rules don't change: understand the mood of your audience, know your subject, open with a laugh, make three short and clear points, and close with a memorable synopsis.

always be concise
He can compress the most words into the smallest idea of any man I ever met.
— Abraham Lincoln

learn some powerful poetry!

Every man should have a quiver of at least a half-dozen classic poems that he can recite flawlessly whenever the right occasion demands. It is superb training for your vocal sense of power, pace and pause. Ladies will love it. Here is a starter, author unknown:

If you think you are beaten, you are,
If you think you dare not, you don't.
If you like to win, but you think you can't,
It is almost certain you won't.

If you think you'll lose, you're lost,
For out in the world we find,
Success begins with a fellow's will —
It's all in the state of his mind.

If you think you are outclassed, you are,
You've got to think high to rise,
You've got to be sure of yourself before
You can ever win a prize.

Life's battles don't always go
To the stronger or faster man,
But sooner or later the man who wins
Is the man who thinks he can!

"Man in the Glass" is a classic. Rudyard Kipling is one of the masters; "Gods of the Copybook Headings" is a favorite of mine.

learn foreign languages!

I consider this vital for growth, experience, and perspective. The earlier you begin, the easier it will be to master a foreign language. (After puberty, you won't be able to develop a native accent.) Author Tim Ferriss of the *4 Hour Workweek* claims that it is possible to become conversationally fluent in any language in 3-6 months (www.fourhourworkweek.com). All it takes is 2-4 hours per day of work. That's cheap for such an invaluable lifelong skill.

use the foreign language options in movies

This is a free way to train your ear to a new language. Beware of too much slang, however.

www.freetranslation.com

Translate text to/from English and a dozen languages.

Spanish

This should probably be your first choice, as it's very useful in the Southwest USA, and Latin America. Spanish is also probably the easiest foreign language for Americans to learn. Spanish TV and radio abound. You can easily meet native speakers to hone the language.

Learn a *quality* form of Spanish (*i.e.,* not some Tex-Mex hybrid), and pick up the differences between the Spanish spoken in Mexico, South America, and Spain.

French

Not a favorite of mine, but very useful in Europe and some parts of the Caribbean and Africa. A rather difficult language for some, but worthwhile. It is still used between diplomats, and it sounds "classy".

German

For usefulness, a bit less than French. In the Middle Ages, German and English were very similar. The grammar is intricate, and enunciation is paramount. (Dutch and Afrikaans are easier after German.) A good language in European business.

Italian

Less useful than German, but much more fun. A personal favorite. It has a wonderful cadence and is very expressive. A fun treat after you have your Spanish (and your Latin!).

Esperanto

An artificial language, very similar to Spanish. Very easy to learn as it purposely has no irregular spellings or grammar. (Little known fact: William Shatner "Captain Kirk" learned Esperanto as a child.) Not widely spoken; learn Spanish, French, or Italian first.

Scandinavian (Norwegian, Swedish, Danish)

Not useful at all, and not even necessary as English is so well spoken in those countries.

Russian
Handy (though possibly not appreciated) in the former captive states of the USSR. Becoming increasingly more important to learn.

Arabic
Potentially very useful if the Middle East fascinates you. Pick an accent least offensive to the most countries.

Chinese
The 21st century will increasingly belong to China (and less to the West). You won't need Chinese unless you visit China, as English is the international language of business.

WRITING

Words are the "software" of human beings, and writing our "code" is a powerful tool. Get the largest dictionary you can find, one that takes both hands to pick up. (Hemingway advised not to become a professional writer until you had read the dictionary *three* times!)

the basics of writing
grammar and punctuation
The only book you need is by Strunk and White. Any used bookstore will have this slender paperback.

advice from a real pro: author/scholar C.S. Lewis
(1) Always try to use the language so as to make quite clear what you mean, and make sure your sentence couldn't mean anything else.

(2) Always prefer the plain direct word to the long vague one. Don't "implement" promises, but "keep" them.

(3) Never use abstract nouns when concrete ones will do. If you mean "more people died," don't say "mortality rose".

(4) Don't use adjectives which merely tell us how you want us to feel about the thing you are describing. I mean, instead of telling us a thing was "terrifying", describe it so that we'll be terrified. Don't say it was "delightful", make us say "delightful" when we've read the description. You see, all those words (horrifying, wonderful, hideous, exquisite) are only saying to your readers "Please will you do my job for me".

(5) Don't use words too big for the subject. Don't say "infinitely" when you mean "very"; otherwise you'll have no word left when you want to talk about something really infinite.

— C.S. Lewis, to a child in America, 1956

> *Never use adjectives or adverbs which are mere appeals to the reader to feel as you want him to feel. He won't do it just because you ask him; you've got to make him. No good telling us a battle was "exciting". If you succeed in exciting us the adjective will be unnecessary; if you don't, it will be useless. Don't tell us the jewels had an "emotional" glitter; make us feel the emotion. I can hardly tell you how important that is.*
>
> *I hope, by the way, you always write by ear and not by eye. Every sentence should be tested on the tongue, to make sure that the sound of it has the hardness or softness, the swiftness or languor, which the meaning of it calls for.*
> — C.S. Lewis, to Miss Jane Gaskell, 1957

in order to write, you must first read . . . a lot

> *The greatest part of a writer's time is spent in reading, in order to write; a man will turn over half a library to make one book.*
> — Samuel Johnson

In a way, I read for a living. The writing is actually the end product of all my study. The reading:writing time ratio is at least 20:1.

keep a notebook of thought and ideas

> *Write down the thoughts of the moment. Those that come unsought for are commonly the most valuable.*
> — Francis Bacon

I can't overemphasize how important it is to always be jotting down your ideas as they come to you. Write out every single one! (I'm still mining stuff I jotted down in 1986!) The editing is for later, when you can see them all together. Certain idea hybrids will jump off the page.

writing an essay

Yes, this is forced down your throat in school, and it's a shame they made it so unpleasant, for essay writing is a sublime joy. You must cultivate the right attitude, and pick fun subjects.

writing letters

Master the art of letter writing, and the world is yours. Letters of: love, business, complaint, condolences, thanks, praise, opinion, inquiry, etc. Learn to reply at once, else you won't reply at all. (Email can do only so much. Keep stamps, postcards, and envelopes handy.)

writing poetry

I've heard it said that poetry is the "highest form of writing" and I can believe it. Passion should always move the pen.

Publishing a volume of verse is like dropping a rose petal down the Grand Canyon and waiting for the echo.
— Don Marqui

writing magazine articles

When writing a magazine article, begin with a snappy lead sentence, then write the piece to match the tone of the lead. Before submitting the article, delete the lead sentence.
— *Rules of Thumb 2*, compiled by Tom Parker

This is a great way to get published as a paid author! Magazines are always looking for quality content, so write some and submit it.

writing books

Fewer than 5% of the 195,000 books published each year sell more than 5,000 copies.
— Tim Ferriss, *4 Hour Work Week*

Book authoring is a very exciting career, and with instant-demand publishing and e-books it is easier than ever to succeed. You will have much more competition, however, so stand above the throng with quality work on interesting subjects.

on handling writing criticism and rejection

Your manuscript is both good and original; but the part that is good is not original, and the part that is original is not good.
— Samuel Johnson

It's difficult not to be defensive about your writing, but you must grow some thick skin if you're to succeed. Besides, your critics probably have some good advice for you, if you can hear it.

good books on writing

The Writer's Book of Wisdom — 101 Rules for Mastering Your Craft, Steven Taylor Gooseberry

On Writing, Stephen King

ON GIVING ADVICE

When a man points a finger at someone else, he should remember that three of his fingers are pointing at himself.
  — Louis Nizer

It's probably an excellent rule to rarely give unsolicited advice. If there is something you believe somebody must know for their own benefit, figure a way to cleverly word it into the conversation. Advise through a parable or analogy, vs. any "*You should do_____*".

If you haven't the time or subtlety for this, then give them some fair warning:. "*I have an idea for you about this, if you want to hear it.*" Most people are naturally curious, and few will refuse to listen.

> *Never communicate your feelings or information you consider to be important without first creating a burning curiosity within the listener.*
>   — Gary Smalley, *If Only He Knew: What No Woman Can Resist*

> *Some people are really looking for help. If someone responds to three valid suggestions with a "Yes, but . . ." he or she is more interested in playing games than solving problems.*
>   — *Rules of Thumb 2*, compiled by Tom Parker

📁 8

PERSUADING

Remember that men will go on doing the same things even if you should burst in protest.
— Marcus Aurelius, *Meditations*, VIII:4

WHY SHOULD PEOPLE DO ANYTHING *YOUR* WAY?

People don't care how much you know, until they know how much you care.
— John C. Maxwell, *The 21 Indispensible Qualities of a Leader*

According to G.M. scientist Charles F. Kettering, 90% of success is getting along with people, and only 10% is job technique. Before anybody does anything for you, they must first have confidence in (what the ancient Greeks called) your *ethos, pathos*, and *logos*:

ethos	your personal credibility of integrity and character
pathos	your empathic connection with others
logos	your logical argument

The sequence is vital: your character, your relationships, and the logic of your presentation. You cannot convince anyone with a logical argument if they first don't believe in you and trust that you understand their needs. Never begin with the *logos*.

A man passes for what he is worth. What he is engraves itself on his face, on his form, on his fortunes, in letters of light which all men may read but himself . . . . Trust men and they will make it their business to trust you; treat them greatly and they will show themselves great.
— Emerson, "Compensation"

To get along well with people, you must first discern where you stand with them, and then work to improve it. Again, William J. Reilly does a fantastic job at simplifying things to core essentials. Here, he makes the point that you are on one of four possible mental levels with everyone you know or deal with:

closed mind	*"To hell with you!"*
open mind	*"Really? What makes you think so?"*
confidence	*"That makes sense — you know your stuff!"*
belief	*"No need to convince me — I trust you!"*

closed mind

These people don't want to hear *anything* you have to say. You probably don't understand them, or think they're odd and unpleasant. Since you don't yet know what "makes them tick", reserve judgment!

> *It's difficult to get someone to understand something when his salary depends upon his not understanding it.*
> — Upton Sinclair

> *The only reason you don't kiss cows and consider snakes holy is because you weren't born in a Hindu family on the banks of the Brahmaputra.*
> *You deserve very little credit for being what you are — and remember, the man who comes to you irritated, bigoted, unreasoning, deserves very little discredit for being what he is. Sympathize with him. Say to yourself what John B. Gough used to say when he saw a drunken man staggering down the street: "There, but for the grace of God, go I."*
> — Norman Vincent Peale

> *The first thing to learn in intercourse with others is non-interference with their own peculiar way of being happy, provided those ways do not assume to interfere by violence with ours.*
> — Henry James

logic will not open a closed mind

You can't even begin with facts or logic or rational argument. Do not be rigid or assertive. Do not oppose, as that's pushing on an already shut door.

> *Always avoid the acute angle. Few people like to listen to truths that reflect on their judgment.*
> — Norman Vincent Peale

Advice is not disliked because it is advice; but because so few people know how to give it.
— Leigh Hunt

You must first find *some* common ground, if only agreement on the weather. (*Tip:* Admit your faults, as he will easily agree!)

to open a closed mind, first open *your* closed mind
Listen, or thy tongue will make thee deaf.
— American Indian proverb

Did you know that *listening* is one of the four forms of communication, along with speaking, writing, and reading? We are trained in the other three, but rarely in listening. This is to our loss.

There are four levels of listening:

pretending	(not hearing anything, but acting like you do)
selective	(hearing only parts of what's said, as with a child)
attentive	(with focus, but from your frame of reference)
empathic	(with focus, but from *their* frame of reference)

Empathy is not sympathy. Sympathy is a form of agreement, a form of judgment. And it is sometimes the appropriate emotion and response. The essence of empathic listening is not that you agree with someone; it's that you fully, deeply, understand that person, emotionally as well as intellectually.

Empathic listening is, in and of itself, a tremendous deposit in the Emotional Bank Account. It's deeply therapeutic and healing because it gives a person "psychological air."

If all the air were suddenly sucked out of the room you're in right now, what would happen to your interest in this book? You wouldn't care about the book; you wouldn't care about anything except getting air. Survival would be your only motivation.

But now that you have air, it doesn't motivate you. This is one of the greatest insights in the field of human motivation. Satisfied needs do not motivate. It's only the unsatisfied need that motivates. Next to physical survival, the greatest need of a human being is psychological survival — to be understood, to be affirmed, to be validated, to be appreciated.

When you listen with empathy to another person, you give that person psychological air. And after that vital need is met, you can then focus on influencing or problem solving. (p. 240)

Because we listen autobiographically, we tend to respond in one of four ways. We evaluate — we either agree or disagree; we probe — we ask questions from our own frame of reference; we advise — we give counsel based on our own experience; or we

interpret — we try to figure people out, to explain their motives, their behavior, based on our own motives and behavior. (p. 245)
— Stephen R. Covey, The Seven Habits of Highly Effective People

To listen empathically, avoid the evaluate/probe/advise/interpret and try to get inside their heart by mimicking and rephrasing content (the words they said) and reflecting emotion (how they said it). A closed minded person must first believe that you care about their feelings and understand their concerns. You must first give them "psychological air" through empathic listening.

If you catch yourself with an evaluate/probe/advise/interpret autobiographical response, quickly acknowledge it and apologize with a *"I'm sorry, I just realized I drifted a bit. Could we start again?"*

help the close minded to be right

Don't hammer him that he is wrong, but help him be right. Start by getting him to agree, to say "Yes".

Remember that the other man may be totally wrong. But he doesn't think so. Don't condemn him. Any fool can do that. Try to understand him. Only wise, tolerant, exceptional men even try to do that.
— Norman Vincent Peale

If there is any one secret of success it lies in the ability to get the other person's point of view and see thing from his angle as well as your own.
— Henry Ford

Never take a flat-footed position from which you cannot retreat. Do not pressure, but graciously retreat and form a vacuum for them to fill. (This works well with women, if you retreat soon enough before she's really dug in her heels against you.) Here is a wonderful example of a beautiful retreat, by the master:

Come to think it over, I don't entirely agree with it myself. Not everything I wrote yesterday appeals to me today. I am glad to learn what you think on the subject. The next time you are in the neighborhood you must visit us and we'll get this subject threshed out for all time. So here is a handclasp over the miles.
— Norman Vincent Peale

your smile will open closed minds

Many minds are closed because you didn't *smile* from the start.

A man with a smile is always welcome. Before entering a man's office, pause for an instant and think of the many things he has to be thankful for, then enter the room with the smile just vanishing from your face.
— Norman Vincent Peale

Whenever you go out of doors, draw the chin in, carry the crown of the head high, and fill the lungs to the utmost; drink in the sunshine; greet your friend with a smile, and put soul into every handclasp. Do not fear being misunderstood and do not waste a minute thinking about your enemies. Try to fix firmly in your mind what you would like to do; and then, without veering of direction, you will move straight to the goal.
— Elbert Hubbard

A man without a smiling face must not open shop.
— Chinese proverb

Practice smiling sincerely at others. It's free, easy, and it works! You will open over half of the normally closed minds against you.

open mind

They don't have a closed mind to you, but they aren't yet confident of you. Here is where evidence is used, but only as you (through continued empathic listening) think of their interests, are cognizant of your timing, and briefly give them a reasonably complete story. Be interesting, and tell them what *they* are going to get out of it.

confidence

These people are cooperative and friendly. Show belief in yourself (and in them), and ask them to believe in you with a "*Please just trust me on this*". Never promise something vague or unrealistic.

belief

You're "there". These people do what you ask without question, needing no evidence or proof. They *believe* in you. However, if you blow it you'll have to work your way up again, if that's even possible.

PERSUASION vs. MANIPULATION

I once knew a high-flying corporate climber who proudly gloated about her manipulation technique through clever phraseology:

> *There were a few persuasion techniques that I've already started using to great effect. For example, the article suggested that when asking people to do something, instead of saying "Please do X" you should instead phrase it as a question that requires an answer, because by providing the answer or even thinking about the answer, the other person is making a verbal and/or psychological commitment to do what you're asking. (Examples: "When will you get a chance to do X?" or "Is there anything else you need from me before you do X?")*
>
> *Another technique is to make sure people have something to lose, even if you have to give them something to make that happen. The classic example used in the article (in the context of a corporate setting) is that if a few people are complaining about something, you should ask them to form a committee to investigate it, because then they'll get so distracted by the committee's budget, status, and administrative matters that they will no longer really be agitating for their cause!*

This sort of thing is often ethically borderline, in my opinion. Yes, such techniques can be effective, but beware becoming an overly sly person who manipulates instead of leading or persuading

ARGUMENT

> *Remember that what pulls the strings is hidden within: this is the power of persuasion, this is life . . .*
> — Marcus Aurelius, *Meditations*, X:38

The highest goal of an argument is not victory, but *illumination.* Hard, cold facts do not convince, as first the hearer must agree to *become* convinced.

> *If you argue and rankle and contradict, you may achieve a victory sometimes; but it will be an empty victory because you will never get your opponent's good will.*
> — Ben Franklin

You cannot convince a closed mind; you must first open it. Be sure you understand the person's motives and concerns. Listen empathically before you speak. People never act upon your perceptions, they always act upon their own.

have a reputation for silence, not for argument

> *Remember what Voltaire says: La paix vaut encore mieux que la verite. (Peace is better still than the truth.) Remember also an*

Arabian proverb which tells us that on the tree of silence there hangs its fruit, which is peace.
— Arthur Schopenhauer, *ibid*

This will be difficult for anyone who enjoys arguing because he must always be "right". (I battle with this myself.) I'm learning that often the best way to be "right" is not to get into it at all. From the Internet I found some very good advice:

My father taught me three rules to arguing:
  ❶   *Make sure it's worth the time and effort.*
  ❷   *Make sure you can win.*
  ❸   *Make sure you have a worthy opponent.*
Those three questions tend to limit your arguments.

choose your argument partner very carefully

*As a sharpening of wits, controversy is often, indeed, of mutual advantage, in order to correct one's thoughts and awaken new views. **But in learning and in mental power both disputants must be tolerably equal:** If one of them lacks learning, he will fail to understand the other, as he is not on the same level with his antagonist. If he lacks mental power, he will be embittered, and led into dishonest tricks, and end by being rude.*

The only safe rule, therefore, is that which Aristotle mentions in the last chapter of his Topica: *not to dispute with the first person you meet, but only with those of your acquaintance of whom you know that they possess sufficient intelligence and self-respect not to advance absurdities; to appeal to reason and not to authority, and to listen to reason and yield to it; **and, finally, to cherish truth, to be willing to accept reason even from an opponent,** and to be just enough to bear being proved to be in the wrong, should truth lie with him. **From this it follows that scarcely one man in a hundred is worth your disputing with him. You may let the remainder say what they please, for every one is at liberty to be a fool** — desipere est jus gentium.*
— Arthur Schopenhauer, *ibid*

views not founded on logic cannot be shifted by reason

This is one of the most important concepts I've ever grasped. You can't convince a German in Portuguese. Since irrationality is usually based on emotion, no logical argument can prevail. The only way to jolt somebody out of a fog of irrationality is to become even more irrational that they. This forces their submerged reasonability to surface and "come to the rescue". *Then,* their mind clears up.

Simply take their premise to an outrageous extreme, with deadpan sincerity. I enjoy doing this to pious vegetarians. "*If meat is murder, then salad is slaughter! Cut down in the prime of their sensient life for bowls of green flesh called 'salads,' we must outlaw these so-called 'gardens' — these killing fields of plantkind!"* After several stunned seconds, they ask me what I do eat, and I reply a bowl of hot steam and styrofoam packing peanuts.

When they realize that I'm being ridiculous, I can then explain to them that Life must consume Life in order to live. Everything is on its way somewhere else, usually to another's dinner plate. We're on our way to the worms, just as deer, cows, chickens and plants are on their way to us. It's just Life. Life is voracious, always consuming Life in a never-ending communion of the recently dead. Animals aren't exempt. Plants aren't exempt. We aren't exempt.

I hunt and kill animals for food (and to fulfill my primal instincts as a hunter) as I grow and kill plants for food (and to fulfill my passion as a gardener). The vegetarian bunny-huggers are hypocritical plant slayers, but you'll never convince them of this through rational argument.

never get emotional

A cool demeanour may, however, help you here, if, as soon as your opponent becomes personal, you quietly reply, "That has no bearing on the point in dispute," and immediately bring the conversation back to it, and continue to show him that he is wrong, without taking any notice of his insults. Say, as Themistocles said to Eurybiades (pataxon men, akouson de) — Strike, but hear me. But such demeanour is not given to every one.
— Arthur Schopenhauer,
   Die Kunst, Recht zu behalten   The Art Of Controversy

In Japan, the first person to raise his voice loses the argument. It's actually the same here, though not as formally recognized.

on being persuasive

Research shows that three characteristics are related to persuasiveness: perceived authority, honesty, and likability.
— Robert Levine

Get on a debate team wherever you can; it is invaluable experience difficult to get elsewhere.

when you are absolutely sure of your facts . . .

As a Junior in military school, I was captain of our rifle team. I knew a lot about guns, and wasn't shy about it. Once, a visiting officer was being shown about the school by our Commandant and they stopped by the rifle range. Kicking around the dirt, the visiting officer scuffed up an unfired round of 9mm. Because of the "44" headstamp he declared it a .44 Magnum, a much larger cartridge with a rimmed case. I knew that to be grossly in error, and without a whiff of tact proceeded to lecture him that the round was a German 9mm manufactured in 1944. (Frankly, I was offended that a military officer couldn't tell the difference between the cartridges.)

The Commandant later told me, very patiently, that even though I was correct in my information, I (16 years old, with zits and braces) had embarrassed the officer. I understood then what I'd done, and never forgot it (though I've not always remembered it in time). What I should have said was something like, "*Pardon me, Sir, and I may be wrong about this, but could the '44' designate the year of production? If so, then perhaps this is a pistol cartridge from World War Two?*" This would have allowed the officer to save face by concluding with a, "*Now that you mention it, that makes more sense.*"

Ironically enough, I had another chance decades later, on a very similar issue. My *Safari Dreams* had just come out and had its debut at the SCI 2008. I had bought a new book by a safari celebrity, and noticed an error he'd made about one of the calibers. I dropped by his booth to tell him that I liked his book, and mentioned offhand that it might, however, have just one error. He initially bristled a bit, but then graciously thanked me for having told him. Most importantly, I had picked a time for all this when he wasn't swarmed with people, thus not embarrassing him in front of fans and readers.

Here are some ways to make the softer approach:

"*I may be wrong, but let's look at the record of all this.*"
"*I thought the same until I took this into consideration.*"
"*Let's take a closer look.*"

arguing on the internet

Arguing with anonymous strangers on the Internet is a sucker's game because they almost always turn out to be — or to be indistinguishable from — self-righteous sixteen-year-olds possessing infinite amounts of free time.
— Neil Stephenson, *Cryptonomicon*

If you still feel that you must respond, do so only indirectly. My favorite tactic is to just drop a pithy quote (such as the above). Or, this:

You can always find some Eskimos ready to instruct the Congolese in how to cope with heat waves.
— Stanislaw Lem

I wish that I were young enough to know everything!

Even your ignorance is encyclopedic.

The difference between genius and stupidity is that genius has its limits.

argument: deductive & inductive

Learn to reason forward and backward on both sides of a question.
— Thomas Blandi

When you have excluded the impossible, whatever remains, however improbable, must be the truth.
— Sir Arthur Conan Doyle

Genius is the ability to reduce the complicated to the simple.
— C.W. Ceram

Statistics are like a bikini. What they reveal is suggestive, but what they conceal is vital.
— Aaron Levenstein

The madman is not the man who has lost his reason. The madman is the man who has lost everything except his reason.
— G.K. Chesterton

To "deduce" is to understand the small from the large. To "induce" is to understand the large from the small — which is much more difficult. Induction describes the whole by inference from a part of the whole. Induction offers probabilities while deduction describes certainties.

what is an "argument"?

An argument consists of one or more premises and one conclusion. A premise is a statement (a sentence that is either true or false) that is offered in support of the claim being made, which is the conclusion (which is also a sentence that is either true or false).
— The Nizkor Project, www.nizkor.org

Premises can be true or false, and so can inferences (how the premises are allegedly connected). For deductive argument, here is the table:

premise	inference	conclusion
true	true	true
true	false	false
false	true	true or false
false	false	false

Clearly you can build a valid argument from true premises, and arrive at a true conclusion. You can also build a valid argument from false premises, and arrive at a false conclusion.

The tricky part is that you can start with false premises, proceed via valid inference, and reach a true conclusion. For example:

* Premise: All fish live in the ocean
* Premise: Sea otters are fish
* Conclusion: Therefore sea otters live in the ocean

There's one thing you can't do, though: start from true premises, proceed via valid deductive inference, and reach a false conclusion.
— The Nizkor Project, www.nizkor.org

So, the fact that an inference is valid doesn't necessarily mean that its conclusion holds, because it may have started from false premises. Thus, it's more important to carefully examine the premises than the inference.

2 types of arguments: deductive & inductive

*There are two main types of arguments: deductive and inductive. A **deductive argument** is an argument such that the premises provide (or appear to provide) complete support for the conclusion. An **inductive argument** is an argument such that the premises provide (or appear to provide) some degree of support (but less than complete support) for the conclusion. If the premises actually provide the required degree of support for the conclusion, then the argument is a good one.*

A good deductive argument is known as a valid argument and is such that if all its premises are true, then its conclusion must be true. If all the argument is valid and actually has all true premises, then it is known as a sound argument. If it is invalid or has one or more false premises, it will be unsound.

A good inductive argument is known as a strong (or "cogent") inductive argument. It is such that if the premises are true, the conclusion is likely to be true.

A fallacy is, very generally, an error in reasoning. This differs from a factual error, which is simply being wrong about the facts. To be more specific, a fallacy is an "argument" in which the premises given for the conclusion do not provide the needed degree of support. A deductive fallacy is a deductive argument that is invalid (it is such that it could have all true premises and still have a false conclusion). An inductive fallacy is less formal than a deductive fallacy. They are simply "arguments" which appear to be inductive arguments, but the premises do not

provided enough support for the conclusion. In such cases, even if the premises were true, the conclusion would not be more likely to be true.
— The Nizkor Project, www.nizkor.org

deductive argument

This is the classic "Sherlock Holmes" indisputable reasoning, whereby a certainty can be deduced from related evidence.

Deductive arguments are supposed to be water-tight. For a deductive argument to be a good one (to be "valid") it must be absolutely impossible for both its premises to be true and its conclusion to be false. With a good deductive argument, that simply cannot happen; the truth of the premises entails the truth of the conclusion.

The classic example of a deductively valid argument is:

> *(1) All men are mortal.*
> *(2) Socrates is a man.*
> *Therefore:*
> *(3) Socrates is mortal.*

It is simply not possible that both (1) and (2) are true and (3) is false, so this argument is deductively valid.
—www.logicalfallacies.info

inductive argument

Inductive arguments needn't be as rigorous as deductive arguments in order to be good arguments. Good inductive arguments lend support to their conclusions, but even if their premises are true then that doesn't establish with 100% certainty that their conclusions are true. Even a good inductive argument with true premises might have a false conclusion; that the argument is a good one and that its premises are true only establishes that its conclusion is probably true.
—www.logicalfallacies.info

Inductive reasoning is a form "generalizing" and is never "valid" (*i.e.,* perfectly true), but only "strong" or "weak". There's nothing wrong with using inductive argument . . . as long as everyone understands it's not deductively "valid".

logical fallacies

A fallacy is a technical flaw which makes an argument unsound or invalid. Arguments which contain fallacies are "fallacious".

Generally, fallacies fall into classes of relevance, of ambiguity, and of presumption.

Inductive argument is fraught with several common errors:

- hasty generalization
- overwhelming exception
- biased sample
- false analogy
- misleading vividness
- conjunction fallacy

fallacy of relevance

Example: "fallacy of composition" ("From Each to All").

In a baseball stadium, if you stand up you will see better. Therefore, if everybody stood up they *all* would see better.

Another is the *argumentum ad hominem* or personal attack fallacy:

Kevin said that Dodge trucks are superior to Ford trucks. Since Kevin is an egomaniac, Ford trucks must be superior.

Many fallacies of relevance are "appeals to _____":

antiquity	("*the ancient Greeks proved it for all time*")
	argumentum ad antiquitatem
authority	("*I am a genius and an expert*")
	argumentum ad verecundiam
consequences	("*it has never worked before*")
emotion	("*because it's a shabby thing to do*")
fear	("*it's too risky and dangerous*")
flattery	("*as a man of your intellect would know*")
force	("*because you have to*")
	argumentum ad baculum
majority	("*Obama is now the president*")
	argumentum ad numerum
novelty	("*it's newer and thus must be better*")
	argumentum ad novitatem
pity	("*because the starving deserve food*")
	argumentum ad misericordiam
popularity	("*everybody is buying them*")
	argumentum ad populum
poverty	("*the poor aren't contaminated by money*")
	argumentum ad lazarum
repetition	("*as I've told you, again and again*")

	argumentum ad nauseam
ridicule	*("only a tin-foil hatty would believe that")*
spite	*("yeah, you would say something like that")*
tradition	*("our family has always voted Democrat")*
wealth	*("it's where the elite go")*
	argumentum ad crumenam

fallacy of ambiguity

The best example is the "straw man" argument where you misrepresent your opponent's position in order to "defeat" it. For a classic example of this, read page 218 of Joel Dyer's *Harvest of Rage*:

> *There are people out there stockpiling food and weapons and watching the skies for the inevitable day when the Jewish bankers will send in the black helicopters full of United Nations storm troopers to attack their farms. These people aren't stupid; they're sick. Many have lost touch with reality to the point that they are no longer in control of their actions. Their potential for anger- and paranoia-induced violence is immeasurable.*

Even as Dyer admits to ample evidence of concerted government and corporate action against the family farm, he then resorts to piling on every excessive fear into a psychological catalog of apparent lunacy.

The "fallacy of accident" (*dicto simpliciter ad dictum secundum quid*) makes a generalization that disregards exceptions (*e.g.*, Cutting people is a crime. Surgeons cut people. Therefore, surgeons are criminals.)

The "converse fallacy of accident" (*dicto secundum quid ad dictum simpliciter*) argues from a special case to a general rule (*e.g.*, If I let you go outside to play, then I'll have to let your brother also go.)

fallacy of presumption

Most of these are fallacies of False Cause or *non sequitur* (Latin for "it does not follow"), which incorrectly assume one thing is the cause of another. Just because A and B occur together does not mean that A makes happen B. Correlation is not causality! (In Latin this is called *cum hoc ergo propter hoc*.) While causality contains correlation, the reverse is not automatically true.

The fallacy of believing temporal succession implies a causal relation is called *post hoc ergo propter hoc*.

38 Ways to Win an Argument
"The Art of Controversy"

This timeless work by German philosopher Schopenhauer drew much from Aristotle's *Topica*. You must learn to argue effectively, for truth being on your side does not alone guarantee victory.

> *For it often happens that in a matter in which a man is really in the right, he is confounded or refuted by merely superficial arguments; and if he emerges victorious from a contest, he owes it very often not so much to the correctness of his judgment in stating his proposition, as to the cunning and address with which he defended it.*
>
> — Arthur Schopenhauer, "Conversational Ethics" preface

defending from deception, without practicing deception

Half of Schopenhauer's 38 strategies I would consider dishonest (and unnecessary, if your position is based on truth), but you must be acquainted with them all for your own self-defense.

Schopenhauer, however, believes one must also *employ* dishonesty to be able to protect yourself against it:

> *But even when a man has the right on his side, he needs Dialectic in order to defend and maintain it; he must know what the dishonest tricks are, in order to meet them; nay, he must often make use of them himself, so as to beat the enemy with his own weapons.*
>
> *Accordingly, in a dialectical contest we must put objective truth aside, or, rather, we must regard it as an accidental circumstance, and look only to the defence of our own position and the refutation of our opponent's.*

How did he arrive at *that* conclusion? Through his deep cynicism:

> *If human nature were not base, but thoroughly honourable, we should in every debate have no other aim than the discovery of truth; we should not in the least care whether the truth proved to be in favour of the opinion which we had begun by expressing, or of the opinion of our adversary. . . .*
>
> *Machiavelli recommends his Prince to make use of every moment that his neighbour is weak, in order to attack him; as otherwise his neighbour may do the same. If honour and fidelity prevailed in the world, it would be a different matter; **but as these are qualities not to be expected, a man must not practise them himself, because he will meet with a bad return**. It is just*

> the same in a dispute; if I allow that my opponent is right as soon as he seems to be so, it is scarcely probable that he will do the same when the position is reversed; and as he acts wrongly, I am compelled to act wrongly too. It is easy to say that we must yield to truth without any prepossession in favour of our own statements; but we cannot assume that our opponent will do it, and therefore we cannot do it either.

The world is full of evil people, they will not reciprocate your honesty, thus you must practice an inverse Golden Rule: *"Do unto others as they might do unto you"*? This is typical German philosopher pragmatic horseshit. (Schopenhauer's *"might makes right"* beliefs, by the way, were very influential on Adolf Hitler.) A primary reason why honor and fidelity do not prevail in the world is because moral cowards will not behave ethically without some direct, instant profit.

The value of ethics is not the expectation of a good return (although such occurs much more often than Schopenhauer believed). Rather, the value of ethics is to create ethical *character*. This is true profit — and one that can never be stolen by another. As the Stoics would say: *"Do good because good is good to do."* That others may do bad to you never justifies the jettisoning of your own ethics.

ethical strategies of Schopenhauer's 38

Some people believe victory more important than truth. No, truth *is* victory, or at least it *should* be. Predictably, Schopenhauer strongly disagrees:

> Hence we make it a rule to attack a counter-argument, even though to all appearances it is true and forcible, **in the belief that its truth is only superficial,** and that in the course of the dispute another argument will occur to us by which we may upset it, or succeed in confirming the truth of our statement. **In this way we are almost compelled to become dishonest; or, at any rate, the temptation to do so is very great.** Thus it is that the weakness of our intellect and the perversity of our will lend each other mutual support; and that, generally, a disputant fights not for truth, but for his proposition, as though it were a battle *pro aris et focis.*

Well, if *"truth is only superficial"* then it really doesn't matter what anybody thinks and does, as long as they "win". This is the creed of bullies who never built up the courage to live correctly.

So, do not use any strategy (however ethically neutral or even positive) solely to "win" at the expense of the truth. If your opponent is right, be willing to accept it through argument. Even Schopenhauer make a nod to this notion:

> . . . *to appeal to reason and not to authority, and to listen to reason and yield to it; **and, finally, to cherish truth, to be willing to accept reason even from an opponent,** and to bring just enough to bear being proved to be in the wrong, should truth lie with him . . .*

So, with all the ethical prologue covered, here are the 38 strategies.

#4: hide your conclusion until the end

If you want to draw a conclusion, you must not let it be foreseen, but you must get the premises admitted one by one, unobserved, mingling them here and there in your talk: otherwise, your opponent will attempt all sorts of chicanery. Or, if it is doubtful whether your opponent will admit them, you must advance the premises of these premises; that is to say, you must draw up pro-syllogisms, and get the premises of several of them admitted in no definite order. In this way you conceal your game until you have obtained all the admissions that are necessary, and so reach your goal by making a circuit. These rules are given by Aristotle in his Topica, bk. viii., c. 1. It is a trick which needs no illustration.
    — Arthur Schopenhauer, *ibid*

Do not A-B-C-D state your premises. Rather, mingle them in no discernible order. (Any good trial attorney knows this.) Get all the admissions from your opponent by a circuitous route.

#5: use your opponent's beliefs against him

This is absolutely fair game. If he won't admit to your premises, try to use his own against him. Most people are hypocrites.

#7: ask many questions to get an opponent's admissions

Propositions are made up of components. Get your opponent to admit to at least some of them.

#8: make your opponent angry

Anger clouds reason, and reason is needed to win an argument. By disarming him through his own emotions, he loses by default.

#10: ask your opponent to concede the opposite of yours

If he will not concede to any of your points, try to box him in by demanding he take the opposite view of yours. Then, you will have something more definable to attack.

#11: if partially agreed with, don't rush the conclusion

Introduce your conclusion later, and many will believe that your opponent had already conceded to it.

#12: use language favorable to your proposition

To control the metaphor is to control the framework of the argument. For example, in the abortion debate, each side has tried to capture the metaphor with either a "pro-life" or "pro-choice" label. In early Russia, the Communists brashly called themselves "*Bolsheviks*" ("the majority") when they were actually in the minority.

#13: offer a glaring counter-proposition to your own

This may force your opponent to accept your argument, to avoid appearing paradoxical. If you place gray next to black, it can look white. If next to white, gray can appear black.

#16: use inconsistencies in his statements and actions

Those who piously sport *Free Tibet!* bumper stickers should be challenged why they buy Walmart products from China (which has militarily occupied Tibet since the 1950s).

#17: use subtle distinctions to avoid conceding his point

Taken too far, however, is just plain evasion.

#20: if your premises are conceded, draw the conclusion

Don't ask him to accept your conclusion; draw it yourself.

#21: refute superficial arguments for their nature

Don't inflate such with any credibility, as they don't deserve to be taken seriously even for a moment.

#22: do not allow yourself to be led A+B+C=D

If you admit to A+B+C, and it leaves you forced to then admit D, then you have lost the argument. Try to redirect or redefine and get off that disastrous track.

#25: undermine generalizations by contrary examples
While broad statements can be valid, they go only so far. Don't allow them to be over-applied.

#26: use your opponent's argument against himself
This includes selectively taking a piece of his proposition and wielding it to his disadvantage.

#27: when your opponent is angered, increase your zeal
If he yelps, you may have discovered the weak side to his case. Finish him off!

#34: an opponent's evasion and silence must be pursued
Urge the point all the more (be careful not to expand it) when your opponent has been reduced to silence. You've found a weak spot!

#35: question your opponent's motive
Ethically, this is a borderline strategy, to be used fairly and only when you sincerely believe that your opponent's motive is suspect or contrary to the one he asserts. People do things generally for MICE: Money, Ideology, Coercion, and Ego. If he's claiming idealogy, but making big profits, then he is vulnerable in argument.

#37: attack a faulty proof of a correct proposition
Bad advocates often lose good cases. Another borderline strategy, to be used honestly. It is more important that an opponent (especially when he is much younger than you) is correct in his proposition than his argument of it.

unethical strategies of Schopenhauer's 38
I would classify the below as inherently "hitting below the belt" and unnecessary. If you've a correct and provable proposition, then ethical strategies should be sufficient.

Most unethical strategies incorporate logical fallacies of relevance, ambiguity, and presumption. If you can recognize the fallacy, the unethical strategy of your opponent will become clear.

#1: grossly exaggerate an opponent's proposition
The "*Extension*" is easy to do against a very general statement. Protect yourself by strictly defining a narrow proposition.

#2: use different meanings of an opponent's argument
The "*Homonymy*" is a cheap, though easy, trick of language.

#3: turn limited propositions into untenable general ones
This is often done while something different (and usually irrelevant) is instead attacked.

#6: confuse the issue by changing an opponent's words
Do not allow yourself to be rephrased and misquoted.

#9: use opponent's answers to reach their opposite
This is blatant chicanery, and unworthy of any truthful proposition.

#14: try to bluff a shy or stupid opponent
Beware of bluster, outrage, insistence, and browbeating. Often used with #28, #29, #36 and #38.

#15: exchange a difficult proposition for an easy one
And when the easy one is conceded, proclaim that the opponent agrees with your "reasoning".

#18: avoid an opponent's devastating conclusion
Cowards from truth will interrupt the dispute, break it off completely, or direct it away from the uncomfortable matter at hand. Stay on track and air your conclusion!

#19: when challenged on the specific, counter vaguely
Once I showed one of my new books to a well-known author and personality, who misunderstood that I had only published it. He exclaimed, "*I sure don't like your author!*" When I claimed authorship and politely asked his meaning, he replied something so vague and nonresponsive that I could not quote it even the next day.

A real master opponent will challenge epistemology (how we "know" knowledge and define reality). This is a philosophical muck that you must avoid get dragged into!

#23: contradict in order to foment an extended premise
Beware of enlarging or exaggerating your original proposition, thus giving your opponent something new to refute (which makes it easier for him to claim that he refuted the original).

Retain your limits with "*That is what I said, no more.*"

#24: state a false syllogism
Birds fly.
Penguins are birds.
Thus, penguins can fly.

Another cheap trick is to make a false inference from a proposition, and then try to use it to indirectly defeat the proposition. You must be sharp on the subject of logic, deduction, and induction.

#28: use the audience's ignorance
Beware of invalid objections by your opponent, who is banking on your audience not being able to discern the truth. Quickly and in very few words dispel the erroneous assertion. Do not be long-winded, else you'll bore the audience.

#29: the beaten will usually try for a diversion
While the diversion may be somewhat related to the matter at hand, a desperate opponent will resort to anything. Call it out for what it is before the diversion gains any traction.

#30: the appeal to authority rather than reason
When your opponent begins to recount his degree, alleged experience, genius, etc. you are witnessing the classic *argumentum ad verecundiam.* Beware of high-sounding references to obscure "experts" and historical "examples".

Another typical appeal to authority is the so-called "universal opinion" which Schopenhauer demolishes:

> *Every man prefers belief to the exercise of judgment, says Seneca;*
> *There is no opinion, however absurd, which men will not readily embrace as soon as they can be brought to the conviction that it is generally adopted. Example affect their thought, just as it affects their action. They are like sheep following the bell-wether just as he leads them. They would sooner die than think. It is very curious that the universality of an opinion should have so much weight with people, as their own experience might tell them that its acceptance is an entirely thoughtless and merely imitative process.*
> *. . . the universality of an opinion is no proof, nay, it is not even a probability, that the opinion is right.*
> *In short, there are very few who can think, but every man wants to have an opinion; and what remains but to take it ready-made from others, instead of forming opinions for himself?*
> *Since this is what happens, where is the value of the opinion even of a hundred millions?*

#31: feign lesser intelligence to the opponent's intellect

This is a really desperate thing, especially when done by an older and wiser opponent: *"Sorry, but I wasn't blessed with your penetrating intellect. You'll have to forgive us simpletons for not being able to match your 'genius'!"*

#32: lump the opponent's proposition with bad company

A truly shabby thing is to falsely label the proposition as:

"paranoid"	*"conspiracy theorist"*
"tinfoil hatty"	*"kooky"*
"neo-Nazi"	*"right wing"*

#33: admit opponent's premises, but not the conclusion

"That's fine in theory, but it won't work in practice."
This actually contradicts logic, for if the theory is valid then it also should work in practice.

#36: bewilder an opponent with bombast

The old *"dazzle them with bullshit!"* ploy. This can be effective with ignorant and shy opponents. Some favorites come to mind:

"The black cat is always the last one off the fence."
"You can't tell where the train went by looking at the tracks."
"To those who understand, no explanation is necessary. To those who don't understand, no explanation is possible."

#38: final ploy of the losers: insult the opponent

A last trick is to become personal, insulting, rude, as soon as you perceive that your opponent has the upper hand, and that you are going to come off worst. It consists in passing from the subject of dispute, as from a lost game, to the disputant himself, and in some way attacking his person. . . . But in becoming personal you leave the subject altogether, and turn your attack to his person, by remarks of an offensive and spiteful character. It is an appeal from the virtues of the intellect to the virtues of the body, or to mere animalism.

While it may be very tempting to descend into the mudpit and start flinging some yourself, keep your high ground. It will infuriate your opponent, while adding to audience respect.

A cool demeanor may, however, help you here, if, as soon as your opponent becomes personal, you quietly reply, "That has no bearing on the point in dispute," and immediately bring the conversation back to it, and continue to show him that he is wrong, without taking any notice of his insults. Say, as *Themistocles said to Eurybiades* — paxton men, akouson de (Strike, but hear me.) *But such demeanor is not given to every one.*

being "hit below the belt"

For three years I was embroiled in an intellectual dispute within the field of an ex-friend's alleged expertise. On his forum, this self-described "*genius*" and "*senior engineer*" avoided any factual rebuttal to his challengers, but instead resorted to many unethical strategies, namely #3, #14, #18, #29, #30, #32, and #38. (Not one ethical strategy did he employ. Anytime an opponent uses predominantly unethical strategies, it is a reliable sign that his position is untenable.)

After much bombast and insult, he slunked off in silence with the parting shot: "*Arguing on the Internet is like being in the Special Olympics. Even if you win, you're still a retard.*" I then publicly offered a $1,000 cash prize to anyone who could confirm his discredited "thesis" (which I had previously published in my book *Safari Dreams*, to my detriment). No takers yet — not even him.

Schopenhauer predicted this kind of behavior:

> *Our innate vanity, which is particularly sensitive in reference to our intellectual powers, will not suffer us to allow that our first position was wrong and our adversary's right.* The way out of this difficulty would be simply to take the trouble always to form a correct judgment. For this a man would have to think before he spoke. *But, with most men, innate vanity is accompanied by loquacity and innate dishonesty.* They speak before they think; and even though they may afterwards perceive that they are wrong, and that what they assert is false, they want it to seem the contrary. The interest in truth, which may be presumed to have been their only motive when they stated the proposition alleged to be true, *now gives way to the interests of vanity: and so, for the sake of vanity, what is true must seem false, and what is false must seem true.*

Be careful when you get between certain people and their egos, for they will chuck truth, friendship, and common courtesy out the window to protect their precious vanity. Such is difficult to weather, but try to remain composed and rational. When somebody uses dishonest and cowardly argument, calmly call him out by coldly describing his Schopenhauer strategies. This will focus the audience on the real issue vs. attempted evasions and diversions.

The Man in the Glass
Anonymous Americas

When you get what you want in your struggle for self
and the world makes you king for a day
Just go to the mirror and look at yourself
and see what that man has to say

For it isn't your father or mother or wife
who judgment upon you must pass
The fellow whose verdict counts the most in your life
is the one staring back from the glass

Some people may think you a straight-shooting chum
and call you a wonderful guy
But the guy in the glass says you're only a bum
if you can't look him straight in the eye

He's the fellow to please never mind all the rest
for he's with you clear up to the end
And you've passed your most dangerous difficult test
if the man in the glass is your friend

You may fool the whole world down the pathway
of life and get pats on the back as pass
But your final reward will be heartaches and
tears if you've cheated the man in the glass.

NEGOTIATING & SELLING

NEGOTIATING (HAGGLING)

learn to negotiate
You don't get what you deserve, you get what you negotiate.

Bargaining (*i.e.*, negotiation) skills are *extremely* important in life — a form of wielding and absorbing power. Remember from the *Understanding* chapter how nearly everything in Life is negotiable? Negotiating for better price or terms is often the easiest way to "make money". The only way you can negotiate effectively on your own behalf is to be willing to walk away unsatisfactory price or terms. Whoever more wants the negotiation to succeed has the lesser bargaining power.

synopsis of *Smart Negotiating* by J.C. Freund
preparation before the negotiation starts
What information do you need, and how to get it?
Use agents or negotiate yourself?
What expectations of price and terms are realistic?
Decide in advance your strategy for the dispute.

once the negotiation begins
Decide who goes first on price and terms.
Buttress your original and subsequent positions on rationale.
Your plausible rationale should serve these three functions:
   a. to establish a helpful bid and asked range
   b. to send the right kind of message
   c. to induce a constructive second proposal from the bidder
Actively manage the concession process for final compromise
   a. reciprocity is crucial; you have to give in order to get

b. send a message: it's meaningful, limited, and maybe last
c. try to get the opponent to bid against himself
d. price concessions: meaningful, and decreasing in size
e. nonprice concessions: rank in importance to you both
Leverage consists of necessity, desire, competition, and time.
When you have leverage, quickly and quietly do the deal.
When you don't, go for reasonableness and conventionality.
Keep quiet about what factors work against you.

bringing the negotiations to a close
Achieve credibility for yourself, and look for their bluffs.
a. use specific and detached information
b. assess the reliability of what you're being fed
Decide what is firm for you, and be staunch on such "blue chips"
let the opponent see some flexible "bargaining chips"
In deciding whether to bluff, what will you do if:
a. you are not believed, and your bluff is called?
b. you are believed, and the other side walks away, even
    though you would have accepted their last offer
If you bluff, choose a worthy issue, and be flexible elsewhere.
Generally avoid threats, which can harden your opponent.
a. warn of negative consequences independent of your will
b. if you do threaten, do not bluff (destroys your credibility)
c. subtle threats: ignore, laugh off, or react strongly
d. overt threats: always reply, but shift elsewhere
Deadlines can create pressure.
a. Keep alert for clues that they are feeling some heat
b. conceal any impending deadline pressure you feel
c. test their deadlines, resist what is unrealistic
Keep yourself in balance, and retain good judgment
a. balance between you *must* get vs. what you'd *like* to get
b. balance persistence with perspective, can't win 'em all!
Your style: natural manner, consistent, conveys right message
Compromise: favorable middle ground, solving his problem
a. find the precise formula that works
b. introduce it in a manner that it becomes the solution
c. don't rush to "split the difference"
d. remember, the split does *not* have to be 50:50
e. will you regret sticking to your guns and losing the deal?
Now, negotiate a written contract
a. there is some advantage to your drafting it
b. If marking up the other's draft, avoid initiating new issues
c. don't skip over significant protections in your haste

There are many other books on negotiating, though beware of wussy titles championing nonconfrontational behavior (such as *Getting to Yes*). **Never be nice about a shabby lowball offer.** Freund's book above exhorts "*even to rise up in righteous wrath in response to a real depredation — so as to reduce the other side's expectations and send a strong message of what's going to be needed for a deal . . . .*"

Read as many negotiation books as you can, and then start practicing at flea markets, gun shows, etc. First practice as a buyer, then as a seller. Regardless of the deal size, the tactics remain the same. (The classic rule is that when both parties are vaguely dissatisfied, a balanced deal was struck.) Here are some basic tips.

how to negotiate, from Michael Powell's *Mind Games*

    goal to achieve win / win situation
    know what you want, while knowing what you'll accept
    look to solve the other's needs
    process of give and take; concessions and requests
    begin with a list of concessions
    take your time
    a concession must get something in return
    always get the other person to name their price
    "*Hmmmm*" is a great reply to many offers or demands
    don't bluff unless you can walk away
    don't be afraid to walk away
    stay objective and maintain an emotional distance
    consider the total package
    don't be greedy
    negotiate only with an empowered decision maker
    try to agree on easy things first, to establish a rapport

"My price, your terms. Your price, my terms."

Never give up the opening gambit for both, and feel free to quote the above maxim. If, for example, terms are more important to you than price, you should first ask his price so that you can then announce your terms. If neither is more important to you, then find out what is more important to him.

as a cash buyer

There are more fools among buyers than among sellers.
    — French proverb

Sometimes, only two minutes is all it takes to knock off $20 from the price, and such a "wage" would be $600/hour! Many discounts and bargains are available simply by *asking* for them, especially when it's a demo model or the last item on the shelf. (The trick is to ask *before* the seller believes that you'll pay full price. You must learn to mask your desire. Always make him sell; never become a buyer until you're handing over the money.) Remember, in any purchase negotiation, you are facing an *opponent*.

Don't appear more prosperous than everybody else. Wear older clothing and no jewelry. Learn to haggle. Never pay the first or second, asking price — and often not even the third. Offer two-thirds and pay three-fourths. Remember, unless buyers are standing in line, there are *always* more sellers than buyers. You have the leverage, and never forget that. If his stuff were so choice, then he'd *keep* it. So, the most important question to smoothly ask is:

"Why are you selling it?"

If he hems and haws, or seems evasive, then *beware*. Remember, he knows more about the item than you do.

Inspect the item very carefully. *Caveat emptor!* Once you've decided to bid on it, *put it back on the table*. This is very powerful psychologically — you haven't yet accepted the goods. Find a palpable defect and mention it in disappointed tones. (Don't go overboard as he'll wonder aloud why you're still interested in it at all.)

Act more uninterested than not, and keep looking about as if searching for a friend. No seller can stand such "iffyness" and will work harder to reel you in.

Before you make your first offer, slowly count your money (inside the wallet) with a scowl, pull out the offered amount and put it on the table. He's tempting you with his displayed goods, so you should tempt him with your displayed money. **Always *show* him the money.** That makes it easily *his* money with a simple *"Yeah, O.K."* If he doesn't bite, then walk away. He'll often call you back. Here are some of my best lines as a buyer:

"What repairs does it need now? What will it need later?"
You'll be amazed at what you can learn by asking these two.

"What's your best cash price, right now?"
Very powerful. It often forces the seller to his bottom dollar.

"Can you work with me on price?"
A very low-key line, as nobody wants to appear inflexible.

"It's something I kind of like, but don't really need."
A great way to explain your modest, yet remaining, interest. It encourages him to make up the gap for you.

"Is there anything you'd like on trade?"
Very interesting transactions can thus derive.

"I'm not sure I can swing it . . ."
This forces the seller to help solve your "dilemma."

"Can you sweeten the pot with something?"
A smooth way to get an extra something thrown in.

Times may be tough and you must stretch your funds, but *do* try to create only Win-Win deals. Don't haggle some old guy down to his bones. Once you've reached a fair price you can happily afford, *pay it.* It's cruel to demand everybody's bottom dollar. Let him make a modest profit. Be *fair* to sellers; you never know when you might be one *yourself.*

Final bit of advice: *Never* divulge how much you paid for something, as doing so might kill the chance of a profit later.

ask to part out the item to break up "package" deals
Never forget that the seller's goal is to *sell.* Which will move more quickly: a $700 item with $300 of accessories for $1,000, *or* the items offered separately? Usually, if offered separately.

how J.P. Morgan bought a piece of custom jewelry
Turn-of-the-century financier J.P. Morgan was known for his "sharp" business practices. He once fancied a piece of custom jewelry, which was priced at $5,000. He asked that it be delivered to him for his inspection. For the jeweler he wrote a note, and had a messenger take it (and the box), "*I like the pin, but I don't like the price.*" In the note, Morgan offered a deal: accept my $4,000 check and return the box unopened, or keep the box and return my $4,000 check. The jeweler, not budging on his $5,000 price, kept the box and returned the $4,000 check. The jeweler then opened the box. It did not contain the custom gold and diamond pin! But it *did* contain Morgan's check for the full $5,000. What a clever bluff attempt!

never let a seller treat you as a buyer

If a seller comes to you, make him try to sell — don't let him try to transform you into a buyer (thus giving away your power).

I was visiting a friend at her pawn shop and smiled at how well she understood this rule. Some guy came in with a rifle to sell, and asked what she'd give for it. Meaning, he (as a seller) was trying to get her to act as a buyer. She didn't fall for it, and kept repeating to him, "*What do you want for it?*" He caved after several weak attempts and named his (very low) price. If you want to learn how to deal with sellers, go spend an hour at any pawn shop!

Now, you may wonder why not lowball him an offer that you'd instantly pay if he accepted? Two reasons. First, you risk insulting him and not only losing the deal, but all future deals with him. Second, what you may imagine as a lowball could be more than what he was going to ask for it! So, always let the seller be the first to mention $.

Basically, whoever *first* expresses interest (either as a buyer or seller) is at an automatic disadvantage. Leave it with him always! If he came to you as a buyer, make him remain a buyer. If he came to you as a seller, keep him there as a seller.

SELLING

Everyone sells. Everyone, regardless of occupation or profession, has something to sell. A person's success in life depends on how well he can get their points across. Sell yourself, sell your ideas, services, concepts or products. A person who does a good job of persuading others to his way of thinking always gets to the top.
— Grant G. Gard, *Don't Just Talk About It — Do It!*

If you don't make it yourself, steal it, or get it as a gift, then *trading* for what you want is your only option. It's also the most common (as well as ethical and practical) way of getting what you want. To trade means to exchange your A for somebody's B. Well, why would he want your A? That's up to you to convince *him*. This act of convincing is called *selling*. Even though every transaction has a buyer and a seller, in truth the buyer is also a seller. (The more desirable his trade goods, the less he must "sell". This is an important function of money: to reduce/eliminate effort for the buyers. People readily take cash, so the buyer's task is easy.)

Selling really boils down to just one thing: perceiving the needs of the buyer as *he* perceives them. Whether his perception of his own needs is based in reality is not the question. You must get out of your own head and into his. What does he *really* want, and *why*? Is he motivated by pride, profit, love, fear, or self-preservation? Some say that selling is about persuasion, but I disagree. Once you've discovered the buyer's perceived wants, no persuasion is required of you! In effect, you've found out what the buyer has allowed to persuade *himself,* which is the highest persuasion. (Also read chapter *Power* in Volume 2 for negotiating tips useful to sellers.)

Finally, selling is the art of adding Love to Trade. The more your customers like you (Love/Affection), the more they will trade. Have you ever schmoozed a clerk into giving you a discount? You added Love into Trade.

develop the graces

Appearance, humor, common courtesy, consideration, empathy and sympathy. Note that all of these relate to other people. When you see a person who is sloven, surly, and rude you can almost always bet that he doesn't command much in earnings. Remember, all money comes from other people! Develop the graces.

you don't *get* more until you *become* more

Greed is an attempt to make up for a lack of self-worth. Concentrate on the becoming vs. the acquiring.

We cannot guarantee success. We can only deserve it.
— Winston Churchill

have a good wardrobe and wear it

You've only one chance to make a first impression. Clothes are assets that inform others how to treat you. (Even just an ironed shirt and shined shoes will get you much of the way there.) Superficial, yes, but there's just no getting around it — and I've certainly tried. (Good manners, quality accent, and rich vocabulary are other things which inform others how to treat you, and they're *free!*)

Fortunately, men's fashion is much more stable and classic than women's fashion. Suit lapels vary only between three basic widths, so your wardrobe investment will last for several years. Do not dress with flash (it comes across as trying too hard), but always insist on fine quality. Quality is always stylish. When shopping for new clothes, rely upon the discriminating eye of a mature 40+ year-old woman (other than your mother) to help you pick. Don't take your girlfriend, and refuse the assistance of a male sales clerk (even if he's swish).

don't try to sell to somebody who hasn't the power to buy

Does your client have the money, *and* the authority to spend it? At gun shows there's always some guy whining that his wife would object to his buying another gun. *"Come back when you're an adult,"* I'm usually tempted to retort.

never let a buyer treat you as a seller

If somebody comes to you interested in something you have, you have a certain power over him — his desire. Don't let him invert it into some buying desire of yours. A great example of this was a 1901 incident where J.P. Morgan was interested in purchasing some iron ore mines from the Rockefeller family. After keeping Rockefeller Jr. waiting, Morgan finally admits him into the office, only to gruffly ask what price they were asking. Junior coolly replied:

> *Mr. Morgan, I think there has been some mistake.*
> *I did not come here to sell. I understood that you wished to buy.*
> — The House the Rockefellers Built

In effect, Morgan tried to get Rockefeller Jr. to bid against himself as a buyer. To the delight of his father, son didn't fall for it, and politely reminded Morgan of the actual nature of their meeting: *You . . . buyer. Me . . . only listening.* The result? A $55 million profit. (In 1901! Today, that would equal $1+ billion.)

some selling tips

An old joke (which could be true) comes to mind:

> *A Jewish optometrist was teaching his son how to charge their customers. "When they ask 'How much?' say '$45.' If they don't balk, follow with 'For the frames. The lenses are $30.' If they still don't balk, say 'Each.'"*

Act fairly disinterested, but not overly so (that's rude). If an offer is not even close, don't mull it over or hesitate to reject it (although halfway politely). Only when an offer is "in the ballpark" do you begin to haggle. Never accept a first bid or the buyer will have immediate "cognitive dissonance" by imagining some hidden defect or cursing himself for not offering less. Make him haggle a bit and he'll be much happier with his purchase.

When he asks why you're *selling* such a treasure, reply that you prefer the money (buying a house, taking a vacation, etc.) and you *"can't keep everything."* Say nothing to even indirectly disparage your goods, and don't imply that you desperately need the cash.

If he doesn't bite and walks off, don't follow him with your eyes or he may notice and correctly figure you to be a motivated seller. He's walked off and you've forgotten all about him — that's your attitude. When he returns acting all disinterested, you only vaguely remember him. My best lines for sellers:

"I'd be losing money at $100."
This politely informs the buyer of your (alleged) "bottom dollar".

"Don't you think $125 is fair?"
This politely encourages the buyer not to be such a tightwad.

"Hey, I'm not here just for the fun of it!"
This reminds the buyer that you need to make a profit, too.

"Can you sweeten the deal with something?"
You never know what else he might toss on your table.

"I just got here. I think I'll hear some other offers, thanks."
A very smooth way to decline, yet not slam shut the door.

Finally, if you manage to get another $50 over what you would have taken, put that $50 into savings! (**Any money saved should *go* into savings.** This is how you will quickly amass wealth.)

never leave the buyer with an excuse to say "No"

Remember, he wouldn't be looking at your stuff if he didn't want it. Assuming that he has sufficient money with him, then your task is to remove all his excuses.

The best example I saw of this principle was in India, on the Dal Lake in the Kashmir district. I was a college student in Europe, later traveling with my mother on a four-week trip to India, Sri Lanka, and Nepal. We were in a water taxi going to look at some hand-woven rugs which are so famous of that area. A boy of about 15 puttered up next to us, his little boat filled with fur, leather, wood, and other trickets. After being in country for 10 days, we'd already bought enough of this stuff, but the kid just wouldn't be dissuaded. He wouldn't shove off, but instead kept asking if we liked this over that, what size did we need, etc. I tried on some fur hat, said that it was very nice, but wished it were in another style. Bingo, he had it, and in my size, too. *Sigh.* This went on for several minutes until he'd come up with some things that interested my mom and I.

Then, I thought of our way out from under this vigorous seller. "*Watch this,*" I whispered to mom. I haggled on a total price for everything, and then dropped my atomic bomb. As I reached for my wallet I asked the kid in my most dead-pan way, "*You do, of course, accept American Express?*"

This was back when VISA was hammering AmEx in TV commercials for not being nearly as common, even in fine hotels. My mom, I think, winced at my line because it was really pretty cruel. After all, he was just some kid on a lake trying to make an honest living in a very remote area. I could have more politely and fairly turned him away than to come up with some cheesy excuse for not buying from him. "*You do, of course, accept American Express?*" What gall.

Not that it ended up mattering.

The boy jumped up as if electrocuted, yanked open the hinged seat lid to a storage compartment. "*Yes, Sir!*" Inside were rows of credit card voucher machines and neat stacks of slips. "*I proudly accept American Express, VISA, MasterCard, and Discover!*" Only the greatest of self-control kept my jaw from falling through the bottom of our boat. Though I suspect the boy knew he'd gotten me, he was, even at 15, too much of a professional to let on.

My mom and I gawked at him as he processed my AmEx card more deftly than a Zurich shopkeeper. We motored away without speaking for a while, and then my mom said to me, "*If we could sponsor him over to America, we'd be millionaires!*"

The funniest part, however, was when the bill arrived. The boy's charge got to AmEx *in front of* charges made at luxury hotels days prior! Genius, pure genius. I have no doubt whatsoever that he is now, years later, a very wealthy man. I have his wares to this day, as a reminder of how never to leave a customer with an excuse to say "*No.*"

avoid questions with *No* answers for *Yes* answer questions

When a person says "No" and really means it, he is doing far more than saying a word of two letters. His entire organism — glandular, nervous, muscular — gathers itself together into a condition rejection. . . . The whole neuro-muscular system, in short, set itself on guard against acceptance.

Where, on the contrary, a person says "Yes", none of the withdrawing activities take place.

— Norman Vincent Peale

most of selling is a successful close

Most buyers subconsciously expect the seller to make the close. If you have a customer who seems to want the item and is willing to pay for it, but is hemming and hawing or shuffling around, you must toss out a "trial close." This will either work as the actual close, or at least show you how near or far the buyer is. Smoke out any remaining objections. Some examples:

So, would you like to take it home today?

Shall I wrap it up for you?

some people cannot be sold — you have to let them buy

With practice you'll learn to spot them and just leave them alone to decide. In fact, trying to sell them will run them off. At a gun show I stopped by a custom knifemaker's table. Having worked in a bladesmith's shop off and on over the years, I knew what was good and what I liked. This guy, however, wouldn't stop pestering me with what knives of his sold the best. I finally replied, "*I don't care what other people prefer in their knives, but what I like.*" Amazingly, he didn't take the hint, so I moved on from this unwelcome seller. Nearby was another bladesmith, and he didn't try to sell me. He didn't have to. His knives were superb. I ended up buying one of his excellent Damascus blades with wood grip, and we became friends.

once they are pulling out their wallet, *stop selling!*

Once they are counting out their money, *quit selling!* Don't say anything except for *Would you like a bag for this?* I've undone several sales in my life by mentioning something that caused the buyer to change his mind *after* he was already reaching for his money. You'll never be able to anticipate what this might be, so take no chances in your exuberance. If you mention that blue is the nicest color, he may reply, "*Oh, it comes in other colors? I should see them before I buy.*" Whoops.

develop a reputation for honest dealing

Have a vision for the long run, not merely the short gain. Yes, it's possible to skin people with shrewd dealing, but you will have to continually seek new victims. Instead, cultivate repeat customers with fair and honest dealing. If a buyer returns unhappy with the deal, try to see any part of yours for some misunderstanding. Offer a refund or exchange if there is any doubt to your integrity.

All That is Gold Does Not Glitter
J.R.R. Tolkien

All that is gold does not glitter,
Not all those who wander are lost;
The old that is strong does not wither,
Deep roots are not reached by the frost.

From the ashes a fire shall be woken,
A light from the shadows shall spring;
Renewed shall be blade that was broken,
The crownless again shall be king.

———

The Covenant
Rudyard Kipling

We thought we ranked above the chance of ill.
Others might fall, not we, for we were wise —
Merchants in freedom. So, of our free-will
We let our servants drug our strength with lies.
The pleasure and the poison had its way
On us as on the meanest, till we learned
That he who lies will steal, who steals will slay.
Neither God's judgment nor man's heart was turned.

Yet there remains His mercy — to be sought
Through wrath and peril till we cleanse the wrong
By that last right which our forefathers claimed
When their law failed them and it stewards were bought.
This is our cause. God help us, and make us strong
Our will to meet Him later, unashamed!

LEARNING & TRAINING

Learning is a treasure which will follow its owner everywhere.
— Chinese proverb

Education is about the only thing lying around loose in the world, and it's about the only thing a fellow can have as much of as he's willing to haul away.
— George Horace Lorimer

Men possess thoughts but ideas possess men.
— Max Lerner

The recipe for perpetual ignorance is to be satisfied with your opinion and content with your knowledge.
— Elbert Hubbard

Education is what survives when what has been learned has been forgotten.
— B.F. Skinner

It's what you learn after you know it all that counts.
— John Wooden, Hall of Fame basketball coach

Learning is the acquisition of useful and relevant knowledge. When *very* young, you aren't a good judge of what is worth learning, and so you must trust your parents, relatives, and teachers. The problem with that is *they* often are not the best judge of what is useful and relevant knowledge. (This is not wholly their fault, as they were guided by similar others.)

So, you will have to strike out on your own, supplementing what is likely a very poor intellectual diet masquerading as "education". Otherwise, you will go through Life mentally malnourished. The next quotations sum up what I call education: being able to teach yourself.

Learning is of two kinds: the one kind being the things we learned and knew, and the other being the training that taught us how to find out what we did not know.
— George S. Clason, *The Richest Man in Babylon* (1926), p. 12

He is educated who knows how to find out what he doesn't know.
— George Simmel

To be educated is to be aware of your own ignorance, and then be able to fill in those gaps for yourself. Your attitude should be: "*If I don't know, I will find somebody who does know!*"

NEWS, FACTS, & FACTOIDS

You don't need to read the news. If anything important happens, far too many people are sure to tell you about it.
— C.S. Lewis

Not all news is information. Information is news that is *relevant* to you; news that you can use, ignorance of which is detrimental. Always start your learning with information. There is hardly enough time even for only that, compared to the trivia and factoids masquerading as "news". If you are clueless about the basic fundamentals of Life, then why spend even one second hearing about what some film celebrity or sports figure is doing?

To be caught up in the world of thought — that is being educated.
— Edith Hamilton

THE WILL *NOT* TO BE IGNORANT

It is impossible for a man to learn what he thinks he already knows.
— Epictetus

Complacent Ignorance is the most lethal sickness of the soul.
— Plato

Sixty years ago I knew everything; now I know nothing; education is a progressive discovery of our own ignorance.
— Will Durant

To be proud of learning, is the greatest ignorance.
— Jeremy Taylor

The one real object of education is to have a man in the condition of continually asking questions.
— Bishop Mandell Creighton

If you don't know any better, then you are ignorant.
If you know better and still don't do it, then you are stupid.
— Larry Winget, *Shut Up, Stop Whining, Get A Life!*

Ignorance is the default of the mind, just as laying on the ground is the default of the body. Meaning, without will and effort, your body cannot stand up and move out. Without will and effort, your mind will not grow. Most working class adults are about as ignorant of larger things (history, philosophy, geography, etc.) as they were in school. Their bodies grew up. Their minds did not. These people never had the will to educate themselves. This is why 60 year old men, after working hard over 40 years, did nothing more than stock shelves or wash cars.

There is nothing wrong with stocking shelves or washing cars. Such is necessary and honorable work. But anybody past high-school should be embarrassed if that's all he can offer. When I was 17, one of my summer jobs was to stack bags of grain at a mill. (A good day was when I was allowed to drive the forklift!) I quit that in order to become an assistant-manager trainee at a Gibson's department store. I quickly realized that unless I increased my skillset, a lifetime of dead-end jobs was ahead — including running a Gibson's. I knew that I could do better for myself.

Now, for *some* men, managing the town's department store would just about max out their potential, and that's fine. (Not all of us can be rocket scientists.) I'm no snob. There is nothing wrong with running a large store *if* that is the best you can do. But if you can do more, you should, and to stop on the way up as merely a store manager would be weak of you.

Learning is like rowing upstream: not to advance is to drop back.
— Chinese proverb

The power of instruction is seldom of much efficacy, except in those happy dispositions where it is almost superfluous.
— Gibbon

*This is a uniquely American form of ignorance. With about half of all Americans ranging from minimally literate to functionally illiterate, truth falls before the scythe or rumor and the lust for spectacle. These Americans have eyes, which is to say the camera to shoot what is around them, **but they have no intellectual software to edit and make sense of it all.***

. . . Uneducated and trapped within the hologram, [the working class] will never be capable of participating in a free society, much less making the kinds of choices that preserve and protect one, unless the importance of full literacy can somehow be made clear to them.

. . . Are these successful but unlettered people functioning in society? No. They are functioning in the economy, which to these driven citizens is society. "Own more stuff" and "Gain and hold territory" are their own imperatives.

. . . So long as [the working class] remain incapable of reading or grasping what the greatest minds have learned and written, or can't tell the difference between a patriotic country song and political truth, we aren't likely to make much human progress, no matter how good the economy is how much stuff we own. To do that, we are going to have to switch off the hologram before economic collapse, Peak Oil, or the rest of the world does it for us.

— Joe Bageant, *Deer Hunting with Jesus*

EDUCATION vs. SCHOOLING

Children who know how to think for themselves spoil the harmony of the collective society which is coming where everyone is interdependent.

— master planner of public schooling John Dewey, 1899

Free education for all children in public [government] *schools.*

— Plank #10 of the Communist Manifesto

If you've suspected that there is something basically very, very wrong with public "education" — you're correct. Hear from *the* expert of our time, John Taylor Gatto (New York "Teacher of The Year"):

A century of lending our children to perfect strangers from an early age — to be instructed in what we aren't quite sure — has made an important statement about modern culture which deserves to be mused upon. (p. 100)

From the first month of my teaching career of 30 years, I realized that intellectual power, creative insight, and good character was being diminished in my classroom and that indeed I had been hired for precisely that purpose. (p. 101)

[Government schools] left [children] sitting ducks for another great invention of the modern ear — marketing.

Now, you needn't have studied marketing to know that there are two groups of people who can always be convinced to consume more than they need to: addicts and children. **School has done a pretty good job of turning our children into addicts, but a spectacular job of turning our children into children. Again, this is no accident.** Theorists from Plato to Rousseau . . . knew that if children could be cloistered with other children, stripped of responsibility and independence, encouraged to develop only the trivializing emotions of greed, envy, jealousy, and fear, **they would grow older but never truly grow up.**

Maturity has by now been banished from nearly every aspect of our lives. . . . We have become a nation of children, happy to surrender our judgments and our wills to political exhortations and commercial blandishments that would insult actual adults. (p. xx-xxi)

That's why I call it the German disease — the artificial extension of childhood. Make no mistake, it works. Once sufficiently infected with the virus the disease is progressive. Its victims become inadequate to the challenges of their existence without help, and that relative helplessness makes them manageable. (p. 133)

The genius lies in setting up a perverse hunger which defies eradication later on as the victim struggles to grow up. This implanted need for simplifications in everything makes self-discipline difficult, and for most of us, only indifferently possible. (p. 134)

Think of it this way: lives assigned to routine work are best kept childish. (p. 41)

"A smattering of learning is a very dangerous thing," [William Playfair] said, not because ordinary people are too dumb to learn; just the opposite, they are too smart to be allowed to learn. People become dangerous when too many see through the illusions which hold [a managed] society together. (p. 107)

Educated people, or people with principles, represent rogue elements in a scheme of scientific management; the former suspect because they have been trained to argue effectively and to think for themselves, the latter too inflexible in any area touching their morality to remain reliably independent. At any moment they may announce, "This is wrong. I won't do it." (p. 126)

— www.JohnTaylorGatto.com, *Weapons of Mass Instruction*

It is a miracle that curiosity survives formal education (schooling).
  — Albert Einstein

Our schools are . . . factories in which the raw products [of children] *are to be shaped and fashioned . . .*
    — Ellwood P. Cubberley, *Public School Administration* (1922), chief of elementary school texts for Houghton Mifflin

It ain't what ya don't know that hurts ya. What really puts a hurtin' on ya is what ya knows for sure, that just ain't so.
    — Uncle Remus

Schooling is *not* education. American 15-year-olds do not even rank in the top half of all advanced nations for math or science literacy. (In Detroit, the public schools have tossed aside all pretense by formally gearing their students for a dead-end job at Walmart!)

As John Taylor Gatto explains, education is self-organized from within, provides a set of bountiful connections amongst a surprising blend of random things, and creates customized circuits of self-correction and cross-fertilization of academic disciplines. By being educated, Gatto continues, you will:

❏ always know what to do with spare time
❏ be able to form healthy attachments anywhere
❏ be keen to your own morality
❏ possess a hard-won personal blueprint of value
❏ enjoy power to create new things.
❏ detect other people's needs
❏ actively seek variety
❏ unite with previous generations
❏ thoroughly examine the physical world
❏ encounter and deal with complex possibilities of association
❏ thoughtfully approach your choices of vocation
❏ invest your Life and Death with meaning

As Gatto so sweetly wrote to his granddaughter:

I want you to have a big, bold, free life, one lived with reckless courage, unquenchable compassion, and full reverence for the truth of things.

None of that you can achieve from *government* schools. The *last* thing they want for you is a "*big, bold, free life*"! For over 100 years they have worked to kill off Americans' individuality:

Ninety-nine [people] *out of a hundred are automata, careful to walk in prescribed paths, careful to follow the prescribed custom. This is not an accident but the result of substantial* [government

schooling] *which, scientifically defined, is the subsumption of the individual . . .*
The great purpose of school [self-alienation] *can be realized better in dark, airless, ugly places . . . .*
— William Torrey Harris, U.S. Commissioner of Education from
1889 to 1906, *The Philosophy of Education,* 1906

What [German philosopher] *Hegel taught that intrigued the powerful then and now was that history could be deliberately managed by skillfully provoking crises out of of public view and then demanding national unity to meet those crises — a disciplined unity under cover of which leadership privileges approached the absolute.*
The tool to build such a society was psychological alienation, said Harris. To alienate children from themselves so they could no longer turn inward for strength, to alienate them from families, traditions, religions, cultures — no outside source of advice could contradict the will of the political state. (p. 12-13)
— John Taylor Gatto, *Weapons of Mass Instruction*

If you stay in your mind-numbing public school, you will likely become an example of that very odd and worthless creature: a self-alienated being driven by coarse selfishness. You won't be able to connect with yourself or others. The world will remain a frightening landscape, full of perpetual problems and seemingly random disasters. You will not be able to escape boredom. You will not be able to cope with Life, and will ironically cry out for help to those very corporate and governmental institutions which so hobbled your soul.

Society is composed of persons who cannot design, build, repair, or even operate most of the devices upon which their lives depend . . . people are confronted with extraordinary events and functions that are literally unintelligible to them.
— Langdon Winner, *Autonomous Technology*

You will resent those who *do* cope with Life and actually produce value. You will vote to steal from them. This is happening now, and has been for nearly 100 years.

people are intentionally being "dumbed down"
But whoever causes one of these little ones to stumble, it would be better for him if a millstone were hung around his neck, and he were thrown into the sea.
— Jesus, in Mark 9:42

I'm typing this book out on a common QWERTY keyboard. It was designed a century ago to replace a keyboard that was efficient for the human hand yet too fast for the mechanical typewriters of the day. The QWERTY keyboard purposely slowed down the typing speeds so the keys wouldn't jam. Since the 1970s IBM Selectric typewriter there was no mechanical reason for such a keyboard layout, yet we still use them everywhere. (Look into the efficient Dvorak keyboard.)

Odds are, you went to a "public" school. Let's be accurate: it's a *government* school paid for by the coercive collection of property taxes, staffed by government employees, training children that government has the answers and thus deserves obedience and respect. On purpose, they will not teach you about money, savings, working, or starting your own business. (Nothing about this is new; the ancient Chinese called it "The Policy of Keeping People Dumb". The 19th century Germans devised modern schooling for that same purpose.) Today, in America, *one job in five* is some form of oversight over the behavior of others. The watchers and the watched.

> The dirtiest lie of our age is the euphemism "education," which refers to our concentration camp for the child. We say that we value family, children, and morality; but we sacrifice all these to urges, to pecuniary gain, to momentary thrills. We want everything to be easy. We want to have our cake and eat it. So we allow our children to become brats. For discipline is hard work. In place of hard work we have words, mere words, nice words, as we drown in words — like "education." Let us own up to the fact that we don't want to be bothered with our children.
>
> Think of it this way: The students are locked in with one another, to corrupt and interfere with one another; to stunt one another's growth; to pester and poke one another; but at all costs, to be kept away from the civilizing influence of adult society, until, at long last, adult society becomes yet another question.
>
> Universal free education means that the government determines which individual is to be educated, who is educator, and what is worth learning. This type of arrangement also becomes mixed up in the governmental machinery. The end result is: 1) a society slavishly adhering to government seals of approval; 2) a society with bureaucratic instincts inculcated from the age of five or younger; 3) a society hardened against culture and riddled with bogus career "goals."
>
> Our solution? — Take away all crutches for the parent. Liquidate the public schools and pull the plug on television. Make the family necessary again. (pp. 114, 116, 117, 118)
> — J.R. Nyquist, *Origins of the Fourth World War*

The government schools were originally designed and are constantly refined to stunt the mind's growth.

In our dreams . . . people yield themselves with perfect docility to our molding hands. The present educational conventions [of intellectual and character foundation] *fade from our minds, and unhampered by tradition we work our own good will upon a grateful and responsive folk. We shall not try to make these people or any of their children into philosophers or men of learning or men of science. We have not to raise up from among them authors, educators, poets or men of letters. We shall not search for embryo great artists, painters, musicians, nor lawyers, doctors, preachers, politicians, statesmen, of whom we have ample supply. The task we set before ourselves is very simple . . . we will organize children . . . and teach them to do in a perfect way the things their fathers and mothers are doing in an imperfect way.*
— 1906, Rockefeller Education Board newsletter

Some who favor the public schools assert that an informed public is necessary to a functioning democracy. True, and beyond doubt. But we do not have an informed public, never have had one, and never will. Nor, really, do we have a functioning democracy.

Any survey will reveal that most people have no grasp of geography, history, law, government, finance, international relations, or politics. And most people have neither the intelligence nor the interest to learn these things. If schools were not the disasters they are, they still couldn't produce a public able to govern a nation.

But it is for the intelligent that the public schools - "schools" - are most baneful. It is hideous for the bright, especially bright boys, to sit year after year in an inescapable miasma of appalling dronedom while some low-voltage mental drab wanders on about banalities that would depress a garden slug. The public schools are worse than no schools for the quick. A sharp kid often arrives at school already reading. Very quickly he (or, most assuredly, she) reads four years ahead of grade. <u>These children teach themselves.</u> They read indiscriminately, without judgment — at first anyway — and pick up ideas, facts, and vocabulary. They also begin to think. . . . These young, out of human decency, for the benefit of the country, should not be subjected to public education — "education." Where do we think high-bypass turbofans come from? Are they invented by heartwarming morons?

The absorptive capacity of smart kids is large if you just stay out of their way. A bright boy of eleven can quickly master a collegiate text of physiology, for example. This is less astonishing than perhaps it sounds. The human body consists of comprehensible parts that do comprehensible things. If he is

interested, which is the key, he will learn them, while apparently being unable to learn state capitals, which don't interest him.
What is the point of pretending to teach the unteachable while, to all appearances, trying not to teach the easily teachable? The answer of course is that we have achieved communism, the rule of the proletariat, and the proletariat doesn't want to strain itself, or to admit that there are things it can't do. . . . If a child has a substantial IQ, expect him to use it for the good of society, and give him schools to let him do it. If a child needs a vocation so as to live, give him the training he needs. But don't subject either to enstupidated, unbearably tedious, pointless, one-size-fits-nobody pseudo-schools to hide the inescapable fact that we are not all equal.
— Fred Reed, A Taste of Realism,
http://archive.lewrockwell.com/reed/reed234.html

Government schools are exactly like QWERTY keyboards. However, if you received your education on the open market (which must produce good results or go out of business), you would be "too fast" for government and similar institutions. Too many free-thinking and independent people would "jam up the keys".

After a long life, and thirty years in the public school trenches, I've concluded that genius is a common as dirt. We suppress genius because we haven't yet figured out how to manage a population of educated men and women. The solution, I think, is simple and glorious. Let them manage themselves.
We need to abandon the notion — and punish those who retain it — that ordinary people are too stupid, irresponsible, and childish to look out for themselves. (p. 69)
— John Taylor Gatto, *Weapons of Mass Instruction*

Such a people would quit using the obsolete QWERTY "typewriter" of government, and fulfill their own needs of education, health care, transportation, self-defense, etc. **The biggest fear of large parasitical institutions is *not to be needed*.** You don't need them! You can Do It Yourself. And you should.

what about "school reforms"?

I urge you to examine in your own mind the assumptions which must lay behind using the police power to insist that once-sovereign spirits have no choice but to submit to being schooled by strangers. Surely this is one of the most radical acts in human history, . . . (p. 46)
I can't escape the conclusion that [teachers] are involved in a social engineering project whose mission is to weaken children's

minds and give them bad characters — all concealed in the sanctimony we exude on parents' night. I heard one principal (a decent man in his own estimation, I'm sure), tell a large audience that the damage to these children had already been done before they came to him in seventh grade, and that his job was to relieve their pain and make them feel good in the here and now because their limited futures were already predetermined.

Can you believe it?! The shameless brass! I couldn't make that up.

The degree of disrespect our nation has assigned its ordinary population wouldn't be possible unless somewhere in the command centers it hadn't been decided that common men and women should be stripped of any power to rebel. And that they could be lied to without compunction, because their dignity didn't count. Or their lives. (pp. 78-79)

. . . as for me, I concluded long ago that some deliberate intent was (and is) at work on the school institution, that it operates far from public access, and until it is confronted the term "school reform" is meaningless. Unless the ends of the operation are put on public trial, and its sexual relationship with economics and social management exposed to the light and ended, each reform effort will only be another illusion, another room added to the national house of mirrors. (p. 179)

— John Taylor Gatto, *Weapons of Mass Instruction*

school as jail — jail as school

The United States [with just 5% of the global population], traditional land of the free, now jails 25% of all prisoners on earth, 90% for non-violent crimes.

Horace Mann himself called school "the best jail" to his financial backers, by which he meant that the jail you sentence your mind to when you go to school is harder to escape than any iron bars.

— John Taylor Gatto, *Weapons of Mass Instruction*, p. 165-166

We can recover from the destruction that may be visited on us by these Islamic radicals. But can we recover from the damage being done by our hideous government schools?

A massive terrorist weapon might destroy a city. Our government schools will destroy a generation.

Our wonderful government educational system produces graduating classes of young Neanderthals with no sense of individuality, no sense of self-worth, and no understanding of what it means to live in a truly free society.

— Neal Boortz, *Somebody's Gotta Say It*

attend a quality private school, if possible!

Two little boys I knew went to a lovely little private school. Their mother considered the $300/month/child a bargain. For just $10/day, those precious ones were kept from the jaws of those concentration camps of government schools.

> *You need finely tuned critical judgement to defend yourself in the dangerous house of mirrors America has become.*
> — John Taylor Gatto, *Weapons of Mass Instruction*, p. 161

have your parents look into homeschooling

> *The art of teaching is not imparting truth but imparting a thirst for truth.*
> — Perry Tanksley

> *The object of teaching a child is to enable him to get along without a teacher.*
> — Elbert Hubbard

> *Good teachers cost much but poor teachers cost more.*
> — Perry Tanksley

A mother dedicated to good and rigorous homeschooling can do a better job until the 5th grade of educating her children than the government schools.

> *Aristotle says that the aim of education is to make the pupil like and dislike what he ought. . . . The little human animal will not at first have the right responses. It must be trained to feel pleasure, liking, disgust, and hatred at those things which really are pleasant, likeable, disgusting and hateful.*
> — C.S. Lewis, *The Abolition of Man*

This initial training is too important to be left in the hands of government employees. It is up to the mother to inculcate "*the right responses*" in her children. If she does not, the government will program the wrong responses:

> *Once you understand the logic behind modern schooling, its tricks and traps are fairly easy to avoid. School trains children to be employees and consumers; teach yours to be leaders and adventurers. School trains children to obey reflexively; teach yours to think critically and independently. Well-schooled kids have a low threshold for boredom; help your own to develop an inner life so that they'll never be bored. Urge them to take on the*

serious material, the grown-up material, in history, literature, philosophy, music, art, economics, theology — all the stuff schoolteachers know well enough to avoid. Challenge your kids with plenty of solitude so that they can learn to enjoy their own company, to conduct inner dialogues. Well-schooled people are conditioned to dread being alone; they seek constant companionship through the TV, the computer, the cell phone, and through shallow friendships quickly acquired, quickly abandoned. Your children should have a more important life, and they can.

Don't let your own children have their childhoods extended, not even for a day. If David Farragut could take command of a captured British warship as a preteen, if Ben Franklin could apprentice himself to a printer at the same age, . . . there's no telling what your own kids could do. (p. xxii)
— John Taylor Gatto, *Weapons of Mass Instruction*

Home-schooling, it seems to me, becomes a towering social responsibility. I have actually seen a teacher saying that parents should not let children learn to read before they reach school. You see, it would put them out of synch with the mammalian larvae that children are now made to be. Bright children not only face enstupiation and hideous boredom in schools taught by complacent imbeciles. No. They are also encouraged to believe that stupidity is a moral imperative.

Once they begin reading a few years ahead of their grade, which commonly is at once, school becomes an obstacle to advancement. This is especially true for the very bright. To put a kid with an IQ of 150 in the same room with a barely literate affirmative-action hire clocking 85 is child abuse.
— Fred Reed, "A Culture in Regression",
http://archive.lewrockwell.com/reed/reed216.html

a family business is the best homeschooling

I personally know this to be true. My step-father bought silver and turquoise jewelry wholesale, and my step-brothers and I would set up a card table selling it at the local mall. Learning how to sell is a vital component to Life, best learned in childhood.

After graduating from high-school, my parents were wise and kind enough to let me live at home while I started, ran, and later sold a successful small business of my own.

if you can't escape government schools

. . . you must cold-bloodedly plan to subvert and sabotage it — all the while pretending with a smile on your face to cooperate. In that way you can inflict substantial damage on the institution

> *which seeks to render you incomplete, without opening yourself to*
> *punishments.* (p. 176)
>   — John Taylor Gatto, *Weapons of Mass Instruction*

"mandatory" school vaccinations

There is solid evidence that not all vaccines are necessary, effective, or safe. The primary example of this is the clear link between thimerosal (a mercury-based preservative in some vaccines) and autism. Robert F. Kennedy Jr. wrote a shattering investigative piece about the long cover-up by the CDC, WHO, and big pharma:

> *In June 2000, a group of top government scientists and health officials gathered for a meeting at the isolated Simpsonwood conference center in Norcross, Georgia . . . [c]onvened by the Centers for Disease Control and Prevention . . .*
>
> *The federal officials and industry representatives had assembled to discuss a disturbing new study that raised alarming questions about the safety of a host of common childhood vaccines administered to infants and young children. According to a CDC epidemiologist named Tom Verstraeten, who had analyzed the agency's massive database containing the medical records of 100,000 children, a mercury-based preservative in the vaccines — thimerosal — appeared to be responsible for a dramatic increase in autism and a host of other neurological disorders among children.*
>
> *But instead of taking immediate steps to alert the public and rid the vaccine supply of thimerosal, the officials and executives at Simpsonwood spent most of the next two days discussing how to cover up the damaging data. According to transcripts obtained under the Freedom of Information Act, many at the meeting were concerned about how the damaging revelations about thimerosal would affect the vaccine industry's bottom line.*
>
> *In fact, the government has proved to be far more adept at handling the damage than at protecting children's health. The CDC paid the Institute of Medicine to conduct a new study to whitewash the risks of thimerosal, ordering researchers to "rule out" the chemical's link to autism. It withheld Verstraeten's findings, even though they had been slated for immediate publication, and told other scientists that his original data had been "lost" and could not be replicated. And to thwart the Freedom of Information Act, it handed its giant database of vaccine records over to a private company, declaring it off-limits to researchers.*
>
> *CDC officials are not interested in an honest search for the truth, [Florida Congressman Dr. David] Weldon told me, because "an association between vaccines and autism would force them to admit that their policies irreparably damaged thousands of*

children. *Who would want to make that conclusion about themselves?"*

As the federal government worked to prevent scientists from studying vaccines, others have stepped in to study the link to autism. In April, reporter Dan Olmsted of UPI undertook one of the more interesting studies himself. Searching for children who had not been exposed to mercury in vaccines – the kind of population that scientists typically use as a "control" in experiments – Olmsted scoured the Amish of Lancaster County, Pennsylvania, who refuse to immunize their infants. Given the national rate of autism, Olmsted calculated that there should be 130 autistics among the Amish. He found only four. One had been exposed to high levels of mercury from a power plant. The other three – including one child adopted from outside the Amish community – had received their vaccines.

The story of how government health agencies colluded with Big Pharma to hide the risks of thimerosal from the public is a chilling case study of institutional arrogance, power and greed. I was drawn into the controversy only reluctantly. . . . It was only after reading the Simpsonwood transcripts, studying the leading scientific research and talking with many of the nation's pre-eminent authorities on mercury that I became convinced that the link between thimerosal and the epidemic of childhood neurological disorders is real.

I devoted time to study this issue because I believe that this is a moral crisis that must be addressed. If, as the evidence suggests, our public-health authorities knowingly allowed the pharmaceutical industry to poison an entire generation of American children, their actions arguably constitute one of the biggest scandals in the annals of American medicine. "The CDC is guilty of incompetence and gross negligence," says Mark Blaxill, vice president of Safe Minds, a nonprofit organization concerned about the role of mercury in medicines. "The damage caused by vaccine exposure is massive. It's bigger than asbestos, bigger than tobacco, bigger than anything you've ever seen."

— www.rollingstone.com/politics/story/7395411/deadly_immunity

Children of the current generation receive 24 mandatory vaccinations. A generation ago, only 10 or less were called for.

Through vaccinations, children receive 400x the amount of mercury deemed safe by the FDA.

The Hep B routinely given to newborns contains so much mercury preservative that it would normally only be considered safe under standard medical guidelines to give to a 275 pound adult.

Why is this going on?
Politics and corruption.

> In the White House, in Congress, in the FDA, in the medical establishment and in the pharmaceutical industry.
> — Mercury in vaccines causes autism
> www.brasschecktv.com/Vaccines_and_Autism.htm

Another harmful component of some vaccines is an adjuvant (a sort of booster to kick off the body's response) is squalene (a form of cholesterol). www.Vaccine-A.com links it to Gulf War Syndrome:

> Both GlaxoSmithKline and Novartis are using the substance squalene in their H1N1 vaccines. According to The American Journal of Pathology, squalene is a cholesterol precursor which stimulates the immune system nonspecifically. One intradermal injection—or shot—of this adjuvant lipid can induce joint-specific inflammation in arthritis-prone rats.
> Novartis' squalene adjuvant was used in the experimental anthrax vaccines for soldiers serving in the Gulf War and has been linked to Gulf War Syndrome, the devastating auto-immune disease suffered by Gulf War veterans who took the anthrax shots.
> Symptoms of Gulf War Syndrome include ulcers, arthritis, chronic diarrhea, fatigue and headaches, dizziness, fibromyalgia, memory loss, mood changes, multiple sclerosis, neuropsychiatric problems, rashes, skin lesions, photosensitive rashes and systemic lupus, according to osteopathic physician Joseph Mercola, M.D.
> — The Great Swine Flu Boondoggle
> www.personalliberty.com/conservative-politics/the-great-swine-flu-boondoggle

Before you allow somebody to inject you with chemicals, why not do your own research into what they are and if they can cause harm? You have the right to refuse objectionable vaccinations:

> Simple guidelines:
> It is NOT the law that you must vaccinate your children (no matter what the doctor or schools tell you), and you can sign a form to make your child exempt.
> The law states that schools must accept your children under 1 of 3 possible exemptions, depending on your state:
>
> 1. Religious - Vaccines are against your religion, no matter what religion your practice. You do not need to list a religion.
>
> 2. Philosophical - You don't believe in vaccines, you don't think they're safe, you don't think they've been tested enough, etc.
>
> 3. Medical - Your child has an autoimmune disease or had a negative reaction to a vaccine in the past.

Under such conditions it is dangerous to vaccinate a child and it states in the vaccine insert not to vaccinate under these circumstances, but doctors and nurses are NOT taught this so you must be firm!
Vaccinations are a school policy, NOT the LAW. If you choose not to vaccinate, the law is on your side.
— Mercury in vaccines causes autism
www.brasschecktv.com/Vaccines_and_Autism.htm

I know several families who did not vaccinate their babies, and every single one of their children are *much* more healthy than the common herd of (over)vaccinated kids. The parents are often asked if their children's "*asthma has come in yet*" — because such has become normal for the vaccinated crowd! (Give them a few more years, and they'll be wondering why families eating organic food don't seem to "come down" with obesity and diabetes.)

My wife now finds it hard to relate to the other young mothers at her workplace because they are in and out of the emergency room and doctors office all the time with ear aches, skin problems, runny noses that never stop, diarrhea, etc. I believe the reason these things don't occur with our son is precisely due to the fact that his immune system was not impaired by vaccines as a newborn.
—www.youroptimal.com/blog/2008/11/16/vaccines-for-my-baby/

Here are a couple of other links about vaccines:
www.naturalnews.com/035163_public_health_unvaccinated_antibiotics.html
www.naturalnews.com/Vaccines_Get_the_Full_Story.html

never take government school drugs, such as Ritalin
If seven-year-old Mozart tried composing his concertos today, he might be diagnosed with attention-deficit hyperactivity disorder and medicated into barren normality.
— The *Washington Post*, quoted by
www.naturalnews.com/028803_psychiatry_disease.html

Paxil, Prozac, Celexa, Zoloft, Luvox, and Effexor are brain-altering SSRIs (selective serotonin reuptake inhibitors) with provable links to violent ideation, murder, and suicide.   www.thesaveproject.com
Their correlation to mass shootings is extremely high (about 9 in 10):

When roughly nine out of every 10 cases in these school shootings and mass shootings involve these drugs being prescribed, then at least a significant proportion of these cases were either caused by

the drugs or the drugs made a significant contribution to the problem.
— psychiatrist Dr. David Healy
www.rxisk.org, www.ssristories.com
www.wnd.com/2013/01/top-psychiatrist-meds-behind-school-massacres/

INCIDENT	MURDERER	KIA / WIA	SSRI
Standard Gravure	Joseph Wesbecker	8K/12W+1	Prozac
Columbine	Eric Harris	13K/25W	Zoloft, then Luvox
Red Lake,MN	Jeffrey Wise	7K/5W+1	Prozac (60 mg/day)
Virginia Tech	Cho Seung Hui	32K/17W+1	prescribed Prozac
	Kip Kinkel	4K/25W	Prozac and Ritalin
Pearl H.S	Luke Woodham	3K/7W	Prozac
Heath H.S.	Michael Carneal	3K/5W	Ritalin
Westside School	Andrew Golden	5K/10W	Ritalin
	Mitchell Johnson	5K/10W	Ritalin

These dangerous drugs were envisioned over 40 years ago:

... the Behavioral Science Teacher Education Project, *BSTEP for short, which clearly sets down government policy intentions for compulsory schooling, outlining reforms to be forced on the US after 1967. Institutional schooling, we learn, will be required to "impersonally manipulate" the future of an America in which "each individual will receive at birth a multi-purpose identification number". This will enable employers "and other controllers" to keep track of the common mass and to expose it to "direct or subliminal influence when necessary"* . . . [*so that*] *"few will be able to maintain control over their own opinions".*

BSTEP tells us that "chemical experimentation" on minors will become normal procedure after 1967, a pointed foreshadowing of Ritalin, Adderol, and other chemical "interventions" which accompany little Johnny to grade school these days.

The document identifies the future as one in which a small elite will control all important matters, a world in which participatory democracy will disappear, reduced to a meaningless voting prerogative in electoral campaigns, campaings in which all serious candidates have been pre-selected to exclude troublemakers. Politicians will still be able to threaten substantial change, but to deliver only token efforts to that end after election. (pp. 5-6)
— John Taylor Gatto, *Weapons of Mass Instruction*

do you *really* need college?

*I thoroughly enjoyed Harvard, and I am sure it did me good, but
only in the general effect, for there was little in my actual studies
which helped me in afterlife.*
— Theodore Roosevelt

*35 percent of the young regret their university experience and
don't consider the time and money invested worth it; more than
half said they learned nothing of use.*
— *Wilson Quarterly*, Autumn 2006

In one study using 14,000 students, at 16 of the 50 American colleges
graduating seniors knew *less* than incoming freshmen! Today,
colleges are just high-schools with ashtrays.

Education can train, but not create, intelligence.
— Edward McChesny Sait

*I call a complete and generous education that which fits a man to
perform justly, skillfully, and magnanimously all the offices, both
private and public, or peace and war.*
— John Milton

*I prefer the company of peasants because they have not been
educated sufficiently to reason incorrectly.*
— Michel de Montaigne

Unless you've dreamed of being a doctor, lawyer, or engineer, you
likely can get by just fine without college. Going into business? Then
go into business, as a bachelor's business degree is generally a waste of
time and money. (I know this personally, as I first had the business
and *then* got the degree! What I learned of any use from college could
have been acquired in 6 months of self-study.)

*A recent graduate handed his diploma to his father and said, "I
finished law school to please you and Mom. Now I'm going to be a
fireman like I've been saying to you since I was six."*
— Gene Brown

If you knew that the path ahead of you was a very steep and tall hill to
climb, it would make sense to start working out your legs and stamina,
now. You'd want to be ready when you finally arrived at the base of the
hill. Next, after strengthening your legs, you'd prefer to get a running
start before the slope. Momentum will help you ascend. You'd also
buy and train in the appropriate shoes for the climb.

Adult life (meaning, after high-school) is that "hill". Your "legs" are your skills and your "stamina" is your determined mindset. Your "running start" could be many things: a college scholarship you've worked for, your savings from all those summer jobs, the right introduction from an adult who believes in you, etc. Appropriate "shoes" would be a conducive lifestyle to succeed in college (*e.g.*, good study habits, like-minded friends, no repetitive partying, etc.).

But look at most young males about to tackle that hill: they have been lazy, so their legs are like twigs. They don't even bother to get a running start. They wear beach party flip-flops and can't get any traction. They ooze out of high-school into college, and then ooze into adult life assuming that their college degree will give them some right to earn a decent living. They didn't appreciate how steep and tall the hill was, and they didn't read the rules of hill climbing.

two author views on going to college

Q: Ann, Where should I go to college?

A:You probably shouldn't. The people who are going to be in the best shape after this collapse are people who know an honest-to-goodness TRADE. 95% of college degrees are utterly useless. Further, the Marxists are trying to gin up a sense of entitlement amongst the young by stating that a college education is a "human right" and that everyone should have a college degree. What they are really trying to do is enslave everyone with student loan debt. If everyone has a college degree, then a college degree will be, by definition, utterly meaningless. If the guy who scrubs the toilets at Burger King has a bachelor's, then what meaning does a bachelor's have? None. I would recommend learning by apprenticeship something like plumbing, welding, engine repair, carpentry, masonry, animal husbandry, petroleum extraction, machining, fishery, etc. College is over. Most degrees are intrinsically useless. Skip it.

— www.Barnhardt.biz, January 16, AD 2012

Another authoress put the matter even more bluntly:

At college, boys are taught to be passive and obedient, and memorize the status quo. Many of them go in clean and come out alcoholics, or positive for herpes. Instead of following the human heard into college, take a few targeted technology classes from a community college—work with your dad on the farm or family business—or go to work for a small or midsize company. The main thing robbing young white men of self-esteem and positive motivation today is stifling corporate drone jobs, where they take orders from their inferiors, with their right hands tied behind their backs, undergoing daily psychological abuse like "sensitivity training," which is aimed at undermining their selfworth, and substituting neurotic "feelings" for rational facts.

In most engineering and science programs, there are only 2-5 classes worth taking. In humanities programs, there are 0-1. Does that sound like a good investment of five years of your life? Forget the degree: take the interesting classes, and get the hell out into the workforce. Bill Gates dropped out and became a billionaire. You can drop out and do at least better than the average college grad.

This young "man" at age 23 enters the world of W-2s and lock-step corporate drones with a nice comfy $40,000 in college debt (the only kind of debt that the Insiders don't let you get rid of by declaring bankruptcy.) He spends his time makin' copies, attending meetings, kissing up to the women and affirmative action hires, and looking for designs to copy — since he's only learned how to memorize formulas — not how to build things.

There is no financial justification in going to college. Statistically, the average college graduate earns over a lifetime after taxes, only about $200,000 more than the average high school graduate. If parents and intelligent young men would only skip the college tuition and invest the money instead, any vigorous, alert guy could own a home and his own business by age 28, and get married. Plus, instead of wasting the best years of his life reading 9th-rate literature and "textbooks," he'd be self-educated in the real modern (and ancient) classics. College is a horrifically poor use of time and money for any future head-of-household.

All I need now to make money is the courage to face rejection over and over again — and social skill. For every 20 doors I knock on, one gives me a $20,000 check. The average dolt needs a college degree to rise above mechanic. The top 5% don't — they're only hampered by college. My boss almost dropped out of the college he hated with his whole heart, when Intel offered him $100,000 a year to work fulltime (he'd done a summer internship), the beginning of his Junior year. Get real. What's stopping you from making a fortune is lack of social skills, positive motivation, and basic commonsense business experience. College hurts, instead of helps, the development of all these things.

Education must be highly targeted to be useful. Good education? DeVry. A good, four-year liberal arts education? Great idea. Not the slightest idea where you find it. . . . Yes, college is essentially a scam these days. But middle-class mom and pop ain't going to pick up on it. "Education" means a piece of paper from a label, and they can't separate the outward form from the content. If you know what you're doing — do it. You have to make yourself, no one can do that for you.

You may have to be your own leader. You can do it. The world

is geared so that when you make the initial surge, things kick in to help you. I don't understand why that is, but it's true."
— Elizabeth Bennett, "How To Marry a High-Quality Woman"

Educate yourself for the Life you truly want to live, and stay away from those boneyards.

a real-world experiment

Alone on a dark gritty street, Adam Shepard searched for a homeless shelter. He had a gym bag, $25, and little else. A former college athlete with a bachelor's degree, Mr. Shepard had left a comfortable life with supportive parents in Raleigh, N.C. Now he was an outsider on the wrong side of the tracks in Charleston, S.C.

But Shepard's descent into poverty in the summer of 2006 was no accident. Shortly after graduating from Merrimack College in North Andover, Mass., he intentionally left his parents' home to test the vivacity of the American Dream. His goal: to have a furnished apartment, a car, and $2,500 in savings within a year.

To make his quest even more challenging, he decided not to use any of his previous contacts or mention his education.

During his first 70 days in Charleston, Shepard lived in a shelter and received food stamps. He also made new friends, finding work as a day laborer, which led to a steady job with a moving company.

Ten months into the experiment, he decided to quit after learning of an illness in his family. But by then he had moved into an apartment, bought a pickup truck, and had saved close to $5,000.

The effort, he says, was inspired after reading "Nickel and Dimed," in which author Barbara Ehrenreich takes on a series of low-paying jobs. Unlike Ms. Ehrenreich, who chronicled the difficulty of advancing beyond the ranks of the working poor, Shepard found he was able to successfully climb out of his self-imposed poverty. (KWR Note: Why did he succeed? Because of attitude and commitment. It's the only "secret" to success.)

He tells his story in "Scratch Beginnings: Me, $25, and the Search for the American Dream." The book, he says, is a testament to what ordinary Americans can achieve.
— "Building a Life on $25 and a Gym Bag; College Graduate
Leaves Comfortable Life for Poverty Experiment"— Peter Smith

After his 10 month experiment, Adam Shepard doesn't believe that a college degree is generally necessary: "*To be honest with you, I think I was disadvantaged, because my thinking was inside of a box. ... You can use your talents. That's why, from the beginning, I set very realistic goals: $2,500, a job, and a car. This isn't a "rags-to-riches million-dollar" story. This is very realistic. I truly believe, based on* *what I saw at the shelter . . . that anyone can do that."* Certainly, such a bare-bones existence would not be sufficient to enjoy many luxuries, or raise a family, but Shepard's point was that one can still climb out of the muck with hard work and solid choices. Think about it: if you have a job, car, apartment, and $2,500 in savings — you are out of the pit. You are on your way! You are poised to keep climbing, as high as you wish. You can get a better job, a nicer apartment, a classier car. You can then begin to mix with more successful people, and get noticed for your talents, integrity, and hard work. You're on your way!

You have but two choices:

write your *own* script
become an actor in somebody *else*'s script.

Don't yet know what you want to do? Then why not hit the road and try a new type of job every month for a year? (One young man did just that, and wrote a book about it.) You'd have great travel and work experience, and no year in college could compare with that!

If you do choose to go to college, don't have unrealistic expectations about your increased earning potential. If you waltz out in the job market bragging about your new BBA or MBA, the world will soon enough teach you the *rest* of Life's alphabet.

There are three keys to avoiding poverty: Stay in school, don't get pregnant, and take any job you can get and work hard at it until you can move to a better one. It's just that simple.
— Neal Boortz, Somebody's Gotta Say It

Just because somebody lives in a home and drives a car does not mean that they are middle class. The actual middle class is only 20-30% of Americans. The working class has been trained to believe that they are middle class, when they are not. While not *"genuine rope-belted mouth breathers*," the laboring *Lumpenproletariat* never has been middle class. They are the Proles in George Orwell's *1984*.

your most valuable attribute: *adaptability*

The top-10 jobs in 2010 did not even exist in 2004. Antiquated college curriculums don't keep up with this speed of change; debt slavery just makes it worse. You must quickly and firmly grasp How Life Works, and use these fundamentals to adapt for opportunities using undiscovered technologies we don't even have yet. To get an idea of what I mean, watch the amazing short video "Speed of Change".

The real secret was the self-study in advance. The strategy paid dividends as soon as I walked into the second session of each course in each semester. Having read ahead, I knew not only what the subject was, but where my misunderstandings lay, and how the material of the today tied into the material of tomorrow. And so, while some of my peers were struggling to stay awake and keep up with he newness, I was listening intently to fill the gaps in what I already knew. (p. 5)
— Tom Baugh, *Starving the Monkeys — Fighting Back Smarter*

GOOD STUDY SKILLS

designate a study-only area, and use only that for study

before a study session, spend 5 minutes clearing your head

establish your optimum concentration plan, and use multiples of this unit with 10 minute breaks; study in short, intensive bursts

BEGIN. It's the best way to finish!

don't over-commit yourself

break your workload into small tasks

set goals by understanding the overall goal of your study

do important, difficult, unpleasant stuff first, while fresh

test yourself

something half-learned isn't learned at all

if you are bored, switch tasks

do rote memory learning before you fall asleep for the night

little but frequent studying gives best recall (vs. an all-nighter)

distinguish what must be learned verbatim vs. conceptual

if your mind wanders, take a 5 minute break (stand up, stretch, leave the room, rebound exercise) to avoid associating the study area with poor concentration

make completion of individual tasks your biggest reward while studying, and only physically reward yourself at end of study session

make a clear distinction between study and relaxation, else they will merge

schedule 7-8 hours sleep into study timetable — write it down

AVOID TV & VIDEO GAMES!

I find television very educational. Every time someone switches it on I go into another room and read a good book.
— Groucho Marx

American males ages 18–34 are now the biggest users of video games, with 48.2% owning a console and playing an average of 2 hours and 43 minutes per day. That doesn't include online games like *World of Warcraft*. TV and video games are for children. Children who insist on *remaining* children. You can not become a self-governing adult if a video entertainment is a significant part of your Life.

In truth, television drives the hologram, creates Americans' reality, regulates our national perceptions and interior hallucinations of who we Americans are — the best and the bravest, the richest and the most powerful, the freest country on the planet. Television promotes the illusion du jour, . . .

. . . Because our consciousness is entirely based in our brain neurology and neurochemistry, and because television is the one voice and one image projected to the many, it regulates the seasons of our national consciousness [such as football, election, Christmas shopping, clothing, etc.]. Television regulates the national mood, stirring patriotic passion during wars and anxious vigilance against the threat of unseen terrorists, . . .

. . . Americans, rich or poor, now live in a culture woven entirely of illusions, and all of us are rendered actors. Television actors portray nonactors in "reality show," and nonactors in Congress perform in front of the cameras, grappling over the feeding tube in Terri Schiavo.

. . . The corporate simulacrum of life has penetrated us so deeply it has become internalized and now dominates our interior landscape. Just as light pollution washes out the nighttime sky, so much of our day-to-day existence has lost its depth and majesty, having been replaced by constellations of commercial images. So marvelous is their glow is that ordinary people will do the most extraordinary to be represented in the constellation for a few brief moments — grovel at the zipper of Donald Trump's trousers, confess to marital infidelities before millions, and do other completely degrading and unimaginable things. We are all watching the hologram and cannot see one another in the breathing flesh. Within the hologram sparkles the culture-generating industry, spinning out mythology like cotton candy. We all need it to survive. Hollywood myths, imperial myths, melting-pot myths . . .

The difficulties of self-expression having been neatly eliminated through standardization, adult yokels and urban

> *sophisticates can choose from a preselected array of possible selves based solely on what they like to eat, see, wear, hear, and drive. . . . When enough of your kind coagulate around anything, you have a "lifestyle" on your hands. . . . **Not one of them made up his or her identity from scratch.***
>
> *We have come a long way since the days when millions of Americans were concerned with actualizing individual potential, looking inward and asking themselves, "What do I have to offer the world, and how do I become that person?"*
> — Joe Bageant, *Deer Hunting with Jesus*

The average American spends about a *third* of their waking life (1,600 hours/year) watching some sort of video screen, releasing brain endorphins which act as opiates. Any how many hours a year does the average American spend reading? Just 323. They watch TV *five* times more than they read *anything* (including all the trash magazines). If that does not explain their intellectually squalid nature, nothing will.

> *Nightmare children are all about us; . . . no vital interests, creatures trained to organize their time around spasm of excitement and amusement, or escape from punishment. The maps of the road they carry are false. The most curious commentary of these kids is the thousands of hours they spend in not exploring, not playing, not seeking opportunities for personal gain — but in watching other people on television, in music videos and computer games. Sane children would never do this — **the arc of anyone's life is too short to accept passivity and fantasy to this degree.** (p. 82)*
>
> *Since the advent of schoolrooms and electronic screens, many of us never grow up. Too much of our precious trial and error period is wasted sitting in the dark. Being a mature being means living with a purpose, your own purpose: it's about welcoming responsibility as the nourishment a big life needs; it's about behaving as a good citizen — finding ways to add value to the community in which you live; it's about wrestling with your weaknesses and developing heart, mind, and spirit — **none of them properties of the spectator crowd.***
>
> *Hitching the body and mind to screens reduces the attention span to quick takes arranged by strangers; **it creates a craving for constant stimulation which reality can't satisfy.** (p. 97)*
> — John Taylor Gatto, *Weapons of Mass Instruction*

> *The genius of television is that, to shape a people as you want, you don't need unrestrained governmental authority, nor do you need to tell people what you want of them. Indeed, if you told them what to do, they would be likely to refuse.*

> *No. You merely have to show them, over and over, day after day, the behavior you wish to instill. Show them enough mothers of illegitimate children heartwarmingly portrayed. Endlessly broadcast storylines suggesting that excellence is elitist. Constantly air ghetto values and moiling back-alley mobs grunting and thrusting their faces at the camera — and slowly, unconsciously, people will come to accept and then to imitate them. Patience is everything. Mold the young and in thirty years you will have molded society. Don't tell them anything. Just show them.*
> — Fred Reed, *Nekkid in Austin*, p. 335-336

If you can avoid what I believe are the worst four things in your diet, you will automatically be twice as far ahead of your peers:

videoscreen entertainment (TV, video games, Wii, etc.)
tobacco (cigarettes, snuff, chewing tobacco, etc.)
soft drinks (especially all "diet" ones with aspartame poison)
white, sugared carbs (cookies, doughnuts, white bread, etc.)

Read books (go to the library or buy bargain used books), don't smoke, and drink water or tea instead of sodas. Avoid all junk food. You will enjoy increased health and intellect, all by avoiding those four major poisons. Also, don't let alcohol get the better of you.

GETTING SERIOUS ABOUT LIFE

Imagine that you lived in a track dorm with your teammates. If you knew it would guarantee your victory over them on the field, would you get up a half hour earlier than the rest of them to train a little harder? Sure you would, if you truly wanted to win. Life is no different. However young or old you are, look around you at your peers, at guys your own age. They are your competition in this world. Against them, you will compete for everything: food, housing, jobs, opportunities, money, girls, and status. Natural talent is pretty evenly disbursed, so yours won't likely trump anybody else's. The only things which will successfully separate you from the others are your good choices in goals and hard work achieving them.
Wisdom. Willpower. That's it.
There is no "secret" to Life but that.
A crude and indelible accounting system runs this world. Generally, **you get out of Life** (yourself, your business, your family, your relationship with God, etc.) **what you have put into it.** A Man

who is in superb physical shape, who has fluid knowledge and many useful skills, has put in the time and energy to earn it. A Life is "spent" just like money; you must choose how to spend this present hour just as a $20 bill. Once that's spent, it's gone. So, did you make a good bargain? Did you spend it wisely? Are you a stronger, smarter, or better Man because of how you spent the last hour? Or, were you careless about it, not valuing its immense worth?

All of us are only culminations of how we spend our time. Put little or nothing into your Life, and your reward is to become a fat, sick, ignorant loser. I recall as a boy pointing out some wheezing 350 lb. lump of guy shuffling down the road. *"He didn't get that way overnight,"* my Mom observed. Poverty or prosperity, illness or health, skilled or unskilled, none of us get anywhere overnight. Spend your day — this very hour! — wisely. One today is worth two tomorrows.

> *Yesterday is a cancelled check.*
> *Tomorrow is a promisory note.*
> *Today . . . is . . . cash.*

BECOME AN AUTODIDACTIC POLYMATH

There is no such thing on earth as an uninteresting subject; the only thing that can exist is an uninterested person.
— G.K. Chesterton

If you teach a man anything, he will never learn.
— George Bernard Shaw

If a man empties his purse into his head, no man can take it away from him; an investment in knowledge pays the best interest.
— Ben Franklin

"What mistakes did I make that time?"
"What did I do that was right — and in what way could I have improved my performance?"
"What lessons can I learn from that experience?"
— Norman Vincent Peale

[Regarding the so-called "honest mistake"] *when an honest but mistaken man learns of his error, he either* [forthrightly] *ceases to be mistaken, or ceases to be honest.*
— Peter E. Hendrickson

The foolish reject what they see, not what they think.
The wise reject what they think, not what they see.
    — Huang Po

"Autodidact" means self-taught, and "polymath" means learned about many different subjects. No school (not even an excellent private one) can teach you what you need to know. When I grew up, there were no personal computers. All we had was the library, but it was enough. Today, you have at your fingertips the largest and most continuously updated library in the world — the Internet.

You can't self-teach without inner strength and a measure of gravity, with opportunities to be alone, to have broad experience with people and great challenges. Most of us who presume to judge schools are fooled by rituals of disciplined behavior, pretty hall displays, and test scores. If we knew what to look for, we'd be horrified and angry at the empty destinies this waste of precious time arranges for us. (p. 74)
    — John Taylor Gatto, *Weapons of Mass Instruction*

In times of change, those who are ready to learn will inherit the world, while those who believe they know will be marvelously prepared to deal with a world that has ceased to exist.
    — Eric Hoffer

Learn to unlearn.
    — Benjamin Disraeli

Learning makes a man fit company for himself.
    — Young

There is an unspeakable pleasure attending the life of a voluntary student.
    — Goldsmith

As you may have guessed, my education was highly autodidactic. No degree in English would have prepared me to write 14 books. No MBA could have shown me how to start a publishing house. I taught myself what I needed to know. So can you. (Read Benjamin Franklin's autobiography as a fascinating case study in precisely this.)

learn/train to do what is *important* vs. obvious

I got this nugget of wisdom from one of the world's best pilot instructors on recovering from aircraft stalls and spins. When an airplane goes into a spin, he urges the student to forget about the

"Hollywood" view through the windshield.   Forget about the screamingly obvious, and do what is important: stopping the spin.

start soon, if not today
You'll never learn it any younger!
— my pastor's father

None of this, however, will matter if you do not *read*. Choosing not to read is the worst form of illiteracy.

reading
There are three kinds of men. The one that learns by reading. The few who learn by observation. The rest of them have to pee on the electric fence for themselves.
— Will Rogers

Experience is a good school. But the fees are high.
— Heinrich Heine

*When I was a child, I lived in a violent household, in a violent neighborhood. But there was a place I could go — a library — and all the librarians did was encourage me to read. I could open a book, and I could be anywhere. I could do anything. I could imagine myself out of a slum. **I read myself out of poverty before I worked myself out of poverty**.*
— Walt Anderson, *Read With Me*

All good books are alike in that they are truer than if they had really happened.
— Ernest Hemingway

Reading is like a bucket lowered into the deep well of human experience. None of us will live long enough to learn from all our own mistakes firsthand, or to gain the wisdom we need. Reading is a must for any Life of variety, depth, accomplishment, and color.

We read to know that we're not alone.
— *Shadowlands*

If you do not like to read, find out *why*. Are the books so far boring? (That can easily be fixed.) Do you have trouble in reading itself? That can be fixed, too. If you cannot read aloud at a normal speaking pace, then you have a reading disability. This is nothing to be ashamed of, and can be corrected. Visit your local library to learn about the soonest literacy course. For speedreading, go to www.pxmethod.com.

A man's library is a sort of harem.
   — Emerson

Books are windows through which the soul looks out. A home without books is like a room without windows. No man has a right to bring up his children without surrounding them with books, if he has the means to pay for them.
   — Henry Ward Beecher

There are shortcuts to learning anything. Discover these shortcuts! With new words, there are shortcuts. Words which begin with a "th" or "ph" are often Greek in origin. Words which end in "age" are usually French in origin. Learn the roots of words (especially Latin and Greek) and then you have the building blocks of language. Words are usually just combinations of roots.

keenly study history
Study the past, if you would divine the future.
   — Confucius

The farther backward you can look, the farther forward you are likely to see.
   — Winston Churchill

To be ignorant of what occurred before you were born is to remain always a child.
   — Cicero

Humans are not all that creative, actually. But, they don't have to be as all the mistakes have already been made. (However, most folks continue to repeat them.) That's one reason to study history: to anticipate the mistakes of tomorrow and thus protect yourself.

vary your reading between old and new works
It is a good rule, after reading a new book, never to allow yourself another new one till you have read an old one in between. If that is too much for you, you should at least read one old to every three new ones . . . Keep the clean sea breeze of the centuries blowing through your mind . . . by reading old books. Not, of course, that there is any magic about the past. People were no cleverer then than they are now; they made as many mistakes as we. But not the same mistakes. . . . Two heads are better than one, not because either is infallible, but because they are unlikely to go wrong in the same direction.
   — C.S. Lewis, Introduction to "The Incarnation of the Word of God" by St. Athanasius

do not avoid mathematics and the sciences!

In his unique book *Starving The Monkeys*, Tom Baugh makes the compelling point that autonomous Americans need to embrace the hard sciences once again:

> The basic crime of poor math education is a gateway act which leads to the more serious offense of failing to teach science to any useful degree. . . . The point is to frame math and science in a form of interest to the student, allowing their natural curiosity to engage.
> — www-StarveTheMonkeys.com

Baugh then recommends the math instruction books by John Saxon:

> Because Saxon uses the military style of education, which means relentless drilling of the basics, you might be tempted to skip past problems which look familiar. Don't. The Saxon technique, borrowed from military instruction, is specifically designed to present you problems from different perspectives, and distributed over time. This approach ensures that you haven't just completed the problems, but truly incorporated the material into your subconscious toolbox. The capstone Saxon course is his physics course.

Home-schooling families have picked up the Saxon courses:

> I'm talking about the famous Saxon Math program, developed by former Air Force officer and high-school math instructor John Saxon. In spite of test after test showing that the use of Saxon Math increases algebra enrollment by up to 400 percent, and that Saxon Math students radically outperform students using other math programs, Mr. Saxon has been fighting an uphill battle to get his program used in the public schools. Opposed by leftist groups such as NOW, on the grounds that his books fail to promote feminism, political correctness, and the New World Order, Saxon was delighted to find out about the homeschooling movement.
> — www.home-school.com/Articles/SaxonEditorial.html

Baugh then recommends *Schaum's Outline Series* in chemistry, probability, statistics, differential equations, and linear algebra.

reading will lead to writing

> The greatest part of a writer's time is spent in reading, in order to write; a man will turn over half a library to make one book.
> — Samuel Johnson

I write because I *have* to. I am crammed with thoughts and ideas, and they must find their way out. Your mileage may vary. Read my *Communicating* chapter on how to write. Even if you haven't any urge to write for fun and profit, quality writing skills remain important for your own success.

daily increase your vocabulary!

Words are one of our chief means of adjusting to all the situations of life. The better control we have over words, the more successful our adjustment is likely to be.
— B. Evans

Dedicate yourself to learning at least 10 new words each day. Write them down with their definitions (classified by noun, verb, and adjective/adverb), and immediately work them into your conversations and letters. Whenever you come across an unfamiliar word, don't' skip over it; look it up and write it down!

Unlearn any bad habits confusing words which sound similar:

it's	its
you're	your
who's	whose
capital	capitol
compliment	complement (to go well with)

There are many words which are confused in meaning:

less	fewer (used with numbers, not in degree)
further	farther (used with geographical distance)
expert	professional (done for money, not love)
continual	continuous (unbroken, like Niagra's roar)
uninterested	disinterested (from interest to uninterest)

learn a new poem every week

This is what actor Anthony Hopkins does. That's an excellent way to keep your mind sharp and your thinking supple. You will seem brilliant and good company to others. Try Henley's *Invictus*:

In the fell clutch of circumstance
I have not winced nor cried aloud.
Under the bludgeonings of chance
My head is bloody, but unbowed.
Beyond this place of wrath and tears
Looms but the Horror of the shade,
And yet the menace of the years
Finds, and shall find, me unafraid.

It matters not how strait the gate,
  How charged with punishments the scroll,
I am the master of my fate:
  I am the captain of my soul.

chat up older and wiser people

A single conversation across the table with a wise man is worth a month's study of books.
  — Chinese proverb

Today, right now, there is an astonishing wealth of information and experiences available to you. Where? At the nearest Senior Center. The largest generation of living history is now in their 60s and 70s, and will be dead in 10-15 years. After that will only be people born in the Computer Age who know nothing of rural life and simpler times when only important things mattered. Living History is dying off!

adopt a wise and famous person

You may doubt that a man of wisdom, wealth, or fame would spend time with a young fellow such as yourself. You'd be surprised, though, if you reached out and tried.

Reading biographies is another way of "conversing" with wise people throughout the ages. I'd start with Theodore Roosevelt.

travel!

Search on YouTube for a remarkable man named Eustace Conway. Appalachian State Univ., straight A's, Anthropology and English, graduated with honors. He's also carved a life for himself out of the forest, making his own clothes and building his own cabin. Plus, he's had numerous traveling epics. "*A college degree is not even a drop in the bucket compared to the education and what I've gotten in all my travels and adventures. Not even a speck!*"

it's easy to become an expert

I am still learning. (Ancora imparo.)
  — favorite saying of Michaelangelo

Pick a field, study it for 30 minutes/day for 6 months, and those in your region will seek your advice. Study for a year, and you will become a national expert. Focus on the core principles (there will be a <12) and have them down cold, as everything else are just combinations of the core principles. Become an amateur expert.

Professionals built the Titanic — amateurs the Ark.
— Frank Popper

the most complete way to learn is to *teach*

After two weeks, we tend to remember:

10% of what we read	(seeing words)
20% of what we hear	(hearing words)
30% of what we see	(seeing still pictures)
50% of what we see and hear	(watching video)
70% of what we say	(giving a speech)
90% of what we say and do	(real experience, simulation)
99% of what we teach	(forces you to fill in the gaps)

Notice that only a max of 50% of knowledge comes from taking in the material, *i.e.*, being "impressed". To know anything more deeply than merely 50%, you must *express* from there, by speaking, demonstrating, doing, and teaching. What went *in* must come *out*.

You don't truly know something until you've taught it. Your students will force you to explain the same concepts from differing angles, which will increase your own supple knowledge and inductive reasoning. You won't realize the holes in your knowledge until you try to teach something you *think* you know. (If you can't teach the basic concepts of something to a 10 year old, you don't really know it yourself.) Start with free tutoring, and then begin to charge for lessons once you feel more solid. Don't forget to *volunteer* teach somewhere.

I hear and I forget.
I see and I remember.
I do and I understand.
I teach and I become.

regarding motor skills and foreign languages

Here is the mantra:

Slow is smooth. Smooth practiced becomes fast.

Start slowly and deliberately. Back in the days of record players, a couple learning a new dance would slow down the song's playing speed to have time for the steps. As they say in martial arts: a black belt is somebody who has mastered the basics. Take it *sloooowwwly* in order to learn it perfectly and smoothly.

LEARNING IS FOR . . . *DOING*

Action is the proper Fruit of Knowledge.
— Thomas Fuller

Verily, when the day of judgment comes, we shall not be asked what we have read, but what we have done.
— Thomas A. Kempis

Only knowledge that is used sticks in your mind.
— Norman Vincent Peale

It's what you learn after you know it all that counts.
— William Griffin

To know and not to do, is not yet to know.
— Zen saying

community education programs

These are great for learning different things. Courses are as varied as the imagination: flying, sausage making, dancing, yoga, GPS nav, and martial arts. The price per course is a bargain, usually under $30. Expand yourself, get out of your rut, and meet new folks. Gain valuable experience with something new, if but for a few hours!

Books are good enough in their way, but they are a mighty bloodless substitute for life.
— Robert Louis Stevenson

Nothing ever becomes real until it is experienced.
— John Keats

One thorn of experience is worth a whole wilderness of warning.
— James Russell Lowell

Experience is not what happens to you; it is what you do with what happens to you.
— Aldous Huxley

TRAINING

We should remember that one man is much the same as another, and that he is best who is trained in the severest school.
— Thucydides

Hardness . . . was the greatest compliment [amongst recon Marines]. *Hardness wasn't toughness, nor was it courage, although both were part of it. Hardness was the ability to face an overwhelming situation with aplomb, smile calmly at it, and then triumph through sheer professional pride.*
— USMC Captain Nathaniel Fick, *One Bullet Away*, p. 145

Pain is temporary. Pride is forever.
Nobody ever drowned in sweat.

practice, practice, practice!

There are no shortcuts to excellence, and only very few to average competence. Dedication and thousands of quality hours in trained practice is the only path. Anybody who claims otherwise is selling something.

Handel practiced on his harpsichord in secret, until every key was hollowed by his fingers to resemble the bowl of a spoon.
— from *Leaders of Men*

GATTO'S REAL LEARNING INDEX

❶	**self-knowledge**	your strengths, weaknesses, etc.
❷	**observation**	processing information accurately
❸	**feedback**	picking up cues, accepting criticism
❹	**analysis**	breaking up a problem into components
❺	**mirroring**	fitting in groups, but remaining yourself
❻	**expression**	having a voice of your own
❼	**judgment**	evaluating dispassionately
❽	**adding value**	adding value to every encounter, group

High Flight
John Gillespie Magee, Jr.

Oh! I have slipped the surly bonds of Earth
And danced the skies on laughter-silvered wings;
Sunward I've climbed, and joined the tumbling mirth
of sun-split clouds, — and done a hundred things
You have not dreamed of — wheeled and soared and swung
High in the sunlit silence. Hov'ring there,
I've chased the shouting wind along, and flung
My eager craft through footless halls of air ...

Up, up the long, delirious, burning blue
I've topped the wind-swept heights with easy grace.
Where never lark, or even eagle flew —
And, while with silent, lifting mind I've trod
The high untrespassed sanctity of space,
Put out my hand, and touched the face of God.

DOING (*ACTION!*)

There is no "try". There is only do, or do not do.
— Yoda

You can't build a reputation on what you're going to do.
— Henry Ford

Life is either a daring adventure or nothing.
— Helen Keller

To change one's life:
    Start immediately.
    Do it flamboyantly.
    No exceptions.
— William James

Get busy living, or get busy dying.
— The Shawshank Redemption

Pray as if everything depended on God, and work as if everything depended upon man.
— Cardinal Francis J. Spellman

Action turns daydreams into memories.
— Kenneth W. Royce, *Safari Dreams* (2008)

living means *doing things*

You are rewarded for effort . . . for work . . . for action. And a lack of action will leave you just sitting in the dust, broke, unhappy, lonely, with nothing to be proud of except your stubbornness for not doing what you knew you were capable of but were too lazy to do. No effort = no reward. Most people do just enough to keep from getting fired.
— Larry Winget, *Shut Up, Stop Whining, Get A Life!*

Well done is better than well said.
— Ben Franklin

After many interviews with the elderly asking "*What would you have done differently?*", one answer was universal. They all wish they'd done things they hadn't, especially when the window of opportunity was briefly open. **Life is no dress rehearsal.** Every minute is your chance to *do* something! If you get into a habit of wasting minutes, you will then waste hours, then days, and then years.

According to a 2011 article by the British *Journal of Sports Medicine*, each hour of TV watching reduces your lifespan by 22 minutes. Well, given the vapid content of TV, your *useful* life is reduced by *one hour and* 22 minutes. Don't forget that.

Time is the one resource that you cannot regenerate.
— Dr. Phil, *Life Strategies*, p. 133

there is a minimum level of action just to maintain

Now, here, you see, it takes all the running you can do, to keep in the same place.
— the Red Queen from Lewis Carroll, *Through A Looking Glass*

I'm not talking about actual success, but just to not fall behind in Life. So, since action is required for even "neutral buoyancy" you might as well learn to do more than just that, and *succeed*.

the 4 wants: love, health, money, ego-food

These are all intertwined, so never lose sight of one while you pursue another. Keep all four in balance. Concentrate on love and health, and you'll begin to notice that the money and ego-food seem to almost take care of themselves as you attract friends and customers. However, if you mistakenly concentrate on the money and ego-food, love and health will suffer.

the more *specific* you are about what you want out of Life, the more likely you are to get it

Just as you can't buy a plane ticket to "Europe" (or even to "Germany"), you can't desire such vague notions as "money" or "love". None of this is actionable. Those who vaguely dream of "*going to Europe*" never do. The mind cannot act on such fogginess. You must define what these four wants mean to *you*. How *much* money? Describe what a successful "love" is to you. What *exactly* do you need for ego-food. What *specifically* does health mean to you?

You are different from anyone else who has every lived, or ever will live. You are not your parents or your brothers or your friends. Your Life is singularly unique. Candidly ask yourself these questions, and write down all your answers (however indistinct at first):

❶ What do I want out of Life? (Understand what is the end versus the means. And, is that end the healthiest thing for me, or does this desire stem from immaturity or neurosis?)

❷ What will it cost me? (Time, energy, money, and sacrifice.)

❸ Am I willing to pay — every moment — the necessary price?

OK, once you've gotten that squared away, you're ready to begin work. There are many books hawking "the secret" to success, but there's really no new "secret" method — only what has always worked.

but first, what is "*success*"?

What's money [as a yardstick of success]? A man is a success if he gets up in the morning and goes to bed at night and in between does what he wants to do.
— Bob Dylan

There is only one success — to be able to spend your life in your own way.
— Christopher Morley

If a multimillionaire businessman really wanted to be a painter all his life, then he did not enjoy *personal* success. He had not been doing what he loved to do. Many people with great wealth are nonetheless very unhappy. If you value other things more, money cannot buy your sense of personal success. What is success to *you*? First understand that, otherwise your wrong paths will create great frustration.

Next, whatever success is to you will require action.

Action may not always bring happiness, but there is no happiness without action.
— Benjamin Disraeli

Every act rewards itself, or, in other words, integrates itself in a two-fold manner — first, in the thing, or in real nature; and secondly, in the circumstance, or in apparent nature. . . . Cause and effect, means and ends, seed and fruit, cannot be severed; for the effect already blooms in the cause, the end pre-exists in the means, the fruit in the seed.
— Emerson, *Compensation*

7 HABITS OF THE HIGHLY EFFECTIVE

These are great books by the Covey family, and I particularly recommend for teenagers *The 7 Habits of Highly Effective Teens.* Although I cover all of the below 7 habits in *Modules For Manhood,* here they are in Covey's order and phrasing. They make a good daily checklist to look over and keep on track.

Habit 1:   be proactive
Take responsibility for your life.

Habit 2:   begin with the end goal in mind
Define your mission and goals in life.

Habit 3:   put first things first
Prioritize, and do the most important things first.

Habit 4:   think win-win
Have an everyone-can-win attitude.

Habit 5:   seek first to understand, then to be understood
Listen to people sincerely.

Habit 6:   synergize
Work together to achieve more.

Habit 7:   sharpen the saw
Renew yourself regularly.

Most self-help books will describe similar nuggets. Again, it's only proof that there are no new tricks and tips in Life. We really don't know anything modern about human nature. What worked 5,000 years ago still works today. OK, I'll now break it down for you:

THE "SECRET" OF SUCCESS

Vision without a task is only a dream. A task without a vision is but drudgery. But vision with a task is a dream fulfilled.
  — Willie Stone

The only difference between Reality and Dreams is inactivity. There is a proven sequence of success, and it goes something like this:

Purpose
> ➡ **Imagination**
>> ➡ **Dreams**
>>> ➡ **Goals**
>>>> ➡ **Commitment**
>>>>> ➡ **Knowledge**
>>>>>> ➡ **Planning**
>>>>>>> ➡ **Passion**
>>>>>>>> ➡ **Action!**
>>>>>>>>> ➡ *Accomplishment!*

Purpose precedes Imagination
The purpose of life is life with a purpose.
   — Robert Byrne

Live by design, not by default. Most people spend more time planning their weekend than planning their life. You don't get what you want out of life until you know what you want out of life.
   — Larry Winget, *Shut Up, Stop Whining, Get A Life!*

You will always gravitate to that which you secretly most love. Men do not attain that which they want but that which they are.
   — James Allen

We act as though comfort and luxury were the chief requirements of life, when all that we need to make us really happy is something to be enthusiastic about.
   — Charles Kingsley

The ideal must be high; the purpose strong, worthy and true, or the life will be a failure.
   — Orison Marden

The great use of life is to spend it for something that outlasts it.
   — William James

Your purpose is the great engine of your Life, powering your imagination as you live for something worthy. Purpose is the foundation upon which everything else is built. Abraham Lincoln's mother said to her gangly young son, "*Abe, be somebody*" — and after decades of repeated failures he became President. Become excited about your Life's purpose. That excitement is infectious!

People often confuse "goal" and "purpose." A goal is something tangible; a purpose is a direction. A goal can be achieved; a purpose is fulfilled in each moment. We can set and achieve many goals; a purpose remains constant for life.
— John-Roger & Peter McWilliams, Do It!, p. 135

Nothing contributes so much to tranquilizing the mind as a steady purpose — a point on which the soul may fix its intellectual eye.
— Mary Wollstonecraft Shelley

Many persons have a wrong idea of what constitutes true happiness. It is not attained through self-gratification but through fidelity to a worthy purpose.
— Helen Keller

The thing always happens that you really believe in; and the belief in a thing makes it happen.
— Frank Lloyd Wright

Find out what you love to do and you will never have to work another day in your life.
— Nietzsche

There is no road to success, but through a clear, strong purpose. Nothing can take its place. A purpose underlies character, culture, position, attainment of every sort.
— T.T. Munger

I can tell you only two things about your purpose: it is *unique* to you alone, and it may likely *evolve* throughout your Life. It's up to you to discover your own current purpose. (It's gradually discovered by first understanding what is *not* your purpose.) Start writing thoughts and ideas down on paper; keep a notebook! "*When it comes to going after what you love in life, don't take no for an answer.*"

You cannot skip the first step of learning your own Purpose. Everything else in Life hangs on it.

*On a public beach, sand is free. On the other hand, sand for a playground costs $25 a bag. That same sand, glued to a piece of paper and sold in a hardware store, may cost $5 a sheet. Sand (silicon) that is manufactured into computer chips is far more expensive. Sand is sand. All that's different is what the sand is used for. **The more specific its purpose, the more valuable it becomes.***
— *Game Plan for Life*, Joe Gibbs

It's also up to you to sense when your purpose evolves or changes. I had a very original purpose from my 30s to mid-40s, and then I sensed that purpose morphing into something more mainstream. This book is one of my first achievements from my newer purpose.

My path to my fixed purpose is laid on iron rails in which my soul is grooved to ride.
— Herman Melville, *Moby Dick*

The world stands aside to let anyone pass who knows where he is going.
— David Starr Jordon

What makes you cry? What pisses you off? What makes you dream? What gives you joy? Basically, what is it that *energizes* you? Inside that is your passion, your purpose — even if it's "only" opening up your own body shop or juice bar.

Every calling is great when greatly pursued.
— Oliver Wendell Holmes Jr.

Imagination precedes Dreams

Creative activity could be described as a type of learning process where teacher and pupil are located in the same individual.
— Arthur Koestler

Imagination is more important than knowledge.
— Albert Einstein

The future belongs to those who see possibilities before they become obvious.
— John Sculley, former CEO of Pepsi and Apple Computer

Your purpose energizes your imagination, and your imagination creates your dreams. Once you have *dreams* (which is the hard part), the rest becomes much easier.

Dreams precede Goals

Desires must be simple and definite. They defeat their own purpose should they be too many, too confusing, or beyond a man's training to accomplish.
— George S. Clason

A goal without a dream behind it is just a gray desire. Even if you accomplish it, it won't be very satisfying. Oh, and dream *big*. You get further by aiming for the stars than for the horizon.

It's lonely at the top. Ninety-five percent of people in the world are convinced they are incapable of achieving great things, so they aim for the mediocre. The level of competition is thus fiercest for "realistic" goals, paradoxically making them the most time- and energy-consuming.
There is just less competition for bigger goals.
— Timothy Ferriss, *4-Hour Work Week*

When I enrolled for flight training, I'd imagined that my instructor would be busy with many other students. Nope, not very many real dreamers out there; I had him all to myself and thus soloed in 14 days.

Not failure, but low aim is crime.
— Lowell

Big dreams can seem a little nutty:

You have everything but one thing — madness. A man needs a little madness or else — he never dares cut the rope and be free.
— Zorba the Greek

One such man with a "crazy" dream was Heinrich Schliemann who dreamed *since age seven* of finding the ruins of ancient Troy (of Homer's *Iliad*). He learned classical Greek and married a Greek woman. He then earned a fortune as a merchant in order to retire in his 40s to search for Troy. With 100 workmen and two years of work, he found it! It had been buried for over two thousand years.

One of the nuttiest of all was Joshua Abraham Norton. His dream was to become Emperor . . . *of the United States!* And, in September 1859, he did. From San Francisco, he issued a proclamation that since the U.S. Congress was corrupt, he was abolishing it to rule in person. (Soon, he proclaimed himself *"Protector of Mexico"* as well.) San Franciscans were delighted, and supported Norton I with free board, meals, and travel. He was greeted in the streets with bows as he inspected his kingdom. When he complained that "*our imperial wardrobe is a national disgrace*" the city council paid for a new outfit. He died in 1880 (after a 20 year "reign") and it took two days for the 10,000 mourners to file past his coffin. A local obituary sommented:

> *The Emperor Norton killed nobody, robbed nobody and deprived nobody of his country — which is more than can be said for most fellows of his trade.*

Goals precede Commitment

> *You better know what you're going to do* [in life] *before somebody knows for you.*
> — movie *Astronaut Farmer*

> *Set clear and detailed goals and break them down into long-term, short-term, and daily goals. Motivation comes from having plenty of good reason for doing something. If you can't come up with good reasons, you're wasting your time.*
> — Michael Powell, *Mind Games*

> *Life begins when we have a goal and it's over when we don't have one.*
> — Grant G. Gard, *Don't Just Talk About It — Do It!*

Never confuse dreams with goals. A goal is a dream . . . but with a *deadline*. Dreams without deadlines are trapped as pitiful fantasies. Until written down with a deadline, a fantasy cannot become a goal. **Have goals, or else work for those who *do*.**

> *You must have long-range goals to keep you from being frustrated by short-range failures.*
> — Charles C. Noble

> *Give me a stock clerk with a goal, and I will give you a man who will make history. Give me a man without a goal and I will give you a stock clerk.*
> — J.C. Penney

Be *specific* in defining your goals. Every race has its ribbon at the end; every goal should have a way to know you've accomplished it. "Making more money" is not a goal, it's a general wish. So is "getting a promotion" or "a new car". Be specific: *i.e.*, how *much* more money over *what* time.

> *Preceding accomplishment must be desire. Thy desires must be strong and definite. Desires must be simple and definite. They*

defeat their own purpose should they be too many, too confusing, or beyond a man's training to accomplish.
— George S. Clason, *The Richest Man in Babylon* (1926), p. 40

Be bold enough to reach for what will truly fill you up, without being unrealistic. Once you have the strength and resolve enough to believe that you deserve what it is that you want, then and only then will you be bold enough to step up and claim it. Remember that if you don't, someone else will.
— from Dr. Phil's Life Law #10, www.drphil.com/articles/article/44

Keep setting bigger goals as you achieve smaller ones.

Long-range goals are 3-5 years
Medium-range goals are 1-3 years
Short-range goals are within 12 months

By the way, most goals fit into one of these areas:

Social/Political
Professional
Marriage/Family
Spiritual/Personal Development

Revising your goals may be in order:

You should change your goals whenever you get significant new information about yourself or your goal that changes the fundamental reason that you chose the goal to begin with.
— John T. Reed

Commitment precedes Knowledge

One person with belief is equal to a force of ninety-nine who have only interests.
— John Stewart Mill

[A]s a general rule, half an ounce of will is more effective than a hundredweight of insight and intelligence.
— Arthur Schopenhauer,
  Die Kunst, Recht zu behalten   *(The Art Of Controversy)*

Until one is committed, there is hesitancy, the chance to draw back, always ineffectiveness. *Concerning all acts of initiative (and creation) there is one elementary truth, the ignorance of which kills countless ideas and splendid plans: that the moment one commits oneself, then Providence moves too. All sorts of things occur to help one that would never otherwise have*

occurred. A whole stream of events issues from the decision, raising in one's favor all manner of unforeseen incidents and meeting and material assistance, which no man could have dreamed would have come his way.
— W.H. Murray, Scottish Himalayan Expedition

People easily fall short of commitment, so you must watch this in yourself. Once you've decided on your Purpose and have worked things through to its Goals, then you must firmly *commit* to seeing them through. Without commitment, everything else will just stall out at the first difficulty. Turn intentions into commitments.

Best-selling author Robert J. Ringer hung this on his wall:

I AM THE MACHINE

I labor the same number of hours, I put forth the same intensity, I tap the same creative powers, and I produce the same quality of work, without regard to circumstances of any kind.

Sickness is not a factor; being tired is irrelevant; all problems are aside and apart from the work that I, The Machine, do.

Because of the self-discipline and regimentation required of me, I have the willpower to avoid being distracted by anybody or anything that does not directly contribute to my project.

No person, activity, or situation can affect the relentless performance of me, The Machine.

Commitment can also be called determination. You're only as big of a man as the smallest problems that will stall you out.

When confronted with a challenge, the committed heart will search for a solution. The undecided heart searches for an escape.
— Andy Andres, The Traveler's Gift

Time and I against any other two.
— Balthasar Gracian

Where the Determination is, The Way Can Be Found.
— George S. Clason, The Richest Man in Babylon

A hero is one who knows how to hang on one minute longer.
— Norwegian proverb

Example: A wealthy merchant, retired at 33, was Cyrus W. Field. In 1854, he had not only the dream of laying a 2,300 mile transatlantic telegraph cable between England and America — he had the sheer determination to make it happen. On the first attempt, 335 miles of cable fell to the sea. The second attempt was also a disaster. The third attempt was a brief success with a laid cable and test message, but the connection somehow broke. (The public, at first ecstatic, then believed it had been a hoax.) The fourth attempt wasn't made until seven years later, and the cable again snapped. The next year, a *fifth* attempt was made with a new design of cable, and that one succeeded.

Abraham Lincoln (whom I don't respect as a President, as the States did, and still do, have the right to secede) was an incredibly determined man. His road to the White House:

> *failed in business in 1831*
> *defeated for Legislature in 1832*
> *second business failure in 1833*
> *suffered nervous breakdown in 1836*
> *defeated for Speaker in 1838*
> *defeated for Elector in 1840*
> *defeated for Congress in 1843*
> *defeated for Congress in 1848*
> *defeated for Senate in 1855*
> *defeated for Vice President in 1856*
> *defeated for Senate in 1858*
> *elected President in 1860*

And Lincoln also somehow persevered with a *very* sharp-tongued wife who constantly lambasted him for his failures. Talk about uphill!

> *When people are not determined, their civilization is not determined. When people do not persevere, their civilization does not persevere.*
> *But it's a blessing — for you . . . because people have been encouraged to be lazy, ignorant, and incompetent, you can expect to have very little competition if you're one of the few who chooses to stand right side up. Likewise, because most people have neither the courage nor the inclination to fight the good fight to the finish, the determined individual has the field pretty much to himself.*
> — Robert J. Ringer, *How You Can Find Happiness During the Collapse of Western Civilization*, p. 120

> *Perhaps there is no more important component of character than steadfast resolution. The boy who is going to make a great man, or is going to count in any way in afterlife, must make up his mind not merely to overcome a thousand defeats, but to win in spite of a thousand repulses and defeats.*
> — Theodore Roosevelt

Example: In 1958, a destitute African boy named Legson Kayira decided that he wanted to go to America for college. He had no money, no passport, no connections, no shoes. His only possessions were a Bible and a copy of *Pilgrim's Progress*. At 17 years old he left anyway, by foot, from what is now Tanzania. (I've flown there to hunt. It's a long way away!) He worked his way from village to village (often rejected, so he had to sleep in the forests, eating herbs and wild fruit). After 14 months and 1,000 miles he reached Uganda, where he found a job making bricks. From there he wrote the Skagit Valley College in Mount Vernon, Washington and received a scholarship offer. Still, he had no travel fare, no passport, and no visa, but these obstacles Legson overcame with great faith and drive. It took Legson two years and 2,500 miles to reach Khartoum in the Sudan. He learned that his college had raised the travel fare of $1,700 through benefit parties. He bought his first pair of shoes. Legson arrived for college in 1960, carrying his two only books and wearing his first suit. Later, he wrote:

> When God has put an impossible dream in your heart, He means to help you fulfill it. I believed this to be true when, as an African bush boy, I felt compelled to become an American college graduate. This became true when I graduated from the University of Washington.
> **It is when we resist God that we remain nothing.** When we submit to Him, whatever the sacrifice or hardship, we can become far more than we dare dream.

If a barefoot African boy can make it to America for college, what's *your* excuse for failure? Legson Kayira proved that *anything* can be done with firm commitment to make it happen. The universe will open up and help you once you give it a "green light" with your determination. Another destitute African boy of 14, William Kamkwamba of Malawi, built a windmill power generator from junkyard scraps to power his family home (and then his village). He is now world famous, and studies under a scholarship.

There are still a million things not yet accomplished. What is waiting for you to do? What will *you* commit to do? Have a "made-up mind" and then watch things happen!

> There is perhaps nothing more conducive to success in any important and difficult undertaking than a firm, steady, unremitting spirit.
> — Nathaniel Emmons

With ordinary talent and extraordinary perseverance, all things are possible.
  — Thomas Buxton

Commitment is the enemy of resistance.
  — David McNally

A small daily task, if it be really daily, will beat the labors of a spasmodic Hercules.
  — Anthony Trollope

Endeavor to persevere.
  — from the movie *Outlaw Josey Wales*

A German named Phillip Reis actually invented the telephone 15 years before Alexander Graham Bell did, but allowed some potential investors to dissuade him. Children's book author Dr. Seuss was rejected by 23 publishers. The legal thriller author John Grisham persevered through 25 rejections. French author Jean-Dominique Bauby after a paralyzing stroke dictated his entire 150-page novel by blinking his left eye. If you believe in yourself, keep at it until you find the right person who also believes in you. It will happen!

My progress has been slow and toilsome, with little about it that was brilliant or spectacular; the result of persistent and painstaking work, which gave it a foundation that was solid.
  — President Calvin Coolidge

Anyone can dabble, but once you've made that commitment, your blood has a particular thing in it, and it's very hard for people to stop you.
  — Bill Cosby

Decide what you want, decide what you are willing to exchange for it. Establish your priorities and go to work.
  — H.L. Hunt

4 types of people — which are you?

❶ Cop-outs   no goals
❷ Hold-outs   goals, but never with commitment
❸ Dropouts   goals, but with lost commitment
❹ All-outs   set goals, commit, and pay the price to win

The haves and the have-nots can often be traced back to the dids and the did-nots.
  — D.O. Flynn

Knowledge precedes Planning

Never confuse basic information with necessary knowledge. You must learn reasonably everything there is to know about your project — especially its costs and downside potential. Understand the entire package of what you are considering. Most important here is to comprehend the opportunity costs involved; what are you giving up?

Planning precedes Enthusiasm

Opportunity is a haughty goddess who wastes no time with those who are unprepared.
— George S. Clason, *The Richest Man in Babylon* (1926), p. 18

The method of the enterprising is to plan with audacity, and execute with vigor; to sketch out a map of possibilities; and then to treat them as probabilities.
— Bovee

Much of what we call good luck, is, in reality, unconscious skill in the arrangement of those elements which go to make up events.
— Stewart Edward White

Action without planning will usually result in failure. Planning first requires your goals, and then information. From *there,* you plan. Planning is breaking your goals down into their components, and then working them forward in order.

> Understand the problem or goal
> Know what results you really *need*
> Know what results you really *want*
> Harmonize these two

pursue real accomplishments that matter

Forget about mere "achievements" based primarily on public misconceptions (and I include all "soft" degrees from college). Real accomplishments (including marketable "hard" degrees, such as engineering) increase your experience and skill-set.

make useful lists (*Do Before, Take With, Do There*)

The above is my travel list which I've used for decades. Even the longest and most complex trip can usually fit on a single page. Another list of mine is the *Buy/Do/Call.*

Author David Allen's books such as *Making It All Work* are fantastic planning tools.

plan with simple and easy steps

Any goal, no matter how big, can be broken down into simple and easy steps. It must be broken down that way, as a step is not a step unless you can climb it. (An unclimbable step is still a wall.)

how to plan

I plan both backwards from the goal, and also forward from where I stand. Somewhere in the middle the two lines will meet, forming a solid path from me to my goal.

Then, I notate all the "milemarkers" of things that need to be done, and in what order. Some tasks have no prerequisites and can be done at any time, while others will rely on several preceding tasks. (Look for software which offers PERT planning and its "critical path".)

What can be done at *any* time, I highlight with their own color. That way, if I get blocked by a task because of its uncompleted prerequisites, I can always keep moving forward by completing small tasks which are unconnected to any other. **Your constant question should be:** *"What can I do right now?"*

Tasks which are prerequisites for other tasks have a special power over your project because they are inherent bottlenecks. Tackle these prerequisites with great vigor, else your plan may stall out.

Some tasks will serve as prerequisites for *multiple* tasks. Start with those immediately. I learned to do this at university, where I got a four-year BBA with a 3.5GPA in just three calender years. It was accomplished by good planning, hard work, and the gracious financial support of my parents. (My semesters were always 18-21 hours, and my final one was 27 hours of nine senior level courses.)

Good planning was crucial in order to work *smart*. I drew out my degree plan as a matrix to identify the most critical prerequisites. Certain courses were key to others, such as Accounting 1 and Finance 1. These I took immediately even though most students waited until their sophomore year. By the end of my freshman year I was eligible to take nearly half of my junior year courses (as far as having their prerequisites out of the way). As a sophomore, I began to do so. This was apparently unheard of, as I had to personally convince the Dean of the business school that I was up for it.

Since I hadn't goofed off my freshman year with all the easy basics (most of which weren't multiple prerequisites), once I got to my junior and senior years I still had some easier freshman courses to take which evened out the work load. My classmates, however, had nothing but the harder courses by that time, having taken it easy their freshman year. In short, I started off with a strong and steady pace maintainable until the end.

My other key to finishing in only three years was that I took full advantage of the available testing credits. I tested out of English 1, Spanish 1, German 1 & 2, and Business Law. A total of 16 hours of credits, which saved me an entire semester!

My BBA degree requiring 130 course hours I completed with 132 hours. No wasted time, no fat, no changing of majors.

In all, though the *planning* was impeccable, I quickly afterwards had retrospective doubts about my *goal* to finish in three years.

always have a *series* of goals

The problem with my college career was that I had not made a single goal for what I would do *after* graduation! (In fact, I had no *dreams* of what to do, much less goals.) No career plans and no entrepreneurial ideas. Nothing. I'd simply forgotten! That first year after university was just a black hole of wasted time. I'd blasted through my studies with nothing waiting for me. I later read that such is typical of Olympic athletes who have focused so ardently on a gold medal that they made no post-Olympic plans at all. Only two years later did I rebound with a new business. But those two years: ugh.

So, have successive goals! **What comes . . . next?**

Passion precedes *Action!*

We are caught up at a particular stage in our national ethos in which we're not only materialistic but worse than that; we're becoming emotionally dead as people. We don't sing, we don't dance, we don't even commit sin with much enthusiasm.
    — Tony Campolo, sociologist

A lack of passion and enthusiasm is a core defect that can't be painted over and ignored. It is the *sine qua non* ("without which, nothing"). As Schjeldahl advised, take an "impersonal joy" in what you do.

Nothing great was ever achieved without enthusiasm.
    — Ralph Waldo Emerson

Motivation is when your dreams put on work clothes.
    — Parkes Robinson

The real secret of success is enthusiasm.
    — Walter Chrysler

The big one is motivation. If [my fighters under training are] motivated, it's just a matter of time before they break through.
    — Greg Jackson, from *The Fighter's Mind*

What gets rewarded gets done.
— Michael LeBoeuf, Ph.D.,
GMP: The Greatest Management Principle in the World

You cannot easily become enthusiastic unless you've first gone through the steps of purpose, imagination, dreams, goals, commitment, and planning.   Once you have, you will find yourself naturally motivated because of all the potential you've created! You are a lake pressing against the dam.   You are an arrow poised in a bowstring at full stretch, ready to be released.

John C. Maxwell on passion

Human beings are so made that whenever anything fires the soul, impossibilities vanish.   How long has it been since you couldn't sleep because you were too <u>excited</u> by an idea?

❶ passion is the fist step to achievement
❷ passion increases your willpower
❸ passion changes you
❹   assion makes the impossible possible
❺ take your passion temperature
❻ return to your first love
❼ associate with people of passion

If you aren't having fun . . . then you're not doing it right!

I use the name of God advisedly, for as previously pointed out, entheos, God within, is a source of enthusiasm not only in semantics but in fact.
— Dr. Norman Vincent Peale, *Enthusiasm Makes the Difference*

Action!

Whatever you can do,
or dream you can, begin it.
Boldness has genius,
power and magic in it.
— Goethe

Never retreat. Never explain. Get it done and let them howl.
— Benjamin Jowett

The world expects results. Don't tell others about the labor pains. Show them the baby.
— Arnold Glasow

There is nothing so fatal to character as half-finished tasks.
— David Lloyd George

Talk is cheap. It's what you do that determines the script of your life. Translate your insights, understandings and awareness into purposeful, meaningful, constructive actions. They are of no value until then. Measure yourself and others based on results — not intentions or words.
— from Dr. Phil's Life Law #5, www.drphil.com/articles/article/44

Action is the proper Fruit of Knowledge.
— Thomas Fuller

Stay focused. Do one job until completion when at all possible. Figure out the most important thing that has to be done today. Then do it. . . . No one ever gets in trouble for doing the things that really matter. Do what you say you are going to do, when you said you were going to do it, in the way you said you were going to do it.
— Larry Winget, *Shut Up, Stop Whining, Get A Life!*

REILLY'S 7 TYPES OF PEOPLE

Your desires must not only be specific and personal, they must be REALISTIC AND ACHIEVABLE — if you are to reach your goals.
In simple terms, the Law of Intelligent Action says that when you are confronted with any kind of problem, you will intelligently solve that problem if you have:
❶ *The* **Desire** *to solve it.*
❷ *The* **Ability** *to solve it.*
❸ *The capacity for handling the* **Human Relations** *involved.*
— William J. Reilly, *How to Get What You Want Out of Life*

D + A + HR = your desired achievements in Life

the "D" type   (the "Hold-outs")

Strong on Desire, but weak on Ability and Human Relations. These are dreamers and procrastinators. At least 30% of people.

I once worked an African safari booth at a show, selling my book *Safari Dreams.* A guy about 30 walked up and inquired how much a Cape Buffalo hunt cost. I quoted him the standard package price, and then asked if he'd already hunted in Africa. He hadn't, but replied that he had just bought a raffle ticket for a new hunting rifle. On a hunch, I then asked if he had ever been hunting at all. Nope. *"Before you even* think about going on African safari, you need to have hunted over here. *Get some deer under your belt first.*" But he hadn't a rifle. Many hunters would lend you one, I replied. I was astonished at his next reflexive excuse: his abode was too small for trophy heads! Well, then just hunt a doe or elk cow for the meat. He was too clever for me, as he hadn't the freezer space! Exasperated, I treated him to a tiny lecture: "*Look, you seem to be waiting for some green light from the universe. It doesn't work that way. You have to give yourself your own green light, and the universe will begin to help you. All your reasons for not hunting are just excuses. You say you can't afford a rifle, but I'd bet your fancy leather Celtics jacket costs more than a used .30-06. You need to get into the game, and stop standing on the sidelines!*" He listened. He looked at me solemnly. There seemed to be hope. Then he next asked me the taxidermy cost for a buffalo shoulder mount. I bid this lost cause *Adieu*, and he shuffled away.

> *Your time, your energy, and your money always go to what's important to you. You are not too busy to clean your garage; it just wasn't a priority to you. If I told you I would give you $5,000 to clean your house completely, play for two hours with your kids, read a book, have dinner with your family, and spend a quality evening with your spouse, along with calling your family to catch up — and you only had 24 hours to do it, could you do it? Sure you could! Simply because the $5,000 was important enough to you to make sure you got it all done. . . . [But] those things are never going to get done until they become a priority to you [in themselves, without a $5,000 reward].*
> — Larry Winget, *Shut Up, Stop Whining, Get A Life!*

the "A" type

Strong on Ability, but weak on Desire and Human Relations. Often perfectionists and bores, these people are lazy and unpleasant.

the "HR" type

Strong on Human Relations, but weak on Desire and Ability. The classic drinking buddy. These folks are lovable, but hopeless.

the "D-A" type

Strong on Desire and Ability, but weak on Human Relations. The well-known "own worst enemy" person who refuses to get along with others. They often have a "chip on their shoulder" and are tetchy.

It is easy to make a noticeable improvement in Human Relations once the D-A type *cares* to do so.

the "D-HR" type
Strong on Desire and Human Relations, but weak on Ability. Charming but impractical dreamers. Most politicians (such as Obama, with no real experience or ability) are D-HRs.

the "A-HR" type (the "Cop-outs" and "Drop-outs")
Strong on Ability and Human Relations, but weak on Desire. Friendly and competent, but with no aim in Life. Often the well-schooled children of the wealthy. They float along, because they can.

the "D-A-HR" type (the "All-outs")
Strong in Desire, Ability, and Human Relations. This person is equipped to solve all problems in all environments at all times. The classic "go-getter". He knows that effort, well-directed, is the formula for achievement. (There is an *eighth* type: those without desire, ability, or human relationship skills. Total losers.)

D + A + HR = your desired achievements in Life

How can *you* become a D-A-HR type of person? Three steps to do:

Learn *specifically* your personal desires. (Half the battle!)
Develop required ability to fulfill these desires. (Takes time.)
Become at least adequate in your human relations. (Easy!)

6 TRAITS OF THE HIGH-PERFORMERS

I once read a 1980s *WSJ* article on Charles A. Garfield of the Peak Performance Center who interviewed 1,200 top achievers in business, education, sports, the arts, etc. He found six characteristics that mark optimal performers. You can learn and hone them yourself!

they can transcend previous levels of accomplishment
They do this by avoiding "comfort zones" of the familiar. They never let themselves feel too much at home in any extended situation. Always strive for bigger and better is their motto.

they solve problems rather than try to place blame
They understand only results matter, and so they don't waste time on whose mess it originally was.

they are masters of delegation and knowing when to relax

They are not workaholics, but pace themselves efficiently while they allow others to take on some of the burdens. They are marathoners in the game of Life who never forget to take vacations.

they practice detailed mental rehearsals

Purposeful daydreaming are vital. The mind doesn't really know the difference between dreaming something vs. having done it.

> *Anyone who doubts the malleability of the adult brain should consider a startling piece of research conducted at Harvard Medical School.*
>
> *There, a group of adult volunteers, none of whom could previously play the piano, were split into three groups.*
>
> *The first group were taken into a room with a piano and given intensive piano practise for five days. The second group were taken into an identical room with an identical piano — but had nothing to do with the instrument at all.*
>
> *And the third group were taken into an identical room with an identical piano and were then told that for the next five days they had to just imagine they were practising piano exercises.*
>
> *The resultant brain scans were extraordinary. Not surprisingly, the brains of those who simply sat in the same room as the piano hadn't changed at all.*
>
> *Equally unsurprising was the fact that those who had performed the piano exercises saw marked structural changes in the area of the brain associated with finger movement.*
>
> *But what was truly astonishing was that the group who had merely imagined doing the piano exercises saw changes in brain structure that were almost as pronounced as those that had actually had lessons.*
>
> *"The power of imagination" is not a metaphor, it seems; it's real, and has a physical basis in your brain.*
>
> — "The REAL brain drain: Modern technology - including violent video games - is changing the way our brains work",
> by Susan Greenfield,
> www.dailymail.co.uk/pages/live/technology/sciencetechnology.ht ml?in_page_id=1965

Mental rehearsals are a form of practice, and a well-proven technique in all sports which can be applied elsewhere. (This also illustrates the awful power of worry, as one replays invented images.)

they work out "catastrophic expectation reports"

Envision a "black sky" scenario with a "*What's the worst that can happen, and how will that affect me?*" By doing so, you can then take risks without any vague sense of impending doom.

they are driven by personally set goals

This is an example of what I mentioned as "competing only with yourself". Not relying solely on the quotas of others, they always have compelling internal goals.

> *If there are no immediate external consequences for nonperformance, I create my own. No, I don't punish myself or ground myself for not doing something. I just create the consequence of disappointment.*
> — Larry Winget, *Shut Up, Stop Whining, Get A Life!*

THE *"but what if?"* EXCUSES

> *If you are going to measure your progress based on results, then you must be willing to question every pattern and every structure in your life. You must be willing to question how and where you spend your time, what you say to yourself, how and why you interact with those you do, and every other aspect of your being. And you must be willing to change it. Resolve to escape the insanity and do something different. Don't intend to do it, actually do it.*
> — Dr. Phil, *Life Strategies*, p. 139

We have programmed ourselves not to act by a myriad of excuses. Most are related to fear. Fear of three ghosts.

the 3 ghosts: time, money, approval

William J. Reilly in *How To Get What You Want Out of Life*, calls these three most common excuses "ghosts".

"I haven't the time."

> *It is generally recognized and accepted that only the busiest people ever have time for anything.*
>
> *You may not have ALL the time you'd LIKE for what you want to do, but you do have enough time TO GET STARTED.*
>
> *[There are] remarkable achievements possible for anyone who will consistently devote even as little as one hour a day to one single purpose. And the unvarnished truth is that every one of us*

who mouths the old excuse, "I haven't the time," wastes much more than an hour every day of his life. (pp. 86-87)

There is always time to begin anything that is truly important to you. You're *already* doing what's truly important to you, even if that means lying around on the couch watching TV. Other people more driven than you are playing ball with their children, learning to fly, dance, etc. Grab ahold of the time in your life, as this soldier does:

> [One of my Delta team leaders] *is the best organized individual on the planet and a master at time management. During a normal day back at Fort Bragg, Pope could accomplish more tasks in a day than most of us could in a month and still find time to shoot and work out. His teammates would arrive in the team room on Monday morning and find that he had repacked each man's gear, shampooed the carpet, and generally cleaned up the entire room. All the kit bags were retagged with not only the proper marking but with some Gucci-looking tags with fancy colors and lamination. . . . It was like he possessed some stolen alien technology to control time.*
> — Dalton Fury, *Kill Bin Laden*, p. 241

"I haven't the money."

> *It's a grave mistake for a young man just starting out to select a job on the basis of how much money it pays; that it's far wiser to seek a job in a business he likes, even though it pays less to start with. For if he likes his job, he'll apply himself more earnestly, he'll get more good ideas, and he'll progress faster.*
>
> *I've been career counseling men and women for a good many years now, and the people I have most trouble with are those who* have *money. For once they find out what they really want to do, they are not pressured enough, by economic necessity, to do anything about it.* (pp. 88-89)

If you shop for bargains or ask to trade out, many things are surprisingly affordable. You'll just have to hustle for it. Sell off some things, quit some of your little luxuries, and get to work.

"My friends and family would not approve."

> *One thing is certain. You will never venture anything or achieve anything worthwhile if you permit yourself to be unduly influenced by others.* (p. 91)

If your goal makes good sense, and if it's something you really want, why let anyone's disapproval stand in your way? Who's Life is it? Your friends and family have their lives to live. You should live your own. If

your father is pressing on you to become a doctor because he "*never had that opportunity*", you can reply, "*I may have the opportunity, but it is not in my heart to do so. I need to live out my own dreams, not anybody else's. Please accept that I am different from you.*"
And never forget the old maxim:

It is easier to obtain forgiveness than permission.

but what if I "*can't decide*"?

The mark of a good action is that it appears inevitable in retrospect.
— Robert Louis Stevenson

Much of Life involves choosing between mutually exclusive choices. Everything involves some sort of a trade-off, however poor or good. But understand this: decisions *will* be made about you and your Life — even if you don't make them yourself. If you are indecisive, others will decide *for* you, and you probably won't like their choices.

Ask yourself these questions:

Is it a need or a want?
Am I really waiting for more information, or just stalling?
Is there a powerful comparative advantage?
Have I balanced out the gains vs. sacrifices?
What's the real downside, and can I live with it?

beware the "Ishmael" — wait for the "Isaac"

In the Biblical story of Genesis 16, Abram and Sarai wanted a son, but Sarai was barren. Through her impatience and suggestion, 85 year old Abram impregnated Sarai's maid Hagar, who bore him son Ishmael (father of the Arab race). Only by waiting another 15 years on God's timing through faith did a 90 year old Sarai (renamed Sarah) give birth to Isaac (father of the Jewish race).

Moral: there is man's best, and then there is God's best. Learn to trust Him, and be patient. Don't fall for the "Ishmael" (which almost always appears just before the Isaac, if you'd only wait).

to not decide is to have it decided *for* you

At some point a decision *will* be made, by others if not by you. It's preferable if you make your own decisions like a Man.

but what if it "*can't be done*"?

Every noble work is at first impossible.
— Carlyle

The future belongs to the discontented. Good things don't just happen. Usually they come to people who are bothered by problems. Grow or go.
— Grant G. Gard, *Don't Just Talk About It — Do It!*

The Wright brothers flew right through the smoke screen of impossibility.
— Charles F. Kettering

The world is moving so fast these days that the man who says it can't be done is generally interrupted by someone doing it.
— Harry Emerson Fosdick

Indeed, "impossibility" (which deserves to be imprisoned within quotation marks) is just a smokescreen. If the doers and creators throughout human history had believed the "*it can't be done*" lie, we'd all still be living in caves today.

The greatest pleasure in life is doing what people say you cannot do.
— Walter Bagehot

Until 1954 it was a known "fact" that the 4-minute mile was not possible. Within a year of Roger Bannister's feat, over a dozen followed. Bannister broke the *mental* barrier, not any physical one.

My first business was a bold new idea, especially in my home town. My 20-year corporate-employee father snidely remarked that it would "*go over like a lead balloon*". (Happily, I'd learned long before not to heed such discouragements.) I started my company and ran it successfully for three years before I sold it and went to university. Although it didn't make me rich, the experience and confidence I gained was priceless. It was the very best thing for me at the time.

I am looking for a lot of men who have an infinite capacity to not know what can't be done.
— Henry Ford

How can you expect the miraculous if you don't attempt the impossible?
— Mother Angelica, EWTN

For an idea which, at first, does not seem absurd, there is no hope.
— Albert Einstein

but what if I've never done this before?

One doesn't discover new lands without consenting to lose sight of the shore for a very long time.
— André Gide

Do not fear death so much, but rather the inadequate life.
— Bertolt Brecht

The past is not our potential.
— Marilyn Ferguson

Everything you can do right now was once something you had never done before. If Life is anything, it's just a series of doing new things. Failing at something new is not failing. Not trying at all is failing. Never pass up a chance to try something new, especially if it's outside of your "comfort zone". The only way to expand your comfort zone is with temporary *discomfort*. **When was the last time you did something for the very *first* time?** To get something you never had, you have to do something you never did. There are no shortcuts. As John T. Reed is fond of saying, "*Avoid 'Little old me-ism'and substitute 'All they can say is no-ism.'*"

Fear is that little darkroom where negatives are developed.
— Michael Pritchard

but what if it's more than *I* can do?

Unless a man undertakes more than he possibly can do, he will never do all he can do.
— Henry Drummond

Reach for something — don't run from something. Be thankful if you have a job that is a little harder than you like. A razor cannot be sharpened on a piece of velvet!
— Grant G. Gard, *Don't Just Talk About It — Do It!*

Focus on your strengths and weaknesses and figure out where your strengths are appreciated and your weaknesses are either insignificant or irrelevant. For example, being facially ugly is irrelevant if you are a radio personality or direct mail entrepreneur or a whole bunch of other occupations.
Choose your goals wisely. Choose goals that reflect your strengths and weaknesses that you cannot correct. But once you have chosen them, attack, attack, attack! When you hit an obstacle, find a way around it.

All around you, people with significant handicaps are finding ways to win and winning. Don't go to your high school reunion with nothing but a long list of excuses for losing only to find that your classmates who could have created even longer lists [for themselves] have found a way to win instead.
— www.johntreed.com/succeedingwaytowin.html

Until you try to do something beyond what you have already mastered, you will never grow.
— Ronald E. Osborn

I hope that I may desire more than I can accomplish.
— Michaelangelo

There's nothing like biting off more than you can chew, and then chewing anyway.
— Mark Burnett

Don't stick with something easily in your current abilities; always stretch for a bit more. It's the only way to grow.

The human individual usually lives far within his limits.
— William James

Big men become big by doing what they didn't want to do when they didn't want to do it.
— Perry Tanksley

but what if I'm not gifted at this?

. . . the closer psychologists look at the careers of the gifted, the smaller the role innate talent seems to play and the bigger the role preparation seems to play.

. . . the elite performers had totaled 10,000 hours of practice. By contrast, the merely good students had totaled 8,000 hours, and the future music teachers . . . over 4,000 hours.

[The study] couldn't find any "naturals", . . . who floated to the effortlessly to the top while practicing a fraction of the time their peers did. Nor could they find any "grinds", people who worked harder than everyone else, yet just didn't have what it takes to break the top ranks. Their research suggests that once a musician has enough ability to get into a top music school, the thing that distinguishes one performer from another is how hard he or she works. That's it.

The emerging picture from such studies is that 10,000 hours of practice is required to achieve the level of mastery associated with being a world-class expert — in anything. . . . no one has yet

> *found a case in which true world-class knowledge was*
> *accomplished in less time.*
> — Malcolm Gladwell, *Outliers*, p. 38-39

Now, a quick aside here about talent. Notice in the above: "*once a musician has enough ability to get into a top music school, the thing that distinguishes one performer from another is how hard he or she works.*" That qualifier "*enough ability*" means talent. While I am musically inclined, sing and play piano, I haven't sufficient talent to get into music school as an aspiring professional.

> *Talent is something you are born with. You cannot acquire talent.*
> *You can only identify it and make the most of it. Talent is*
> *something you can do almost effortlessly, others cannot do no*
> *matter how hard they try, and you are mystified as to why they*
> *cannot do it.*
> — John T. Reed

Not anybody can become a concert pianist after 10,000 hours. One must first have a high degree of natural ability (talent), and you should ask multiple experts if you have it. Then, after that, one must put in the time. 10,000 hours means about 10 years (averaging 20 hours/week). That's 4 hours a day, 5 days a week — the equivalent of a part-time job. For 10 years. As author Stephen King remarked, "*Talent is cheaper than table salt. What separates the talented individual from the successful one is a lot of hard work.*"

But, since the average youth watches or listens to over 40 hours/week of media and music, it really boils down to a matter of priorities and then the discipline to *grind*. Gladwell makes the fascinating point that Asians are currently outsucceeding Whites because of their entrenched culture of wet-rice cultivation, which requires 3,000 hours/year of work. That's a 60 hour workweek! I recall the high-school cashier at a Chinese restaurant, diligently studying behind her register between customers. She competently settled the bill, and then was back into her book before I hit the door. (You don't see that in a BBQ place.) One South Chinese proverb states:

> *No one who can rise before dawn 360 days a year fails to make his*
> *family rich.*

We have forgotten how to *work*. Our school year is 180 days long. The South Korean school year is 220 days, and the Japanese school year is 243 days. Is it any wonder that Asian children can typically focus 40% more time on a puzzle than American children? Americans are lazy.

Play to your strengths, but above all, focus on improving your weaknesses.   . . . Percentage-wise you can make bigger improvements on a weakness than on a strength.   . . . for example, if you feel you are a poor communicator, you could improve your ability in this area by 20% by, say, buying a book and teaching yourself to be better at it.   If you really are such a disaster in that area, think of the improvement you could make!
   — Michael Powell, *Mind Games*

but what if I'm not extremely smart?

The relationship between success and IQ works only up to a point. Once someone has reached an IQ of somewhere around 120, having [more] doesn't seem to translate into any measurable real-world advantage.
   — Malcolm Gladwell, *Outliers*, p. 79

Certainly, you must be "smart enough" for the task:

at least IQ 75	can master elementary school
at least IQ 105	can master high school and college prep
at least IQ 115	can graduate from college, qualify for grad

What becomes much more important after IQ 120 are sociability and character. You don't have to be brilliant, just smart enough. (Actually, *too* smart is often compromises ones sociability. I knew somebody with a 156 IQ who mistook herself not overly smart in that regard, but was actually a walking disaster with loved ones.)

   Good social skills and sheer determination will carry you through with decent intelligence. I've known many bona-fide geniuses in my life, and many of them were very unbalanced and socially dysfunctional. Most had very little "practical intelligence" and were quite unhappy. One genius committed suicide, and his high-school genius friend is in prison. (Back in 12th grade, teachers would fawn over these two guys, opining what great futures they had ahead of them.) If you've ever heard the phrase "*C-students run the world*", now you understand why.

but look at my competition!

   Why scratch yourself from the race before it even starts? Show up and compete — you may be surprised. Never assume they are better than you. The only way to find out is to go up against them. It is OK to try and fail, but it's not OK to fail to try. Get on the field!

When an archer is shooting for nothing, he has all his skill. If he shoots for a brass buckle, he is already nervous. If he shoots for a prize of gold, he goes blank or sees two targets – he is out of his mind! His skill has not changed. But the prize divides him. He cares. He thinks more of winning than of shooting – and the need to win drains him of power.
> – Chuang Tzu

Untested means unproven. I recall an annoyingly pompous 4th grader who thought he was "too cool for school". At his first track-meet he was so out of his X-Box league that he was puking on the sidelines before his race had even started. He couldn't compete and scratched. Get out on the field and learn to steady your nerves to run your race.

but what if people oppose me?

Let's hope that people *do* oppose you! I would be very wary about any venture that met with unanimous approval. (If the masses could think for themselves, then they wouldn't be the masses.) Individuals follow the beat of a different drummer, whereas the masses follow to beat the different drummer. Oh, of course, after the different drummer has long since been buried in an unmarked grave will his originality be praised by the masses. As Jesus remarked in Matthew 13:57 after returning to minister in his homeland of Nazareth, "*A prophet is not without honor, save in his own country, and in his own house.*"

Great spirits have always encountered violent opposition from mediocre minds.
> – Albert Einstein

Our wretched species is so made that those who walk on the well-trodden path always throw stones at those who are showing a new road.
> – Voltaire

The one who insists that it cannot be done should never interrupt the one who is doing it.
> – Barrett Tillman

Jonas Hanway, in 1750, was the first man to publicly use an umbrella (then carried only by women), and he was jeered for it. Johannes Kepler – the man who utterly proved that planets orbited the Sun in elliptical paths – was placed under surveillance and people even spat on him in the streets.

All truth passes through three stages. First, it is ridiculed, second it is violently opposed, and third, it is accepted as self-evident.
— Arthur Schopenhauer

First they ignore you, then they ridicule you, then they fight you, then you win.
— Mohandas K. Gandhi

I am more concerned when nobody opposes me than when they do. The masses are almost always wrong, and about nearly everything. (Whenever I see the crowd doing something, I tend to look in the opposite direction!) 19 out of 20 Americans, even though they were born here, healthy, and of 100 IQ will end up in old age with little/no net worth, surviving on monthly Social Security checks.

And *that* is your "opposition"? If they were strong enough to actually thwart your plans, they'd be doers and creators themselves with dreams and goals of their *own*. They wouldn't have the time to routinely oppose new things because they'd be too busy having a Life. Remember: a person who is kicking you in the ass must be behind you. Rejoice when slandered, for cannibals never dine on gangrenous flesh.

It is not the critic who counts: not the man who points out how the strong man stumbles or where the doer of deeds could have done better. The credit belongs to the man who is actually in the arena, whose face is marred by dust and sweat and blood, who strives valiantly, who errs and comes up short again and again, because there is no effort without error or shortcoming, but who knows the great enthusiasms, the great devotions, who spends himself for a worthy cause; who, at the best, knows, in the end, the triumph of high achievement, and who, at the worst, if he fails, at least he fails while daring greatly, so that his place shall never be with those cold and timid souls who knew neither victory nor defeat.
— Theodore Roosevelt, "Citizenship in a Republic,"
Speech at the Sorbonne, Paris, 1910

Criticism is part of the price paid for leaping past mediocrity.
Criticism, condemnation, and complaint are creatures of the wind. They come and go on the wasted breath of lesser beings and have no power over me.
— Andy Andrews, *The Traveler's Gift*

Generally, the only way losers can actually oppose you is when they have some *de jure* monopoly power (through Government, of course) to stand in your way.   A planning board, zoning commission, regulatory agency, etc.

speak only to those who are in a position to help you

No matter what new project a man or woman attempts, there is always a crop of gapers ready to laugh or to criticize.   And sometimes those nearest and dearest may laugh the loudest or criticize the most.

*So instead of squandering your early enthusiasm in a futile attempt to excite the world about you and your plans, preserve that enthusiasm within yourself.   Instead of letting your enthusiasm flow out through your mouth like a weak shallow creek, dam it up.   **Let it accumulate and gradually gain the power of a deep reservoir.**   That power will give you the necessary confidence to get started on your first step.   (p. 113)*
— William J. Reilly, *How to Get What You Want Out of Life*

You must begin to ignore laymen friends and relatives who lack confidence in you.   Freedom activist and author George Donnelly has it exactly right:

I have to be blind, deaf and dumb to the negative.

I'm on a mission. This is between me and the universe. It's not about anyone else. I'm taking this to the wall whether I have someone next to me or not.
— www.georgedonnelly.com/libertarian/why-voluntaryist

Keep your face toward the sunshine and the shadows will fall behind you.
— Walt Whitman

but what if I have nobody to help me?

Well now, that *is* a problem.   Nobody ever succeeded on their own.   *"It's not what you know, but who you know"* is usually true.   If you are lacking in Human Relations (an "A + D" type), then start making more friends. Help others first, and they will then help you.

try to meet others' needs before you meet your own

The rare individual who unselfishly tries to serve others has an enormous advantage.   He has little competition.
— Dale Carnegie, *How To Win Friends and Influence People*

My friend Ragnar Benson, a colleague author of many books, always answers the phone with *"How may I help you?"* And he means it!

The man who can put himself in the place of other men, who can understand the workings of their minds, need never worry about what the future has in store for them.
— Owen D. Young

If you believe that you have not been helped enough by others, perhaps that is true because you haven't been all that helpful yourself?

but what if there are obstacles?

Men do not stumble over mountains, but over molehills.
— Confucius

Difficulties are the things that show what men are.
— Epictenus

There are *always* obstacles, because Life is an obstacle course. (Many obstacles, however, exist only in your mind.) Nearly everything in Life begins by needing a push, and usually uphill. There is a natural inertia to overcome, including even simple gravity when you get up every morning. So what? Get over it! "*Inconvenience is temporary. Regret is permanent.*" If you can find a path without obstacles, it probably doesn't lead anywhere you'd want to be.

Nothing will ever be attempted if all possible objections must be first overcome.
— Dr. Samuel Johnson

Always bear in mind that your own resolution to succeed is more important than any one thing.
— Abraham Lincoln

Obstacles are those frightful things you see when you take your eyes off the goal.
— Hannah Moore

Skillful pilots gain their reputation from storms and tempests.
— Epicurus

Doing the easy thing is rarely about doing the right thing. If the wind is at your back, you are going in the wrong direction.
— Larry Winget, *Shut Up, Stop Whining, Get A Life!*

Flying an airplane is a great example of this, as a pilot should takeoff and land into the wind. Always into the resistance. One of the most important things on an airfield is the windsock. It shows the pilot the direction and strength of wind, so that he can put that mostly on his airplane's nose. Pilots are well acquainted with resistance.

but what about my "bad luck"?

Luck is what happens when preparation meets opportunity.
    — Elmer G. Leterman

On its own, there is no such thing as "luck" — good or bad. Good habits attract "good luck". Bad habits attract "bad luck". That's it.

how to be "lucky"
> *create opportunities*
> *recognize opportunities*
> *listen to your intuition*
> *have self-belief and positive expectations*
> *resiliency to learn from your mistakes, and to persevere*
> — Michael Powell, *Mind Games*

but what if it's "*unrealistic*"?

It is a fact that great leaders — great achievers — are rarely realistic by other people's standards. Somehow, these successful people, often considered strange, pick their way through life ignoring or not hearing negative expectations and emotions. Consequently, they accomplish one great thing after another, never having heard what cannot be done. That is precisely why one should never tell a young person that something cannot be done. God may have been waiting centuries for someone ignorant enough of the impossible to do that very thing!
    — Andy Andrews, *The Traveler's Gift*

"Unrealistic" is most likely either your own fear talking, or someone else's envy. Ignore both. Every notable accomplishment in history was derided beforehand as "unrealistic".

but what if it's "*risky*"?

Don't worry too much about yourself and about getting hurt. People who go through life being cautious miss a great deal. Take your chances wherever you have to. It's better luck, you'll see more, and you'll probably live as long anyway.
    — quoted from Dr. Peale's *Enthusiasm Makes the Difference*

He that leaveth nothing to chance will do few things ill, but he will do few things.
    — Charles Baudelaire

Well, good, I hope it is indeed risky! Nothing impressive occurs outside of risk. If everything were safe, everyone would be doing it. Just take your calculated risks head on. Commit and thereafter don't dwell on the risk, but only your task at hand.

but what if "*the timing is not right*"?

That's usually just an excuse. You can nearly always come up with a reason why the timing is wrong, and this just programs yourself for failure. Conditions and timing are *never* perfect for anything. (No price is ever perfect, either.) You just have to make do with what you've got, and proceed anyway.

> *Sometime ain't never now.*
> — All The King's Men

> *Indecision limits the Almighty and His ability to perform miracles in your life. He has put the vision in you — proceed! To wait, to wonder, to doubt, to be indecisive is to disobey God.*
> — Andy Andres, *The Traveler's Gift*

> *The lure of the distant and difficult is deceptive.*
> *The great opportunity is where you are.*
> — John Burroughs

I knew a guy who was the biggest "*Yeah, but . . .*" whiner I'd ever met. A friend gave him — *gave* him! — a very nice mobile hot-dog stand to start a new business with, and the guy immediately came up with a dozen reasons why it wouldn't work. To such people, I reply, "*Hey, you've convinced me!*" and then I drop the subject (and them).

> *Procrastination is the fear of success. People procrastinate because they are afraid of the success that they know will result if they move ahead now. Because success is heavy, carries a responsibility with it, it is much easier to procrastinate and live on the "someday I'll" philosophy.*
> — Denis Waitley

but what if it's "*too late*"?

> *Every passing moment is another chance to turn it all around.*
> — from the movie *Vanilla Sky*

It is very, very *rarely* "too late". Even if you imagine that it is, what have you got to lose, anyway?

Tomorrow is the most important thing in life. Comes into us at midnight very clean. It's perfect when it arrives and it puts itself in our hands. It hopes we've learned something from yesterday.
— John Wayne

but what if I can't do it all at once?

No one could make a greater mistake than he who did nothing because he could do only a little.
— Edmund Burke

One of the greatest reasons people cannot mobilize themselves is that they try to accomplish great things. Most worthwhile achievement are the result of many little things done in a single direction.
— Nido Quebin

We cannot do everything at once, but we can do something at once.
— Calvin Coolidge

You can drive 500 miles at night with headlights that shine only 200' ahead of you. How? You take the road 200' at a time.

Do *what* you can, *while* you can. At least you're operating at current capability. It's more than others do. And who knows, maybe it will become completed faster or easier than you imagined? Rouse yourself now, and do something!

Do what you can, with what you have, where you are.
— Theodore Roosevelt

In Elmer Bendiner's book, *The Fall of Fortresses*, a B-17 bomber got hit with eleven 20mm cannon flak shells over Germany, none of which exploded. The pilot Bohn Fawkes asked his crew chief to investigate. All shells were empty of explosive charge! One contained a rolled up note, written in Czech, "*To je vše, co mužeme udelat pro vás nyní.*" **"This is all we can do for you now."** Some munitions factory workers performed a quiet feat of deliberate sabotage, saving the lives of ten airmen. So, you never know what effect your actions may have!

Do not despise these small beginnings, for the Lord rejoices to see the work begin.
— Zech. 4:10 NLT

but what it it's not "*perfect*"?

Have no fear of perfection — you'll never reach it.
— Salvador Dali

A good plan, executed now, is better than a perfect plan executed next week.
— Gen. George S. Patton

We cannot direct the wind, but we can adjust the sails.
— Bertha Calloway

Well, what *is* perfect? Time is short, and the eventually perfect is the enemy of the presently useful. Learn to discern when near-perfection is called for vs. when it approaches diminishing marginal returns.

Don't allow "perfection" to be your excuse for not acting and thus for failure. The perfect is the enemy of the (very) good. **Half of Life is *just showing up* in the first place.** I once took a basic Salsa dancing class for four weeks. The first week had 30 students. Then 18. Then 7. By the last week, I was the *only* single person who showed up. I wasn't a brilliant student and there were at first better dancers, but I had the advantage of *being there* to the end.

but what if I "*fail* "?

Great opportunities come to all, but many do not know they have met them. The only preparation to take advantage of them is simple fidelity to what each day brings.
— A.E. Dunning

If you're going to fail, you might as well fail at a difficult task. Failure causes others to downgrade their expectations of you in the future. The seriousness of the problem depends on what you attempt.
— Yale School of Organization and Management

Probably he who never made a mistake never made a discovery.
— Samuel Smiles

In great attempts it is glorious even to fail.
— Longinus

The greatest mistake one can make in life is to be continually fearing you will make one. There is no failure except in no longer trying.
— Elbert Hubbard

Failure is an event, never a person.
— William D. Brown

"The ball has no memory."

This is a mantra in professional tennis. Rod Laver and Jimmy Connors were famous for playing matches point by point. Being down in a set didn't matter. Making a mistake doesn't matter for the next shot. *"The ball has no memory."* It doesn't know the score or who's hitting it. Most failures are not that damaging, so press on.

The responses and results that you receive from anyone, in any situation, are triggered by the stimuli you provide. The stimuli are your behaviors. This is the only way people can get to know you, and decide whether to reward or punish you. If you behave in a purposeless, meaningless, unconstructive way, you get inferior results. If you behave in purposeful, meaningful, constructive ways, you get superior results. That is how you create your own experience. When you choose the behavior (the action), you choose the consequences.
— Dr. Phil, *Life Strategies*, p. 127

The secret key to being successful is to Ignore Past Failures and Forge Ahead.
— John Schindler, M.D.

You simply cannot drive forward if you're focused on what's happening in the rearview mirror.
— Steve Harvey

Failure is often the line of least persistence.
— Zig Ziglar

Fall down seven times, stand up eight.
— Japanese proverb

Defeat is not bitter if you don't swallow it.
— Ben K. O'Dell

failure is part of succeeding

You always pass failure on the way to success.
— Mickey Rooney

If you don't make mistakes, you're not working on hard enough problems. And that's a big mistake.
— Frank Wilczek

Learn how to fail intelligently, for failing is one of the greatest arts in the world.
  — C.F. Kettering

If one does not fail at times then one has not challenged himself sufficiently.
  — Dr. Ferdinand Porsche

The man who makes no mistakes does not normally make anything.
  — Edward John Phelps

To conquer without risk is to triumph without glory.
  — Pierre Corneille (1605-1684)

The way to succeed is to double your failure rate.
  — IBM founder Thomas Watson

You may indeed fail. In fact, you're almost guaranteed to fail at something in the beginning. Most entrepreneurs fail *four* times in business before their fifth attempt succeeds.

In the Mexico City 1968 Olympics, the marathon runner from Tanzania limped and wheezed past the finish line dead last — over an hour after the gold-medal winner. Asked why he bothered, he replied, "*I come from a small, poor country. Many people made sacrifices for me to go to Mexico City to run in the marathon. They didn't send me to start the race; they sent me to finish the race.*" This is the attitude of a champion, regardless of his ranking. Finish . . . your . . . race.

> *What I'd say, especially to young people, is that you're not going to be anything in life . . . you're not going to be a great athlete, you're not going to be great in any profession unless you learn to commit your life to that. You have to reach deep within yourself to see if you are willing to make the sacrifices. And even when you commit your life to whatever that desire is, you're going to run into problems. But I was taught years ago that you don't accept anything as a problem but, rather, as a challenge.*
> *. . . But even if you're not prepared for it, use common sense, for the last thing in life you want to do is give up on anything. You set your goals, work on your objectives to achieve those goals, and no matter how great the problems are, just accept that problem as a challenge and go for it. You're not always going to have your dreams come true. You can't set your life goal on one thing. Suppose you don't have what it takes to be a great athlete. I think you should have an alternative in case your dreams burst on you.*

> *I believe the same is true of making a living today; you should
> have a primary objective in making a living, you should have a
> vocation, but you should also have an alternative.*
> — Louis Zamperini,
> www.la84foundation.org/6oic/OralHistory/OHZamperini.pdf

failure means at least that you're risking

> *Defeat is not the worst of failures.*
> *Not to have tried is the true failure.*
> — George Edward Woodberry

> *You miss 100% of the shots you never take.*
> — Wayne Gretzky

> *What would you attempt to do if you knew that you could not fail?*
> — Dr. Robert Schuller

> *Life is too short to be little.*
> — Disraeli

What's much worse than failure is regret. So, what if you do "*fail*"? Then at least (as Theodore Roosevelt said) you've been "*in the arena*". I had a friend who once began his own private beer label. He made a good go at it, but after a few years demand fizzled out (probably through lack of sustained marketing, as beer is all about the marketing). We all admired him for the great attempt, even though he didn't become the Samuel Adams of Texas.

By the way, what do you call a guy who finished *last* in the Olympics? **A guy who competed in the *Olympics!*** He was in the game — in the arena. He was no mere spectator. (Thanks to my great good friend Terence for this view. When I bemoaned my ratty old Cessna at Oshkosh, he rhetorically asked, "*What do you call a guy with a ratty old Cessna at Oshkosh? A guy who flew to Oshkosh!*")

failure can almost always be instructive

> *Even a mistake may turn out to be the one thing necessary to a
> worthwhile achievement.*
> — Henry Ford

> *We often discover what will succeed by finding out what will not.*
> *Probably he who never made a mistake never made a discovery.*
> — author unknown

"Failure" is just a state of mind, as everything is something to learn by or enjoy. It's all about how *you* see things. OK, something didn't work out the way you planned: what of that can you *make* work for you? Where is the *positive* you can use?

Besides, you never know when a mistake will turn out to be something *useful*. Many, many inventions were stumbled across by accident: the microwave oven, the Slinky, Play-Doh, Super Glue, Teflon, the Pacemaker, Velcro, styrofoam, Corn Flakes, dynamite, champagne, anesthesia, penicillin, X-rays, and many others.

there is no such thing as "failure" anyway!
When a hoped-for result does not happen, we call it a "failure". Every result is technically a success, in the sheer realm of "Action A causes Result A" causality. Although a particular result may not be what you desired or what matters, it was the (successful) result of *that* action. Learn from it, as Edison did (with over 1,000 light bulb tries).

The only real failure is when you expect Result B from Action A. For Result B, you must do Action B.

author Harold Sherman's 6 ways to reverse failure
I will never give up, so long as I know I'm right.
I will believe that all things will work out if I hang on.
I will be courageous and undismayed by poor odds.
I will not permit anyone to deter me from my goals.
I will fight to overcome all physical handicaps and setbacks.
I will try again and yet again, to accomplish my desire.

Excellent advice! I would add some final bits:

I will always seek to learn from my attempts and failures.
I will continually ask myself: *"What is it that I am trying to do?"*

no more excuses!
The way to do things is begin.
— Horace Greely

Every time a man puts a new idea across, he finds ten men who thought of it before he did — but they only thought of it.
— Henry Grady Weaver

Occasionally, there may be insurmountable *reasons* for not succeeding, but there should never be a single *excuse*. Proceed until someone says you're trespassing.

You either make it or you don't.
— movie *Pushing Tin*

START, AND THEN FINISH

Who has begun has half done. Dare to be wise; begin!
— Horace, c. 65 B.C.

It is no use saying, "We are doing our best."
You have to succeed in doing what is necessary.
— Winston Churchill

The world does not care what you know, or even what you can do, but what you have *done*. Only . . . results . . . matter. Flee that putrid land of *shoulda-coulda-woulda*. Allow yourself no excuses. Start it, do it well, and finish the job! Here is the healthy order:

Feared Things 1st.
Unpleasant Things 2nd.
Fun Things 3rd.

start with the basics; don't get ahead of things

The Wrights developed a series of gliders while experimenting with aerodynamics, which was crucial to developing a workable control system. Many historians, and most importantly the Wrights themselves, pointed out that their game plan was to learn flight control and become pilots specifically by soaring, whereas all the other experimenters rushed to add power without refining flight control. By 1903, Orville and Wilbur Wright had achieved powered flight of just over a minute by putting an engine on their best glider design.
— FAA-H-8083-13, *Glider Flying Handbook*

The Wright brothers were smart to focus first on control vs. power. Power without control means a crash, and that's just what the others did (with better motors).

3 Positive Rules of Accomplishment

Write up a very specific list of what you want, and re-read it three times a day — morning, noon, and night. Dwell on what you want as often as possible. Discuss with no one your plan.

start early, such as today, or even right now!

The time to repair the roof is when the sun is shining.
— John F. Kennedy

Dig the well before you are thirsty.
— Chinese proverb

Start wherever you are, however you are.
  — Vernon Howard, *Pathways to Perfect Living*

Why right now? Because you can't start any sooner!

"*Never confuse motion with action.*" — Hemingway

One of the easiest ways for people to fool themselves is being *busy* instead of being *productive.* Learn to daily ask yourself:

Are you *goal* oriented, or merely *process* oriented?

the power of "focused inattention"

This means not wanting something *too* badly, but learning how to relax more and letting it happen.

keep track of your results along the way

Measuring success or failure purely as a function of results means that you are taking a hard-nosed, bottom-line approach to self-evaluation. You might as well do it that way, because that's how the world is measuring you. You can't make your own rules or laws: the world already has its own. More importantly, the world has the ability to enforce them. . . . Only with results can we be sure that the changes are real.

The time-honored formula for taking purposeful action goes like this:
> Be
> Do
> Have

What the formula says is BE committed, DO what it takes, and you will HAVE what you want. *The difference between winners and losers is that winners do things that losers don't want to do.*
  — Dr. Phil, *Life Strategies*, p. 133

One of the best examples I've personally experienced for keeping track of results is going through flight training. It is a sequential building block program, and it requires very thorough records of the student's progress. Even if must change instructors midway, the new one could glance at your chart and immediately grasp where you were in the program and how to continue. After about 20 hours you can solo. Between 60-75 hours, you will be ready for the flight test checklist. It is very clear and logical; if you can pass each maneuver with your checkride examiner along, you will then become a Private Pilot!

not only finish, but complete your goal with excellence
A great man leaves clean work behind him, and requires no sweeper up of the chips.
— Elizabeth Barrett Browning

"Getting something done is an accomplishment. Getting something done right is an achievement."

To give anything less than your best is to sacrifice the gift.
— Steve Prefontaine

ON BEING BOLD

Our doubts are traitors, and make us lose the good we oft might win by fearing to attempt.
— Shakespeare

Und setzest Du nicht das Leben ein,
nie wird Dir das Leben gewonnen sein.
(If you don't risk your life, you will never win the life.)
— Schiller

The very best way to predict the future is to create it.
— Michael Kami

Boldness means doing something that you would normally fear. With personal goals, good information, and solid planning, it will become easier to act boldly because you've reduced your own uncertainty. You are sure of what you *want* and *how* to achieve it. The rest is just getting used to successes! Fate serves those who seize it by the tail.

The #1 cause of failure is <u>fear</u> of failure. Fear paralyzes action.
— Steve Harvey

confront your problem ("*grasp the nettle firmly*")
A nettle is a kind of thistle with tiny needle-like thorns. If you gently touch it, it will prick you. However, if you grasp it firmly, its spines crumble into dust. As Edna Mode of *The Incredibles* urged:

Go! Confront the problem! Fight! WIN!

pulling the tooth
Sometimes, you just have to do The Big Thing, like pulling a tooth. No half-measures or delay will work.

> *Don't be afraid to take a big step if one is indicated. You can't cross a chasm in two small jumps.*
> — David Lloyd George

Once you've decided that a big step is indicated, just do it. Stopping at third base adds nothing to the score. For big changes, "yank the Band-Aid off". There's no shortcut; just do it. Yes, it may be scary, but:

> *Courage is doing what you're afraid to do. There can be no courage unless you're scared.*
> — Eddie Rickenbacker

> *Nine-tenths of tactics are certain, and taught in books: but the irrational tenth is like the kingfisher flashing across the pool and that is the test of generals. It can only be ensured by instinct, sharpened by thought practicing the stroke so often that at the crisis it is as natural as a reflex.*
> — T.E. Lawrence

> *The very determined person finds a way, the other kind finds an excuse. You get back exactly what you have sent out . . . bad or good, constructive or destructive.*
> *We either produce results or we produce excuses, and there is no in between.*
> *Three types of people in the world:*
> *The Wills. The Won'ts. The Can'ts.*
> — Grant G. Gard, *Don't Just Talk About It — Do It!*

> *People don't lack strength, they lack will.*
> — Victor Hugo

> *I hate a thing done by halves. If it be right, do it boldly; if it be wrong, leave it undone.*
> — Bernard Gilpin

if there is no leader, then lead it yourself

A leader is somebody with followers. In effect, by choosing leadership you deserve it. If a situation requires leadership, and nobody has taken it on, then it's up to you! A Real Man steps up.

FINAL WORD

If you don't like the crop you are reaping,
check the seed you are sowing.
— sign on a feed store

Growing old is no more than a bad habit which a busy man has no
time to form.
— Andre Maurois

Remember that there are only three kinds of things anyone need
ever do. (1) Things we ought to do. (2) Things we've got to do.
(3) Things we like doing.
— C.S. Lewis, to his godchild

If you shouldn't be doing it, don't have to do it, or don't like doing it . . .
then why are you doing it at all?

The essential conditions of everything you do must be choice, love,
passion.
— Nadia Boulanger

> *Choose* to do what you do.
> *Love* what you are doing.
> Do it with *passion.*
> *Finish* the job.

How many people live that way? Very few, and *all* of them stand above
the crowd; all are a success in their fields no matter how small.

When love and skill work together, expect a masterpiece.
— John Ruskin

Ambition and love are the wings of great actions.
— Goethe

The future never just happened. It was created.
— Will and Ariel Durant, *The Lessons of History*

Action This Day.
— Winston Churchill

Ladder of Achievement
100%	I *did* it!
90%	I'm doing it now.
80%	I will do it.
70%	I might do it.
60%	I think I might do it.
50%	I can do it.
40%	I think I can do it.
30%	I wish I could do it.
20%	I don't know how to do it.
10%	I can't do it.
0%	I won't do it.

There are no greater words to hear yourself say than: "*I did it!*"

In Andy Andrews' remarkable book *The Traveler's Gift*, a depressed family man is taken through time and history to meet seven famous personalities, each of them with a particular message. For me, the most powerful chapter was when the man awoke in a giant warehouse filled with photos of people and pets. Also stacked without end were the everyday things of life, as if the belongings of an entire city were stored there. Some things, however, were very odd, such as inventions the man had never seen before. Explaining the room was the archangel Gabriel:

> *This, my friend, is the place that never was.*
> *This is the place where we keep all the things that were about to be delivered just as a person stopped working and praying for them. The contents of this warehouse are filled with the dreams and goals of the less courageous.*

Seeing a photo of two children that he and his wife never had because they "couldn't afford" them, he asked to keep the photo. Gabriel replied, "*Jason and Julia do not exist. The time for their arrival has passed. The opportunity is missed. There are no second chances.*"

What children, inventions, books, songs, and accomplishments of yours are in that sorry warehouse of the "*less courageous*"? Every passing moment is but another chance to turn it all around. Forget about your missed opportunities, and concentrate on the opportunities you still have right now.

Carpe diem!

You must always *Seize the day!* Your Life began with 29,000 days ahead, and every one must be grabbed ahold of and lived to its fullest. The best *Carpe diem!* example was undoubtedly Theodore Roosevelt.

I have been fulfilling a boyish ambition of mine [to live, ranch, and hunt in the West]. *We are so very rarely able to, actually and in real life, dwell in our ideal "hero land."*
— Theodore Roosevelt

He was so alive at all points, and so gifted with the rare faculty of living intensely and entirely in every moment as it passed.
— Edith Wharton

Study T.R.'s amazing Life for inspiration. He once explained, "*I am only an average man, but, by George, I work harder at it than the average man.*" His secret was simple, as one friend famously commented:

You must understand that Theodore is about six.

T.R. never lost the heart of a boy. Boys *do* things. When asked why he went on a dangerous Brazilian river expedition, 55 y/o T.R. replied:

Youth will be served, Tom. It was my last chance to be a boy.

After T.R.'s death in 1919, a young child remarked:

He was a fulfiller of good intentions.

It is difficult to imagine a better epitaph. T.R. was all action. You can be all action, too!

Thanks for reading, and I'll see you for in Volume 2!

prayer by an unknown Soldier

I asked God for strength, that I might achieve.
I was made weak, that I might learn humbly to obey.

I asked for health, that I might do greater things.
I was given infirmity, that I might do better things.

I asked for riches, that I might be happy.
I was given poverty, that I might be wise.

I asked for power, that I might have the praise of men.
I was given weakness, that I might feel the need for God.

I asked for all things, that I might enjoy life.
I was given life, that I might enjoy all things.

I got nothing that I asked for — but everything I had hoped for.
Almost in spite of myself, my unspoken prayers were answered.

I am among all men, most richly blessed.

by Kenneth W. Royce (Boston T. Party)

Modules for Manhood   (2014)
What Every Man Must Know (Volume 1)
What do women want? What does America need? *Men!* Do you want to become a capable well-rounded man? Learn your unique Purpose in Life, and how to achieve it? Start your exciting journey today!

    360 pp. softcover (2014) $27 + $7 s&h (cash, please)

Hologram of Liberty   (revised for 2012)
The Constitution's Shocking Alliance
with Big Government
The Convention of 1787 was the most brilliant and subtle *coup d'état* in history. The nationalist framers *designed* a strong government, guaranteed through purposely ambiguous verbiage. Many readers insist that it's Royce's best book. A jaw-dropper. Revised for 2012 and Obamacare.

    360 pp. softcover (2012) $27 + $7 s&h (cash, please)

You & The Police!   (revised for 2009)
    The definitive guide to your rights and tactics during police confrontations. When can you refuse to answer questions or consent to searches? Don't lose your liberty through ignorance! This 2009 edition covers the *USA PATRIOT Act* and much more.

    168 pp. softcover (2009) $16 + $5 s&h (cash, please)

One Nation, Under Surveillance   (2009)
Privacy From the Watchful Eye
Explains precisely how to lay low from snoops of all types. Extremely thorough on computers, data, Internet, VoIP, digital gold, and prepaid cellphones. This is the huge replacement of his 1997 *Bulletproof Privacy.* Boston retired in 2009; this was his last new title.

    480 pp. softcover (2009) $27 + $7 s&h (cash, please)

Boston's Gun Bible   (new text through 2009)
    A rousing how-to/why-to on our modern gun ownership. Firearms are "*liberty's teeth*". No other general gun book is more thorough or useful! Indispensable! Covers the *D.C v. Heller* case. Our best seller.

    848 pp. softcover (2002-2009) $33 + $7 s&h (cash, please)

Molôn Labé!   (a novel)
    If you liked *Unintended Consequences* by John Ross and Ayn Rand's *Atlas Shrugged*, then Boston's novel will be a favorite. It dramatically outlines an innovative recipe for Liberty which could actually work! A thinking book for people of action; an action book for people of thought. It's getting people moving to Wyoming! **www.freestatewyoming.org**

    454 pp. softcover (2004) $27 + $7 s&h (cash, please)

Safari Dreams   (2008)
A Practical Guide To Your Hunt In Africa
Possibly the most useful "one book" for making your first safari. Thoroughly covers: rifles, calibers, bullets, insurance, health, packing and planning, trip prep, airlines, choosing your PH, shot placement, and being in the bush. Don't go to Africa without it!

    352 pp. softcover, 100 color photos (2008) $30 + $5 s&h

www.javelinpress.com

www.javelinpress.com

NOTE: Please verify pricing *and address* from our website *before* ordering!

Prices <u>each</u> copy:	Retail	<40%>	<44%>	<50%>
Boston's Gun Bible 5½"x8½" 848 pp. 1/2009	1-5 copies $33	6-7 $20	8-15 $18.50	*case 16 or more* $16.50
Modules for Manhood - 1 5½"x8½" 360 pp. 3/2014	1-5 copies $27	6-13 $16	14-27 $15	*case 28 or more* $13.50
Molôn Labé! 5½"x8½" 454 pp. 1/2004	1-5 copies $27	6-13 $16	14-27 $15	*case 28 or more* $13.50
One Nation, Under Surv. 5½"x8½" 480 pp. 6/2009	1-5 copies $27	6-13 $16	14-27 $15	*case 28 or more* $13.50
Hologram of Liberty 5½"x8½" 360 pp. 5/2012	1-5 copies $27	6-13 $16	14-27 $15	*case 28 or more* $13.50
Boston on Surviving Y2K 5½"x8½" 352 pp. 11/1998	1-5 copies $11	6-17 $10	18-35 $9	*case of 36 or more* $8
Safari Dreams 5½"x8½" 352 pp. 1/2008	1-5 copies $30	6-17 $18	18-39 $17	*case of 36 or more* $15
You & The Police! 5½"x8½" 168 pp. 1/2009	1-5 copies $16	6-37 $10	38-75 $9	*case of 76 or more* $8

Mix titles for any quantity discount. This is easiest done as ¼ case per title:
¼ case of: BGB 4   MfM 7   ML! 7   ONUS 7   HoL 7   BoSY 9   SD 9   Y&P! 19

Shipping and Handling are *not* included!   Please add below:

non-case S&H within USA for (*BGB   MfM   Molôn   ONUS   Hologram*):
First Class (or UPS for larger orders) add: $7 for first copy, $2 each additional copy.

non-case S&H within USA for other titles (*Y&P!   BoSY   Safari Dreams*):
First Class (or UPS for larger orders) add: $5 for first copy, $1 each additional copy.

CASE orders (straight or mixed) UPS Ground: $35 west of the Miss.; $40 east.

Overpayment will be refunded in cash with order. Underpayment will delay order!
If you have questions on discounts or S&H, please email us through our website.

These forms of payment only:

Cash (Preferred. Cash orders receive pre-signed copies when available.)
payee <u>blank</u> M.O.s (Which allows negotiability.)
silver 1oz. bullion (At today's spot price, found at: www.kitco.com)

Unless prior agreement has been made, *we do <u>not</u> accept and <u>will</u> return* checks,
C.O.D.s, or any other form of tender. (Many of our distributors take credit cards.)
Prices and terms are subject to change without notice (check our website first).
Please send paid orders to the address on **www.javelinpress.com**